SAS® Guide to Macro Processing, Version 6, Second Edition

SAS Institute Inc.
SAS Campus Drive
Cary, NC 27513

The correct bibliographic citation for this manual is as follows: SAS Institute Inc., *SAS® Guide to Macro Processing, Version 6, Second Edition*, Cary, NC: SAS Institute Inc., 1990. 319 pp.

SAS® Guide to Macro Processing, Version 6, Second Edition

1st printing, June 1990
2nd printing, January 1991
3rd printing, August 1991
4th printing, January 1993
5th printing, January 1994

Note that text corrections may have been made at each printing.

The SAS® System is an integrated system of software providing complete control over data access, management, analysis, and presentation. Base SAS software is the foundation of the SAS System. Products within the SAS System include SAS/ACCESS; SAS/AF; SAS/ASSIST; SAS/CALC; SAS/CONNECT; SAS/CPE; SAS/DMI; SAS/EIS; SAS/ENGLISH; SAS/ETS; SAS/FSP; SAS/GRAPH; SAS/IML; SAS/IMS-DL/I; SAS/INSIGHT; SAS/LAB; SAS/NVISION; SAS/OR; SAS/PH-Clinical; SAS/QC; SAS/REPLAY-CICS; SAS/SHARE; SAS/STAT; SAS/TOOLKIT; SAS/TUTOR; SAS/DB2; SAS/GIS; SAS/IMAGE; SAS/PETRO; SAS/SESSION; SAS/SPECTRAVIEW; and SAS/SQL-DS software. Other SAS Institute products are SYSTEM 2000® Data Management Software, with basic SYSTEM 2000, CREATE; Multi-User; QueX; Screen Writer; and CICS interface software; NeoVisuals® software; JMP; JMP IN; JMP Serve; and JMP *Design®* software; SAS/RTERM® software; and the SAS/C® Compiler and the SAS/CX® Compiler; and Emulus™ software. MultiVendor Architecture™ and MVA™ are trademarks of SAS Institute Inc. SAS Video Productions™ and the SVP logo are service marks of SAS Institute Inc. Books by Users™ and its logo are service marks of SAS Institute Inc. SAS Institute also offers SAS Consulting; Ambassador Select; and On-Site Ambassador™ services. *Authorline; Observations; SAS Communications; SAS Training; SAS Views;* the SASware Ballot; and *JMPer Cable™* are published by SAS Institute Inc. All trademarks above are registered trademarks or trademarks of SAS Institute Inc. in the USA and other countries. ® indicates USA registration.

The Institute is a private company devoted to the support and further development of its software and related services.

Other brand and product names are registered trademarks or trademarks of their respective companies.

DOC SS1 Ver110.1N060590

Contents

INTRODUCTION

MACRO FACILITY REFERENCE

SPECIAL TOPICS

MACRO APPLICATIONS

APPENDICES

iv

Illustrations

Displays

Figures

Tables

Credits

Documentation

Composition

Mary Cole, Cindy A. Hopkins, Lee N. Lai, Craig Sampson, Pamela A. Troutman, Denise Truelove, P. Darlene Watts

Graphic Design

Creative Services Department

Proofreading

Gwendolyn T. Colvin, Carey H. Cox, Beth A. Heiney, Hanna P. Hicks, Jeffrey Lopes, Josephine P. Pope, Toni P. Sherrill, John M. West, Susan E. Willard, Anna B. Williams

Technical Review

Gloria N. Cappy, Oita C. Coleman, Greg Cooper, Jodie Gilmore, Linda C. Helwig, Christina A. Keene, Fritz Lehman, Jeffrey A. McDermott, Lynn Patrick, Denise M. Poll, Caroline Quinn, Lisa M. Ripperton, Joseph G. Slater

Writing and Editing

Rick Cornell, Jr., Rick Early, Stacy A. Hilliard, Brenda C. Kalt, Len Olszewski

Software

Development

Product development includes design, programming, debugging, support, and providing source material for documentation. In the following list, the SAS Institute staff member whose name is followed by an asterisk has primary responsibility for the feature; others give specific assistance.

Credits for host-specific features appear in the SAS documentation for that operating system.

Macro Facility

Bruce Tindall,* Susan M. O'Connor

%DISPLAY and %WINDOW Statements

Jeff Polzin

%KEYDEF Statement

Jeffrey A. Shaughnessy

Support

Technical Support

Greg Cooper, Lynn H. Patrick

Using This Book

PURPOSE

SAS Guide to Macro Processing, Version 6, Second Edition provides complete documentation on portable features of the Release 6.06 SAS macro facility that are used with base SAS software. In this context, the term portable includes features that work the same across all host operating systems. (In contrast, host-specific features are those which are meaningful only under specific host operating systems or which work differently under different host operating systems.) It includes an introductory tutorial, reference material, a chapter of examples that provide usage material, and a glossary.

SAS Guide to Macro Processing, Version 6, Second Edition replaces the following books:

- *SAS Guide to Macro Processing, Version 5 Edition*
- *SAS Technical Report P-175, Changes and Enhancements to the SAS System, Release 5.18, under OS and CMS.*

It does *not* replace *SAS Guide to Macro Processing, Version 6, First Edition*. That book (previously titled *SAS Guide to Macro Processing, Version 6 Edition*) is used with Releases 6.03 and 6.04 of the SAS System for Personal Computers and the SAS System under UNIX® and derivative operating systems.

"Using This Book" is your guide to using *SAS Guide to Macro Processing*. It describes what you should know in order to benefit from using this manual; how the book is organized; which sections you should read if you have specific goals; and the typographical, syntax, and coding conventions used. In addition, the final section describes other SAS documentation that may be helpful to you.

AUDIENCE

SAS Guide to Macro Processing, Version 6, Second Edition is written for users who either have previous experience using the SAS System or who have at least an intermediate level of experience with another programming language and understand the fundamentals of programming logic. Such users may include end users, applications developers, or systems programmers.

The SAS macro facility has many features ranging from simple to complex. You can begin to use the simple macro features almost immediately and work up to the more complex ones as your experience and needs grow.

UNIX is a registered trademark of AT&T.

PREREQUISITES

The following table summarizes the SAS System concepts you need to understand in order to use *SAS Guide to Macro Processing*.

You need to know how to . . .	Refer to . . .
invoke the SAS System at your site	instructions provided by the SAS Software Consultant at your site
use base SAS software. You need varying amounts of familiarity with the SAS System depending on which features you want to use.	*SAS Language and Procedures: Introduction, Version 6, First Edition* for a brief introduction; *SAS Language and Procedures: Usage, Version 6, First Edition* for a more thorough introduction; *SAS Language: Reference, Version 6, First Edition* and *SAS Procedures Guide: Version 6, Third Edition* for reference information on the SAS programs shown in this book.
manage files on your operating system	SAS documentation for your host operating system or vendor documentation for your system

HOW TO USE THIS BOOK

This section provides an overview of the information in this book and describes what you should read in particular situations.

Organization

This book begins with the changes and enhancements between Release 5.18 and Release 6.06 of the macro facility. The parts of the book contain a tutorial for the macro facility; background material on the macro language and reference entries for individual items in the language; a section on special topics for the advanced user; examples of utility macros; and appendices. Each of these parts is described briefly here.

Part 1: Introduction

This part contains a tutorial that introduces major parts of the macro facility. The structure proceeds from simple features to more advanced features. You can read part of the material, put what you need into practice, and read later parts of the material as you become more experienced.

Chapter 1, "A Macro Facility Overview"

Part 2:   Macro Facility Reference

This part contains reference information for features in the SAS macro facility. Chapters include the following:

Chapter 2, "Macro Variables"
Chapter 3, "Macro Program Statements"
Chapter 4, "Macro Functions"
Chapter 5, "Macro Windows"
Chapter 6, "DATA Step Interfaces"
Chapter 7, "The Autocall Facility"

Part 3:   Special Topics

This part introduces topics that are helpful in understanding the background of how the SAS System in general and the macro facility in particular process programs. The topics are intended for users who want to program more complex macro applications than those shown in this book.

Chapter 8, "How the SAS System Processes a Program"
Chapter 9, "Macro Compilation and Execution"
Chapter 10, "Macro Quoting"

Part 4:   Macro Applications

This part contains examples of macros that can be included in a toolkit for use in general programming.

Chapter 11, "Writing Utility Macros"

Part 5:   Appendices

Appendices include the following:

Appendix 1, "SAS System Options Used with the Macro Facility"
Appendix 2, "Reserved Words in the Macro Facility"
Appendix 3, "Macro Efficiency and Debugging"

What You Should Read

Depending on your level of experience with the macro facility, you should read different parts of this book first. The following table shows the experience levels and the suggested reading for users of that level.

If you are . . .	You should read . . .
an experienced macro user	the "Changes and Enhancements" section in the front of this book to find the summary of changes and enhancements for Release 6.06. You should then look at the reference chapters to find more details on the new features and overall explanations of the items you are interested in.
new to macro programming: experienced SAS programmer	Chapter 1, which serves as an overview of the macro facility; then the references indicated in the section **For More Information** at the end of each topic in Chapter 1. Then read Chapter 7, which describes a way to store the source code for macros and retrieve the macros as needed in your programs. Also read Chapter 11, which contains examples of useful macros.
new to macro programming: inexperienced SAS user	the introductory material and the section **MACRO VARIABLES** in Chapter 1 to use the simplest portion of the macro facility, macro variables. For background on macro variables, read **DEFINING MACRO VARIABLES** and the first part of **MACRO VARIABLE REFERENCES** in Chapter 2. Using more complex features depends on your understanding of DATA and PROC step processing. You can learn to use more features of the macro facility as your experience with the SAS System grows.

Reference Aids

SAS Guide to Macro Processing will be easier to use if you are familiar with the following features of the book. They are listed in order of appearance within the book:

inside front cover graphic
   illustrates the different parts of the SAS System, organized by function.

Contents
   lists the parts of the book, chapters, and their page numbers.

Illustrations
> lists the figures in the book and their page numbers.

Tables
> lists the titled tables and their page numbers.

Changes and Enhancements
> provides information about changes and new features in the macro facility between Releases 5.18 and 6.06.

chapter tables of contents
> give the titles and page numbers of main sections within chapters.

Glossary
> defines the major terms used in this book.

Index
> provides the page numbers where specific topics are discussed. Page ranges indicate discussions that cover several pages.

inside back cover graphic
> illustrates the parts of base SAS software and the major categories of features within each.

CONVENTIONS USED IN THIS BOOK

This section explains the various conventions used in presenting text, macro language syntax, file and library references, examples, and printed output in this book. The following terms are used in discussing syntax:

keyword
> is a literal that is a primary part of the macro language. (A literal must be spelled exactly as shown although it can be entered in uppercase or lowercase.) Keywords in this book include names of macro program statements, macro functions, and automatic variables.

argument
> is an element that follows a keyword. It is either literal or user-supplied. It has a built-in value or has a value assigned to it.
>
> Arguments that you must use are *required arguments*. Other arguments are *optional arguments*, or more simply, *options*.

value
> is an element that supplies a quantity for an argument. It may be a literal or a user-supplied value.

Typographical Conventions

SAS Guide to Macro Processing uses several styles of type and related conventions in presenting information. The following list explains the meaning of the conventions in general. Conventions used in presenting syntax appear in the following section.

roman
> is the standard type style used for most text in this book.

UPPERCASE ROMAN
> is used for literal and user-created elements of the macro language in text.

italic
> is used to define new terms and to emphasize important information.

`lowercase black monospace set off from the text`
> is used to show examples of macro language and SAS code entered by the user. (However, words that usually receive capital letters, such as words in titles, are capitalized.)

`UPPERCASE BLACK MONOSPACE SET OFF FROM THE TEXT`
> is used to show the way the SAS System sees code created by the user. (As a general rule, the SAS System changes all source statements entered to uppercase, except for values enclosed in single or double quotes.)

`RED MONOSPACE SET OFF FROM THE TEXT`
> is used to show code generated by the macro facility. (Because the code is shown at the point at which the SAS System sees it, most of the generated code appears in uppercase.)

`black monospace within text`
> is used to show the values of macro and DATA step character variables in text.

Although this book follows the conventions listed here, you can enter your own code in lowercase, uppercase, or a mixture of the two. In addition, the following conventions are used in referring to user-created elements of the macro language in text:

- Names of macro variables do not begin with an ampersand.
- Macro variable references begin with an ampersand.
- Names of macros do not begin with a percent sign.
- Macro invocations, by default, begin with a percent sign. (This type of macro invocation is also called a name-style invocation.)

The following examples illustrate these typographical conventions:

- The %MACRO statement begins the definition of a macro, assigns the macro a name, and optionally includes a parameter list of macro variables. A *macro invocation* causes the macro processor to begin executing a macro.
- The second %LET statement attaches the string `work.` to the value of DSN from the first %LET statement and assigns the result to the macro variable LONGNAME:

```
%let dsn=testdata;
%let longname=work.&dsname;
```

The value of LONGNAME is `work.testdata`.

- Suppose you enter the following program:

```
%let dsn=Newdata;
proc print data=&dsn;
   title "Subset of Data Set &dsn";
run;
```

DSN is the name of the macro variable, and `Newdata` is its value. The SAS System sees these statements:

```
PROC PRINT DATA=NEWDATA;
   TITLE "Subset of Data Set Newdata";
RUN;
```

Syntax Conventions

Type styles have special meanings when used in the presentation of macro language syntax in this book. The following list explains the style conventions for the syntax sections:

UPPERCASE BOLD
> identifies macro language keywords such as the names of statements and functions (for example, **%LET**).

UPPERCASE ROMAN
> identifies arguments and values that are literals and names of automatic macro variables (for example, %TO, GROUP=, SYSBUFFR).

italic
> identifies arguments or values that you supply. Items in italic can represent user-supplied values that are either
> - nonliteral values assigned to an argument (for example, GROUP=*group-definition*)
> - nonliteral arguments (for example, *keyword-parameter=value*).
>
> In addition, an item in italics can be the generic name for a list of arguments from which the user can choose (for example, *attribute-list*). If more than one of an item in italics can be used, the items are expressed as *item-1* through *item-n*.

The following symbols are also syntax conventions:

< > (angle brackets)
> identify optional arguments. Any argument not enclosed in angle brackets is required.

| (vertical bar)
> indicates that you can choose one item from a group. Items separated by bars are mutually exclusive.

. . . (ellipsis)
> indicates that the argument or group of arguments following the ellipsis can be repeated any number of times. If the ellipsis and the following argument are enclosed in angle brackets, they are optional.

The following examples illustrate the syntax conventions described in the preceding section. These examples contain selected syntax elements, not complete syntax.

- **%LET** *macro-variable=value;*
- **%MACRO** *name* <(*parameter-list*)> </ <STMT> <PARMBUFF>>;
- ATTR=*attribute* | (*attribute-1* <, . . .*attribute-n*>)

Conventions for Referencing SAS Data Libraries and External Files

Many SAS statements and other elements of the SAS language refer to SAS data libraries and external files. In Release 6.06 you can usually choose whether to make the reference through a logical name (a libref or fileref) or to use the physical file name enclosed in quotes. If you use a logical name, you usually have a choice of using a SAS statement (LIBNAME or FILENAME) or the operating system's control language to make the association. As a result, many methods of referring to SAS data libraries and external files are available, and some of them depend on the host operating system.

In examples that use external files, this book uses either of the following conventions:

- the italicized phrase *file-specification*. You should refer to the SAS documentation for your operating system for the rules for referencing external files on your host.
- a fileref. You should assume the fileref is assigned correctly for your host operating system.

Examples refer to SAS data libraries with one of these conventions:

- the phrase *SAS-data-library* in italics. You should refer to the SAS documentation for your operating system for the rules for assigning librefs under your host operating system.
- a two-level SAS data set name. You should assume the libref is assigned correctly for your host operating system.

Conventions for Examples and Output

Output in this book was produced using the following SAS system options:

- NODATE
- LINESIZE=76
- PAGESIZE=60
- NOSTIMER.

Programs that use only these options do not contain an OPTIONS statement. However, any program that uses other options or specifies different values for these options includes an appropriate OPTIONS statement.

Your output may differ from the output shown in the book if you run the example programs with different options or different values for those options.

ADDITIONAL DOCUMENTATION

SAS Institute provides many publications about products of the SAS System and how to use the SAS System on specific host operating systems. For a complete list of SAS publications, you should refer to the current *Publications Catalog*. The catalog is produced twice a year. You can order a free copy of the catalog by writing to

SAS Institute Inc.
Book Sales Department
SAS Campus Drive
Cary, NC 27513

Base SAS Software Documentation

You will find these other documents helpful when using base SAS software:

- *SAS Language: Reference, Version 6, First Edition* (order #A56076) provides detailed reference information about all portable aspects of the SAS language that are not procedures.
- *SAS Procedures Guide, Version 6, Third Edition* (order #A56080) provides detailed reference information about procedures in base SAS software.
- *SAS Language and Procedures: Usage, Version 6, First Edition* (order #A56075) provides task-oriented examples of the major features of base SAS software.

- SAS documentation for your host operating system provides information about the operating-system-specific features of the SAS System for your operating system.
- *SAS Language and Procedures: Introduction, Version 6, First Edition* (order #A56074) provides information for users who are unfamiliar with the SAS System or any other programming language

Documentation for Other SAS Software

The SAS System includes many software products in addition to the base SAS System. Several books that may be of particular interest to you are listed here:

- *SAS/ASSIST Software: Your Interface to the SAS System, Version 6, First Edition* (order #A56086) provides information on using the SAS System in a menu-driven windowing environment that requires no programming.

- *SAS/FSP Software: Usage and Reference, Version 6, First Edition* (order #A56001) provides information on using interactive procedures for creating SAS data sets and entering and editing data or for creating, editing, and printing form letters and reports.

- *SAS/AF Software: Usage and Reference, Version 6, First Edition* (order #A56011) provides information on building windows for your own applications.

- *SAS/GRAPH Software: Reference, Version 6, First Edition, Volume 1* and *Volume 2* (order #A56020) provides information on creating presentation graphics to illustrate relationships of data.

Changes and Enhancements

Introduction

This section summarizes the major changes and enhancements to the macro facility for Release 6.06 since Release 5.18. If you are familiar with the SAS macro facility, read this section to get an overview of the differences between Release 5.18 and Release 6.06.

Changes and enhancements are grouped here by chapter. The last section contains topics found only in the SAS documentation for your operating system. Complete information on any of these topics can be found in either the related chapter or in the SAS documentation for your operating system.

Note: Some of the features listed here are available in Release 6.03.

Chapter 2, Macro Variables

The following automatic macro variables are documented and available in Release 6.06:

SYSCMD	SYSLAST
SYSERR	SYSLIBRC
SYSINFO	SYSMSG

All automatic variables beginning with the prefix DMS in Release 5.18 are obsolete in Release 6.06.

Chapter 3, Macro Program Statements

There are four new macro program statements available in Release 6.06:

%DISPLAY   displays windows you define with the %WINDOW statement from within a macro or in an interactive SAS session.

%KEYDEF   redefines function keys from within a macro, in an interactive SAS session, or in open code.

%SYSEXEC   executes operating system commands from within a macro, in an interactive SAS session, or in open code.

%WINDOW   defines windows from within a macro, in an interactive SAS session, or in open code.

In Release 6.06, the macro processor does not allow command-style macro invocations. (You can use a name-style invocation for macros defined with the CMD option in the %MACRO statement in Release 5.18. Command-style invocations will be available in a future release of the SAS System.)

Chapter 4, Macro Functions

The following new functions are available:

%SUPERQ   removes the significance from all special characters, including ampersands, percent signs, and mnemonic operators. The %SUPERQ function was previously an autocall macro.

%SYSGET   returns the value of operating system variables and symbols from within a macro, in an interactive SAS session, or in open code. The %SYSGET function is described in the SAS documentation for your operating system.

The following Release 6.06 functions, in addition to performing the same tasks as in Release 5.18, now return values with the significance of mnemonic operators removed:

%BQUOTE
%NRBQUOTE
%QSCAN
%QUPCASE
%QSUBSTR

In Release 5.18, these functions did not affect the significance of mnemonic operators. As before, the %QUOTE and the %NRQUOTE functions remove the significance of mnemonic operators.

Chapter 6, DATA Step Interfaces

Function RESOLVE and call routine EXECUTE are not available in Release 6.06. They will both be implemented in a future release.

Chapter 7, The Autocall Facility

The autocall facility provides a more flexible means of specifying aggregate storage locations as autocall libraries with the SASAUTOS= system option. The syntax now accepts filerefs, quoted physical names, or a list containing both filerefs and quoted physical names in any order.

The %SUPERQ macro is now a macro function that works the same way the %SUPERQ autocall macro did in Release 5.18.

Chapter 10, Macro Quoting

In general, using macro quoting is easier in Release 6.06 than it was in Release 5.18. Quoting functions, and character functions that return quoted results, all quote mnemonic operators. You can use the %SUPERQ function, previously a SAS autocall macro, without specifying any autocall options.

Appendix 1, SAS System Options Used with the Macro Facility

The MLOGIC,* MPRINT, and SYMBOLGEN system options provide more information with greater clarity in Release 6.06. Using the MACROGEN system option is no longer necessary.

---

* The MLOGIC system option provides the same output in Release 6.06 as the MTRACE system option in Release 6.03.

The following SAS System options are obsolete in Release 6.06:

MLEAVE=	MSYMSIZE=
MSIZE=	MWORK=

The following SAS System options are obsolete in Release 6.06 but generate no warnings or errors if you specify them:

DQUOTE	MCOMPILE

The CMDMAC system option has no effect in Release 6.06 but will be implemented in a future release.

Features Documented Elsewhere

The following macro features do not appear in this guide because their behavior is operating system dependent:

- %CMS statement - see *SAS Companion for the CMS Environment, Version 6, First Edition*
- %TSO statement - see *SAS Companion for the MVS Environment, Version 6, First Edition*
- %SYSGET function - see the SAS documentation for your operating system.

The %CMS and the %TSO statements have no effect on operating systems other than CMS or MVS, respectively.

INTRODUCTION

A Macro Facility Overview

Chapter 1
A Macro Facility Overview

The *macro facility* is a tool for extending and customizing the SAS System and for reducing the amount of text you must enter to do common tasks. The macro facility allows you to package small or large amounts of text into units that have names. From that point on, you can work with the names rather than with the text itself.

When you use a macro facility name in a SAS program, the macro facility generates SAS statements and commands as needed. The rest of the SAS System receives those statements and commands and uses them in the same way it uses the ones you enter.

The macro facility has two components:

- the *macro processor* is the portion of the SAS System that does the work.
- the *macro language* is the language that you use to communicate with the macro processor. The macro language has variables, program statements, expressions, and functions—the same kinds of pieces that make up the SAS DATA step language. However, the macro language uses the patterns *%name* and *&name* to trigger macro processor activity.

This chapter introduces you to the parts of the macro facility and the way they work together. It moves from simple ideas to more complex ones. You do not need to read the entire chapter at once—you can stop at any point and use what you have learned. (Even simple macro facility features will help you extend your SAS programming.) When you are ready, resume reading the chapter to see how more advanced features fit in with what you have learned. At the end of each topic, you are directed to the reference chapter in Part II that covers the material in detail.

Contents

MACRO VARIABLES

Macro variables (sometimes called *symbolic variables*) belong to the SAS macro language and are different from DATA step variables. You can define and use macro variables anywhere in a SAS program, except within data lines. Whereas a DATA step variable is associated with a SAS data set, a macro variable is independent of a SAS data set. The value of a DATA step variable depends on the observation being processed, but a macro variable contains one value that remains constant until explicitly changed.

Defining a Macro Variable

The simplest way to define and assign a value to a macro variable is to use the macro program statement %LET, as in the following:

```
%let dsn=Newdata;
```

DSN is the name of the macro variable; macro variable names follow the rules for SAS names. **Newdata** is the value of the macro variable DSN. The value of a macro variable is simply a string of characters. The characters can include any letters, numbers, or printable symbols found on your keyboard (though some characters, such as unmatched quotes, require special treatment). The macro processor treats all characters alike; it does not make a distinction between character and numeric values as the rest of the SAS System does.*

Referring to a Macro Variable

To refer to the value of a macro variable, place an ampersand (&) in front of its name, as shown here:

```
&dsn
```

The pattern *&name* is called a *macro variable reference*. After you create a macro variable, you can reference it in SAS programs, as in the following:

```
%let dsn=Newdata;
title "Display of Data Set &dsn";
```

The macro processor resolves the reference by replacing &DSN with the value of DSN; the SAS System sees the following TITLE statement:

```
TITLE "Display of Data Set Newdata";
```

The title is enclosed in double quotes rather than single quotes because the macro processor resolves references in double quotes but not in single quotes. Note that the keyword TITLE is uppercase when the SAS System reads it,** but the title itself remains as you entered it. By default, the SAS System converts all input except data lines and items enclosed in quotes to uppercase before processing them.

---

* The %EVAL function, used explicitly or implicitly, assigns numeric properties to integers. See Chapter 4, "Macro Functions," for more information.

** The portion of the SAS System that sees the statement is usually the SAS compiler. The SAS compiler is discussed in Chapter 8, "How the SAS System Processes a Program."

Referring to a Macro Variable Several Times

You can refer to a macro variable as many times as you need to in a SAS program; the value remains constant until you change it. This program refers to macro variable DSN twice:

```
%let dsn=Newdata;
data temp;
   set &dsn;
   if age>=20;
run;

proc print;
   title "Subset of Data Set &dsn";
run;
```

Each time the reference &DSN appears, the macro processor replaces it with **Newdata**. Thus, the SAS System sees these statements:

```
DATA TEMP;
   SET NEWDATA;
   IF AGE>=20;
RUN;

PROC PRINT;
   TITLE "Subset of Data Set Newdata";
RUN;
```

Changing the Value of a Macro Variable

You can change the name of the SAS data set each time it occurs in the program simply by changing the value of the macro variable once:

```
%let dsn=In.Permdata;
data temp;
   set &dsn;
   if age>=20;
run;

proc print;
   title "Subset of Data Set &dsn";
run;
```

The SAS System now sees these statements:

```
DATA TEMP;
   SET IN.PERMDATA;
   IF AGE>=20;
RUN;

PROC PRINT;
   TITLE "Subset of Data Set In.Permdata";
RUN;
```

Creating Macro Variable Values Containing SAS Statements

You can create macro variable values that contain entire sections of a SAS program:

```
%let plot=%str(
   proc plot;
      plot income*age;
   run;
   );
```

In this case you enclose the value of the macro variable in the %STR function so that semicolons within the value are part of the text, not the end of the %LET statement.

You can reference the section later in the program as &PLOT, as shown here:

```
%let dsn=In.Permdata;
data temp;
   set &dsn;
   if age>=20;
run;

&plot

proc print;
   title "Subset of Data Set &dsn";
run;
```

After macro variable resolution, the SAS System sees these statements:

```
DATA TEMP;
   SET IN.PERMDATA;
   IF AGE>=20;
RUN;

PROC PLOT;
   PLOT INCOME*AGE;
RUN;

PROC PRINT;
   TITLE "Subset of Data Set In.Permdata";
RUN;
```

To execute the program without the PROC PLOT step, assign a *null value* to PLOT:

```
%let dsn=In.Permdata;
%let plot=;
data temp;
   set &dsn;
   if age>=20;
run;

&plot

proc print;
   title "Subset of Data Set &dsn";
run;
```

A null value has a length of 0, and the macro processor replaces a reference to a null value with 0 characters. The SAS System sees these statements:

```
DATA TEMP;
    SET IN.PERMDATA;
    IF AGE>=20;
RUN;


PROC PRINT;
    TITLE "Subset of Data Set In.Permdata";
RUN;
```

The two blank lines that separate the steps represent the two blank lines that surrounded the reference &PLOT in the program.

Nesting Macro Variable References

You can nest macro variable references to change a long macro variable value without redefining the variable. For example, if the plotting variables in the PROC PLOT step can change, replace them in the value of PLOT with macro variable references. Then assign the values in %LET statements:

```
%let dsn=In.Permdata;
%let yvar=income;
%let xvar=age;
%let plot=%str(
   proc plot;
       plot &yvar*&xvar;
   run;
   );
data temp;
   set &dsn;
   if age>=20;
run;

&plot

proc print;
   title "Subset of Data Set &dsn";
run;
```

After macro variable resolution, the SAS System sees these statements:

```
DATA TEMP;
    SET IN.PERMDATA;
    IF AGE>=20;
RUN;

PROC PLOT;
    PLOT INCOME*AGE;
RUN;

PROC PRINT;
    TITLE "Subset of Data Set In.Permdata";
RUN;
```

Displaying Macro Variable Values

The simplest way to display macro variable values is to use the %PUT statement, which writes text to the SAS log. For example, the statements

```
%let a=first;
%let b=macro variable;
%put &a !!!&b!!!;
```

write

```
first !!!macro variable!!!
```

For More Information

See Chapter 2, "Macro Variables," for a complete discussion of macro variables. See the sections **%LET Statement** and **%PUT Statement** in Chapter 3, "Macro Program Statements," for information on those statements.

MACROS

A *macro* is stored text identified by a name.* The simplest type of macro works much like a macro variable, but more complex macros can do many things that macro variables cannot.

Defining a Macro

Here is a very simple macro definition:

```
%macro dsn;
    Newdata
%mend dsn;
```

The %MACRO statement must begin every macro and must contain a name for the macro. Macro names follow the rules for SAS names; this macro is named DSN. `Newdata` is the text of the macro. A string inside a macro is called *constant text* or *model text* because it is the model, or pattern, for the text that becomes part of your SAS program. The %MEND statement must close every macro; this %MEND statement also repeats the macro name for clarity.

Invoking a Macro

To *invoke*, or *call*, a macro, place a percent sign (%) in front of its name, as shown here:

```
%dsn
```

The pattern *%macro-name* is called a *macro invocation* or a *macro call*. After you define a macro, you can invoke it in a SAS program, as in the following:

```
title "Display of Data Set %dsn";
```

The macro processor executes macro DSN, which substitutes the constant text in the macro into the TITLE statement. Thus, the TITLE statement becomes

```
TITLE "Display of Data Set Newdata";
```

(Notice that the title is enclosed in double quotes; the macro processor resolves macro invocations within double quotes but not within single quotes.)

---

* A macro is an entry in a utility catalog in the WORK library. The SAS System does not currently support copying or renaming macros.

A SAS program can contain any number of macros, and you can invoke a macro any number of times in a program. To change the text of a simple macro like DSN, simply redefine the macro. For simple text substitution, using a macro variable is more efficient than defining a macro. However, macros have advantages over macro variables as the tasks become more complex.

Creating Macros That Contain SAS Statements

You can create macros that contain entire sections of a SAS program:

```
%macro plot;
   proc plot;
      plot income*age;
   run;
%mend plot;
```

Later in the program you can invoke the macro as

```
data temp;
   set in.permdata;
   if age>=20;
run;

%plot

proc print;
run;
```

to produce these statements:

```
DATA TEMP;
   SET IN.PERMDATA;
   IF AGE>=20;
RUN;

PROC PLOT;
   PLOT INCOME*AGE;
RUN;

PROC PRINT;
RUN;
```

Changing Values within Macros

Suppose that the plotting variables in the PROC PLOT step can change. You can replace the names of the PLOT statement variables with macro variable references. Then supply the values in %LET statements before you call the macro:

```
%macro plot;
   proc plot;
      plot &yvar*&xvar;
   run;
%mend plot;

data temp;
   set in.permdata;
   if age>=20;
run;
```

```
%let yvar=income;
%let xvar=age;
%plot

%let xvar=yrs_educ;
%plot

proc print;
run;
```

The SAS System sees these statements:

```
DATA TEMP;
    SET IN.PERMDATA;
    IF AGE>=20;
RUN;

PROC PLOT;
    PLOT INCOME*AGE;
RUN;

PROC PLOT;
    PLOT INCOME*YRS_EDUC;
RUN;

PROC PRINT;
RUN;
```

For More Information

See the sections **Macro Invocations**, **%MACRO Statement**, and **%MEND Statement** in Chapter 3, "Macro Program Statements," for information on macro definitions.

MACRO PARAMETERS

Combining macro variables and macros gives you a powerful set of tools for macro facility programming. This section and the next one introduce more ways to use macro variables with macros.

Creating Parameters

As programs become longer, like the one in **Changing Values within Macros** earlier in this chapter, it becomes inconvenient to keep entering %LET statements. Therefore, define the macro variables as part of the %MACRO statement:

```
%macro plot(yvar,xvar);
    proc plot;
        plot &yvar*&xvar;
    run;
%mend plot;
```

A macro variable defined in parentheses in a %MACRO statement is a *macro parameter*. You give values to the parameters when you invoke the macro:

```
%plot(income,age)
```

The macro processor matches the first value to the first macro variable name, the second to the second, and so on. (Thus, these parameters are called *positional parameters*). Macro execution produces the following code:

```
PROC PLOT;
   PLOT INCOME*AGE;
RUN;
```

You can now invoke macro PLOT in the SAS program shown here:

```
data temp;
   set in.permdata;
   if age>=20;
run;


%plot(income,age)
%plot(income,yrs_educ)
```

As the macro processor executes the macros, the SAS System sees these statements:

```
DATA TEMP;
   SET IN.PERMDATA;
   IF AGE>=20;
RUN;


PROC PLOT;
   PLOT INCOME*AGE;
RUN;
PROC PLOT;
   PLOT INCOME*YRS_EDUC;
RUN;
```

Note: You assign values to both parameters each time you invoke PLOT, even though the value of YVAR does not change. However, the examples in **MACRO VARIABLES** earlier in this chapter reassigned a value to a macro variable only when the value changed. Why do you reassign the parameter values?

The value you assign to a parameter exists only during the current execution of the macro. Thus, for example, the next invocation of PLOT always assigns YVAR and XVAR the values in the new call. Macro parameters are an example of *local* macro variables. Macro variables that exist from the time you create them until the end of the SAS job or session, such as the ones shown earlier in **MACRO VARIABLES**, are *global* macro variables.

Using parameters has several advantages. First, you can write fewer %LET statements. Second, using parameters ensures that the variables never interfere with parts of your program outside the macro. In fact, in some cases you do not need to know the names of the parameters when you invoke the macro; you only need to know the kind of values to supply (in this case the value for the Y axis followed by the value for the X axis).

Assigning a Default Value to a Parameter

If the plotting variables in macro PLOT are usually INCOME and AGE, you can assign these default values when you create the parameters:

```
%macro plot(yvar=income,xvar=age);
   proc plot;
      plot &yvar*&xvar;
   run;
%mend plot;
```

To use the default values, invoke the macro as follows:

```
%plot()
```

The macro processor generates the following SAS code:

```
PROC PLOT;
   PLOT INCOME*AGE;
RUN;
```

To assign a new value, give the name of the parameter, an equal sign, and the value:

```
%plot(xvar=yrs_educ)
```

Because you do not change the value of YVAR, it retains its default value. Macro execution produces the following code:

```
PROC PLOT;
   PLOT INCOME*YRS_EDUC;
RUN;
```

A parameter defined with an equal sign is called a *keyword parameter* because you must give the keyword (the variable name and equal sign) along with the value. You can give values for keyword parameters in any order. If you define positional and keyword parameters for a macro, the positional parameters must come first, both in the %MACRO statement and in the macro call.

For More Information

See the **%MACRO Statement** and **Macro Invocations** in Chapter 3, "Macro Program Statements," for more information on macro parameters. The section **REFERENCING ENVIRONMENTS** in Chapter 2, "Macro Variables," discusses global and local macro variables.

MACROS WITH BRANCHING

The macros shown so far have generated statements that varied only because the value of a macro variable changed. In this section you learn other ways to change the text a macro generates.

Macros That Invoke Macros

Suppose you regularly create data set TEMP and produce a plot. You can put the DATA step into one macro and the PROC step into another macro, then nest both invocations inside a third macro. Be sure to include comments to document what you have done.

```
%macro create;
   data temp;
      set in.permdata;
      if age>=20;
   run;
%mend create;

%macro plot;
   proc plot;
      plot &yvar*&xvar;
   run;
%mend plot;
```

```
%macro analyze(yvar,xvar);
   %*create the data set;
   %create
   %*plot the variables selected;
   %plot
%mend analyze;
```

In macro ANALYZE, the statements that begin with %* are macro comment statements. They document each action that occurs within ANALYZE. As you write longer macros, it is important to document them.

After you have defined the macros, you can run the complete program by invoking ANALYZE:

```
%analyze(income,age)
```

The SAS System sees these statements:

```
DATA TEMP;
   SET IN.PERMDATA;
   IF AGE>=20;
RUN;
PROC PLOT;
   PLOT INCOME*AGE;
RUN;
```

If you need to change one of the other macros, such as CREATE, simply redefine it:

```
%macro create;
   data temp2;
      set in.permdata(obs=100);
      if age>=20;
   run;
%mend create;
```

Then invoke ANALYZE as before:

```
%analyze(income,age)
```

The SAS System sees the following new program:

```
DATA TEMP2;
   SET IN.PERMDATA(OBS=100);
   IF AGE>=20;
RUN;
PROC PLOT;
   PLOT INCOME*AGE;
RUN;
```

Constant Text in a Macro versus Nested Macro Invocations

Of course, you can put the entire program into macro ANALYZE instead of invoking other macros:

```
%macro analyze(yvar,xvar);
   data temp;
      set in.permdata;
      if age>=20;
   run;
   proc plot;
      plot &yvar*&xvar;
   run;
%mend analyze;
```

However, the advantage of defining CREATE and PLOT is that you can redefine and test each of them separately, before you invoke ANALYZE. In large macros, modular construction is important.

Conditional Execution

When you use macro ANALYZE, suppose that sometimes you need the DATA step in macro CREATE and sometimes you want to start with the PROC PLOT step. Define ANALYZE to use a %IF-%THEN statement:

```
%macro analyze(getdata,yvar,xvar);
   %if &getdata=yes %then %create;
   %plot
%mend analyze;
```

You can then use ANALYZE in a program such as this one:

```
%analyze(yes,income,age)
%analyze(no,income,yrs_educ)
```

Invoking ANALYZE generates this code:

```
DATA TEMP;
   SET IN.PERMDATA;
   IF AGE>=20;
RUN;
PROC PLOT;
   PLOT INCOME*AGE;
RUN;
PROC PLOT;
   PLOT INCOME*YRS_EDUC;
RUN;
```

When you assign GETDATA the lowercase value **yes**, as in the first invocation, the %IF condition is true, and the macro processor executes the %THEN clause. When the value of GETDATA is *anything other than* the lowercase string **yes**, as in the second call, the %IF condition is not true. (Note: This example uses the original version of macro CREATE, not the redefined version.)

Placing More Than One Item in a %THEN Clause

Suppose that when you create a data set with macro CREATE, you also want a title explaining that fact to appear on the third line of the plot. Thus, the %THEN clause contains both the invocation of CREATE and the TITLE3 statement. First,

you put a null TITLE statement at the beginning of ANALYZE to cancel any existing titles; then you enclose the macro call and the TITLE3 statement in a
%DO-%END group:

```
%macro analyze(getdata,yvar,xvar);
    title;
    %if &getdata=yes %then
        %do;
            %create
            title3 "Data Set Created for This Plot";
        %end;
    %plot
%mend analyze;
```

Now use these invocations:

```
%analyze(yes,income,age)
%analyze(no,income,yrs_educ)
```

They generate this program:

```
TITLE;
DATA TEMP;
    SET IN.PERMDATA;
    IF AGE>=20;
RUN;
TITLE3 "Data Set Created for This Plot";
PROC PLOT;
    PLOT INCOME*AGE;
RUN;
TITLE;
PROC PLOT;
    PLOT INCOME*YRS_EDUC;
RUN;
```

Comparisons between Uppercase and Lowercase Characters

In macro ANALYZE, the %IF statement allows you to choose whether to execute
macro CREATE to create the data set TEMP, as shown here:

```
%macro analyze(getdata,yvar,xvar);
    %if &getdata=yes %then %create;
    %plot
%mend analyze;
```

Suppose you invoke ANALYZE as follows:

```
%analyze(YES,INCOME,AGE)
```

This invocation generates the following SAS code:

```
PROC PLOT;
    PLOT INCOME*AGE;
RUN;
```

The macro processor does not invoke macro CREATE to create a data set
because the %IF condition contains the lowercase value **yes**, but you enter the
value of parameter GETDATA as the uppercase value **YES**. Therefore, the %IF
condition is

```
YES=yes
```

and the comparison is not true. To ensure that the comparison is made correctly, regardless of whether the invocation is typed in lowercase or uppercase, define ANALYZE as follows:

```
%macro analyze(getdata,yvar,xvar);
    %if %upcase(&getdata)=YES %then %create;
    %plot
%mend analyze;
```

The %UPCASE function converts lowercase text to uppercase. Now all of these calls cause the %IF condition to be true:

```
%analyze(yes,income,age)
%analyze(Yes,Income,Age)
%analyze(YES,INCOME,AGE)
```

Generating Repetitive Pieces of Text

Suppose you want to create a series of names to be used in a SAS statement such as a DATA or VAR statement. You can write a macro that generates a numbered series of names with a common prefix. The macro NAMES creates names in an iterative %DO loop:

```
%macro names(name,number);
    %do n=1 %to &number;
        &name&n
    %end;
%mend names;
```

Macro NAMES creates a series of names by concatenating the value of parameter NAME and the value of macro variable N. You supply the stopping value for N as the value of parameter NUMBER. Thus, invoking NAMES in the DATA statement

```
data %names(dsn,5);
```

produces the following complete DATA statement:

```
DATA DSN1 DSN2 DSN3 DSN4 DSN5;
```

   Note: You can also execute a %DO loop conditionally with %DO %WHILE and %DO %UNTIL statements.

Generating a Suffix for a Reference

Suppose that, when you generate a numbered series of names, you always want to put the letter X between the prefix and the number. Macro NAMESX inserts an X after the prefix you supply:

```
%macro namesx(name,number);
    %do n=1 %to &number;
        &name.x&n
    %end;
%mend namesx;
```

The period is a delimiter at the end of the reference &NAME. The macro processor uses the delimiter to distinguish the reference &NAME followed by the letter

X from the reference &NAMEX. Thus, invoking macro NAMESX in the DATA statement

```
data %namesx(dsn,3);
```

causes the SAS System to see this statement:

```
DATA DSNX1 DSNX2 DSNX3;
```

For More Information

Chapter 2, "Macro Variables," discusses using a period as a delimiter in a macro variable reference. Chapter 3, "Macro Program Statements," discusses the macro program statements shown here as well as other macro program statements. Chapter 4, "Macro Functions," discusses the %UPCASE function and other macro functions.

INPUT AND OUTPUT IN THE MACRO FACILITY

When you are working in a SAS session, you can have the macro facility prompt you at the terminal and accept your input. For example, suppose you want to decide, while macro ANALYZE is executing, whether to use macro CREATE to generate the DATA step. One method is to define ANALYZE as follows:

```
%macro analyze(yvar,xvar);
    %put Do you want to execute the DATA step?;
    %input getdata;
    %if %upcase(&getdata)=YES %then %create;
    %plot
%mend analyze;
```

Invoke ANALYZE:

```
%analyze(income,age)
```

The macro processor displays the following message and waits for your response:

```
Do you want to execute the DATA step?
```

You key in an answer:

```
yes
```

The macro processor assigns macro variable GETDATA the value **yes**. The macro processor then tests the value in the %IF condition and invokes macro CREATE to generate the statements needed. (This method is most useful in interactive line-oriented or noninteractive sessions.)

Another method is to create a macro window that prompts you and accepts your response. The following %WINDOW statement defines a macro window called ASKIT:

```
%window askit
        #10 @12 "Do you want to execute the DATA step?"
            @50 getdata 3 attr=underline
        #12 @12 "Press ENTER to continue.";
```

The window ASKIT displays the question and an underlined field for your response. To display ASKIT, define macro ANALYZEW to contain a %DISPLAY statement, as shown here:

```
%macro analyzew(yvar,xvar);
    %display askit;
    %if %upcase(&getdata)=YES %then %create;
    %plot
%mend analyzew;
```

Invoke ANALYZEW as you do ANALYZE:

```
%analyzew(income,age)
```

The macro processor displays the ASKIT window as shown in **Display 1.1** and waits for you to fill in the blank.

Display 1.1   Macro Window That Asks for Information

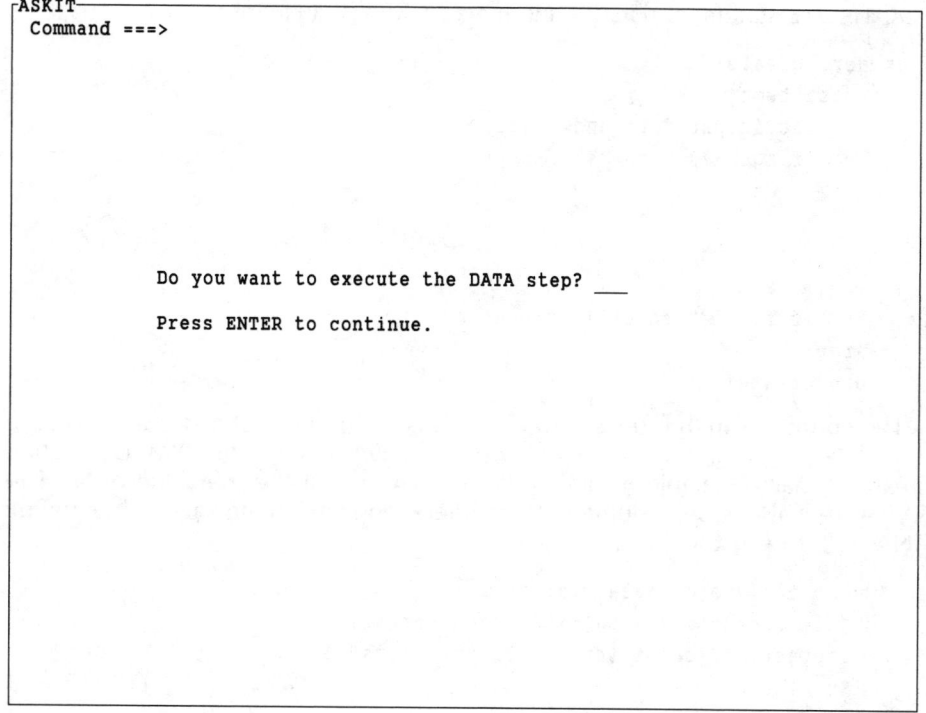

When you fill in the blank (for example, with **yes**), the macro processor assigns the value to macro variable GETDATA and continues executing macro ANALYZEW to generate the rest of the program.

Note: You can also place the %WINDOW statement inside macro ANALYZEW before the %DISPLAY statement. However, when you plan to invoke a window repeatedly, it is more efficient to define the window outside the macro that displays it. (In that case, the macro processor does not redefine the window each time you invoke the macro.)

For More Information

Chapter 3, "Macro Program Statements," describes the %INPUT, %PUT, %WINDOW, and %DISPLAY statements. Chapter 4, "Macro Functions," describes the %UPCASE function. Chapter 5, "Macro Windows," discusses creating and using macro windows in detail.

DATA STEP INTERFACES

Until this point, the examples have shown macro processor activity that takes place while the DATA or PROC step is being compiled (constructed), not while the step is executing. However, you can also program DATA steps that create macro variables based on values within the DATA step—that is, during DATA step execution.

Creating Macro Variables from DATA Step Values

Suppose you want to put the number of observations in a data set into a FOOTNOTE statement. First define macro CREATE as follows:

```
%macro create;
   data temp;
      set in.permdata end=final;
      if age>=20 then
         do;
            n+1;
            output;
         end;
      if final then call symput('number',n);
   run;
%mend create;
```

The counter N in the sum statement counts the number of observations in the new data set. During the last execution of the DATA step, the SYMPUT routine creates a macro variable named NUMBER whose value is the value of N. (The SAS System also issues a numeric-to-character conversion message.) Then define ANALYZE to use CREATE as follows:

```
%macro analyze(getdata,yvar,xvar);
   %if %upcase(&getdata)=YES %then %create;
   footnote "Plot of &number Observations";
   %plot
%mend analyze;
```

The macro call

```
%analyze(yes,income,age)
```

generates this program:

```
DATA TEMP;
   SET IN.PERMDATA END=FINAL;
   IF AGE>=20 THEN
      DO;
         N+1;
         OUTPUT;
      END;
   IF FINAL THEN CALL SYMPUT('NUMBER',N);
   RUN;
```

```
FOOTNOTE "Plot of          26 Observations";
PROC PLOT;
   PLOT INCOME*AGE;
RUN;
```

The number of observations appears in the FOOTNOTE statement, but there is a problem: the value of NUMBER is shifted to the right because the SYMPUT routine writes the value of N using the BEST12. format. To left-align the value, use the LEFT function in the SYMPUT routine:

```
%macro create;
   data temp;
      set in.permdata end=final;
      if age>=20 then
         do;
            n+1;
            output;
         end;
      if final then call symput('number',left(n));
   run;
%mend create;
```

Now the same program generates this FOOTNOTE statement:

```
FOOTNOTE "Plot of 26 Observations";
```

Note: This example assumes that the value of GETDATA is **YES** the first time you call macro ANALYZE; thus, macro CREATE generates the data set TEMP and determines the number of observations in it.

For More Information

Chapter 6, "DATA Step Interfaces," describes the SYMPUT routine. The same chapter describes the SYMGET function, which retrieves a macro variable's value during DATA step execution rather than while the SAS System is constructing the DATA step.

ADDITIONAL TOPICS

This section describes some additional features that do not require detailed introduction. Each example points you to the reference section that describes the topic.

Automatic Macro Variables

Base SAS software provides several *automatic macro variables* that are available in every SAS program. You can refer to them anywhere in the program. For example, to put today's date into a TITLE statement, write the following:

```
title "Report for &sysdate";
```

SYSDATE is an automatic macro variable that contains the current date in DATE7. format. If you run the program on October 17, 1990, the SAS System sees this TITLE statement:

```
TITLE "Report for 17OCT90";
```

Chapter 2 describes automatic macro variables.

Additional Macro Functions

The macro facility contains many functions not described in this chapter. For example, the %SUBSTR function creates a substring of another string. Suppose you want to create a SAS data set whose name is the day of the week. The automatic macro variable SYSDAY gives the day on which the SAS program began execution, but the name Wednesday is too long for a SAS name. Therefore you decide to produce a three-character abbreviation of SYSDAY with the %SUBSTR function, as shown here:

```
data %substr(&sysday,1,3);
```

Depending on the day of the week, the DATA statement becomes

```
DATA MON;
```

```
DATA TUE;
```

```
DATA WED;
```

and so on.

Chapter 4 describes the functions in the macro facility.

Macros That Generate Display Manager Commands

When you are working in the SAS Display Manager System, you can have macros that generate display manager commands as well as those that generate SAS statements. For example, suppose that when you recall previously submitted statements into the PROGRAM EDITOR window, you want to zoom the window to fill the entire display. The following macro issues the ZOOM ON and RECALL commands:

```
%macro rz;
   zoom on; recall;
%mend rz;
```

Invoke macro RZ from the command line of the PROGRAM EDITOR window:

```
%rz
```

The macro processor submits these display manager commands:

```
ZOOM ON; RECALL;
```

For additional convenience, you can assign the macro invocation to a function key with the display manager KEYS window, the display manager KEYDEF command, or the %KEYDEF statement.

See Chapter 3 for information on the %KEYDEF statement. See *SAS Language: Reference, Version 6, First Edition* for information on the SAS Display Manager System.

MACRO
FACILITY
REFERENCE

Macro Variables

Macro Program Statements

Macro Functions

Macro Windows

DATA Step Interfaces

The Autocall Facility

Chapter 2

Macro Variables

Macro variables (also called *symbolic variables*) are part of the SAS macro language; they are different from DATA step variables. You can define and use macro variables anywhere in a SAS program, except within data lines. Whereas the value of a DATA step variable depends on the observation being processed, a macro variable has a single value that remains constant until explicitly changed.

You can define any number of macro variables in a program. Base SAS software also provides some automatic macro variables whose names begin with the letters SYS. Those variables are described in **AUTOMATIC MACRO VARIABLES** in this chapter. In addition, some other products in the SAS System provide automatic macro variables; those variables are described in the documentation for the product that uses them.

Contents

Tables

Figures

DEFINING MACRO VARIABLES

You can define a macro variable in several ways. For simplicity, this chapter concentrates on macro variables created with the %LET statement. However, the principles discussed here apply to all macro variables, regardless of how you create them. The following list shows the macro facility features that can create macro variables:

> iterative %DO statement
> %GLOBAL statement
> %INPUT statement
> %LET statement
> %LOCAL statement
> %MACRO statement
> SYMPUT routine
> %WINDOW statement

All of these features except the SYMPUT routine are discussed in Chapter 3, "Macro Program Statements." The SYMPUT routine is discussed in Chapter 6, "DATA Step Interfaces."

Creating Macro Variables

The simplest way to create and assign a value to a macro variable is to use the macro program statement %LET, as in

%LET *name*=<*value*>;

where

> *name*   follows the rules for SAS names. *Name* must have a length of one to eight characters and must begin with a letter or underscore. The remainder of *name* can only be letters, numbers, and underscores.

> *value*   is any string or macro expression. *Value* can represent text to be generated or to be used by the macro processor. The value can range in length from 0 bytes up to the amount of memory currently available to the SAS System. If you omit *value*, the value is null (0 characters). Leading and trailing blanks are not stored with the value; **Some Special Cases** later in this chapter shows how to store them.
>
>   To retrieve the value of a macro variable, use a *macro variable reference*, that is, the pattern &*name*. (Macro variable references are described in **MACRO VARIABLE REFERENCES** later in this chapter.) In a few special cases, you may need the DATA step function SYMGET (described in Chapter 6) for a specific application.

You can use a %LET statement at any point in a SAS program, either inside a macro or in open code, except within data lines. You can use some other methods only in particular situations; for example, you must define a macro parameter as part of the %MACRO statement.

Assigning Values to Macro Variables

The following examples show how the macro processor assigns values to macro variables.

Constant Text

In the following statement, the value is a simple string:

```
%let street=maple;
```

You can also write this statement in the following ways:

```
%let street=          maple          ;
%let street=
            maple;
```

In each case, the macro processor stores the five-character value **maple** as the value of STREET.

The following example assigns the three-character string **123**:

```
%let num=123;
```

Likewise, this statement assigns the seven-character string **100+200**:

```
%let tot=100+200;
```

The macro processor does not treat **123** as a number or evaluate the expression **100+200**. The macro processor treats digits, characters, and other keyboard symbols alike: it handles them as strings. To treat digits temporarily as numbers (for example, to produce the sum of 100 and 200), use the %EVAL function (described in Chapter 4, "Macro Functions.")

Null Value

The following statement assigns CITY the value of null, that is, zero characters:

```
%let city=;
```

Macro Expressions

In the following program, the third %LET statement contains references to the values of macro variables NUM and STREET (&NUM and &STREET) and some additional text:

```
%let street=maple;
%let num=123;
%let address=&num &street avenue;
```

The macro processor attempts to resolve macro expressions before it makes the assignment. Thus, the macro processor stores the value of ADDRESS as **123 maple avenue**.

This example contains the %SCAN function, which retrieves the *n*th word (second argument) from the source (first argument):

```
%let frstword=%scan(&address,1);
```

Because the macro processor executes the function before it stores the value, the macro processor stores the value of FRSTWORD as **123**. (The %SCAN function is discussed in Chapter 4.)

Some Special Cases

The following examples show some special kinds of values and how to assign them:

```
%let state=%str(   North Carolina);
%let town=%str(Taylor%'s Pond);
%let title=%str(title "Survey of North Carolina";);
```

The value of STATE is stored with leading blanks, the value of TOWN is stored with an unmatched quote, and the value stored for TITLE contains a complete SAS statement.

All these values use the %STR function, which treats special characters such as the semicolon as text. The macro processor does not store the characters %STR() or the percent sign beside the quote in `Taylor's Pond` as part of the value; it simply marks the value internally as needed. See Chapter 4 for a description of the %STR function.

The next section shows how to use the value of a macro variable; **REFERENCING ENVIRONMENTS** later in this chapter shows how a macro variable's referencing environment affects the way you use it.

MACRO VARIABLE REFERENCES

The most common way to use the value of a macro variable is through a *macro variable reference*. (The other way is the SYMGET function in the DATA step.) Replacing a macro variable reference with the value of the macro variable is known as *resolving a macro variable reference* or *symbolic substitution*.

Using Simple Macro Variable References

The simplest type of macro variable reference consists of an ampersand and a macro variable name, as in

&name

When the macro processor encounters a macro variable reference, it retrieves the value of that macro variable and replaces the reference with that variable's value.

Suppose you have these statements:

```
%let vname=Price;
title "Study of &vname over Time";
```

When the macro processor encounters the reference &VNAME, it searches its macro variable storage areas, called *symbol tables*, for the variable VNAME and replaces &VNAME with `Price`. The SAS System sees this statement:

```
TITLE "Study of Price over Time";
```

Note: The macro processor resolves macro variable references within double quotes; it does not resolve references within single quotes or in SAS comment statements.

If you assign a new value to VNAME, the new value replaces the old one, and the macro processor retrieves the new value. The statements

```
%let vname=Tax Total;
title "Study of &vname over Time";
```

produce this TITLE statement:

```
TITLE "Study of Tax Total over Time";
```

If the value of the variable is null, the macro processor replaces the reference with 0 characters. The statements

```
%let vname=;
title "Study of &vname over Time";
```

produce this TITLE statement:

```
TITLE "Study of  over Time";
```

The two blanks between OF and OVER are the blanks that surrounded the reference &VNAME.

What if you reference a macro variable that has not been defined? For example, consider these statements:

```
%let vname=Price;
title "Study of &vnam over Time";
```

You defined variable VNAME, but because of a typing error you reference VNAM. If the macro processor cannot locate a macro variable that has been referenced, it leaves the reference unresolved and allows the reference to pass into the rest of the SAS System. Thus, the TITLE statement becomes the following:

```
TITLE "Study of &vnam over Time";
```

In addition, the macro processor generates the message

```
WARNING: Apparent symbolic reference VNAM not resolved.
```

If a macro variable reference passes unresolved into a SAS statement or command, the reference usually causes a syntax error (because few SAS statements or commands accept the ampersand). These are the most common causes of an unresolvable reference:

- referring to the variable before you define it.
- misspelling the variable name.
- having text in the program that looks like a macro variable reference but is not, as in WASHENKO&JONES.
- referring to a macro variable created by the SYMPUT routine before that variable is available. (The SYMPUT routine is discussed in Chapter 6.)

Combining Macro Variable References with Prefixes and Suffixes

Suppose you keep track of the SAS data sets in your programs by giving them related names. For example, in a program about sales figures you use SALES as part of all the data set names, as shown here:

```
data newsales;
   set save.sales;
   if units>100;
run;
```

You decide to write a program with macro variable references representing the common element so that you can change all the data set names with a single %LET statement. You write this new program:

```
%let name=sales;
data new&name;
   set save.&name;
   if units>100;
run;
```

After macro variable resolution, the SAS System sees these statements:

```
DATA NEWSALES;
   SET SAVE.SALES;
   IF UNITS>100;
RUN;
```

The macro processor resolves the reference &NAME into **SALES** so that the data set names become NEWSALES and SAVE.SALES. Notice that you do not have to use a concatenation operator with macro variable references as you do in the DATA step; the SAS System forms the resulting words automatically.

Now you need another DATA step that uses the names SALES1, SALES2, and INSALES.TEMP. You add the following step to the program:

```
*first attempt to add suffixes;
data &name1 &name2;
   set in&name.temp;
   if status='ok' then output &name1;
   else output &name2;
run;
```

After macro variable resolution, the SAS System sees these statements:

```
DATA &NAME1 &NAME2;
   SET INSALESTEMP;
   IF STATUS='OK' THEN OUTPUT &NAME1;
   ELSE OUTPUT &NAME2;
RUN;
```

None of the macro variable references have resolved as you intended. The macro processor issues warning messages, and the SAS System issues syntax error messages. Why?

Because NAME1 and NAME2 are valid SAS names, the macro processor searches for those macro variables rather than for NAME, and the references pass into the DATA statement without resolution.

To cause the macro processor to recognize the end of the word NAME, use a period as a delimiter between &NAME and the suffix, as shown here:

```
data &name.1 &name.2;
```

The SAS System now sees this statement:

```
DATA SALES1 SALES2;
```

In the SET statement, the macro processor treats &NAME. as a reference ending in a delimiter and resolves the reference into **SALES**. The SAS System concatenates IN, SALES, and TEMP into the single name INSALESTEMP.

Because the macro processor uses a period after a reference as a delimiter, put another period after the delimiter to produce a period in the text, as shown here:

```
set in&name..temp;
```

After macro variable resolution, the SAS System sees this statement:

```
SET INSALES.TEMP;
```

Therefore, the correct DATA step is as follows:

```
*correct way to add suffixes;
data &name.1 &name.2;
   set in&name..temp;
   if status='ok' then output &name.1;
   else output &name.2;
run;
```

After macro variable resolution, the SAS System sees these statements:

```
DATA SALES1 SALES2;
   SET IN SALES.TEMP;
   IF STATUS='OK' THEN OUTPUT SALES1;
   ELSE OUTPUT SALES2;
RUN;
```

You can end any macro variable reference with a delimiter, but the delimiter is necessary only if the characters that follow can be part of a SAS name. For example either of the TITLE statements

```
title "&name.--a report";
title "&name--a report";
```

produce this statement:

```
TITLE "sales--a report";
```

Using Indirect Macro Variable References

The macro variable references shown so far have begun with one ampersand: &name. This section discusses indirect references, which begin with more than one ampersand. It is also closely related to the next section, **Scanning Macro Variable References**.

Using a Double Ampersand

The double ampersand (&&) is a special reference that always resolves into a single ampersand. For example, consider these statements:

```
%let c=compare;
%put &c &&c;
```

The macro processor resolves the first reference into **COMPARE**. In the second reference, the macro processor resolves && into & and then scans the letter C. Next, because the macro processor always rescans an item resulting from a resolution, it scans &C and resolves the reference. The %PUT statement writes the following:

```
compare compare
```

Using a double ampersand at the beginning of a simple macro variable reference produces the same result as using a single ampersand. However, the macro processor scans the reference twice. In particular situations, the second scan is necessary.

Generating a Series of Macro Variable References

Suppose you have five groups of data set names in your program. You define each set as the value of a macro variable, as shown here:

```
%let d1=jan feb mar;
%let d2=apr may jun;
%let d3=jul aug sep;
%let d4=oct;
%let d5=nov;
```

For most of the program, you work with one or another group of data sets, and you reference the macro variable that contains those names as needed. Finally you use all five sets at once, as shown here:

```
data dec;
    set &d1 &d2 &d3 &d4 &d5;
run;
```

After macro variable resolution, the SAS System sees these statements:

```
DATA DEC;
    SET JAN FEB MAR APR MAY JUN JUL AUG SEP OCT NOV;
RUN;
```

You decide to write a macro with an iterative %DO loop that generates all those references with a single macro call. First you write macro NUM as follows:

```
%macro num;
    %*first try--incorrect;
    %do i=1 %to 5;
        &d&i
        %end;
    %mend num;
```

The index variable of the iterative %DO loop is a macro variable named I that takes on the values 1 to 5, depending on the iteration of the loop. When you call NUM in the SAS program

```
data dec;
    set %num;
run;
```

the SAS System sees these statements:

```
DATA DEC;
    SET &D1 &D2 &D3 &D4 &D5;
RUN;
```

The macro processor issues warning messages that a symbolic reference was not resolved, and SAS issues error messages for invalid data set names. Why did the references not resolve?

In each execution of the %DO loop, the macro processor first encounters the reference &D. Because no macro variable named D exists, the macro processor releases the reference and issues a warning message. Then the macro processor encounters &I, resolves it into its current value, and releases it. The macro processor never sees a complete reference such as &D1 and therefore never searches for macro variable D1.

To cause the macro processor both to generate the reference and to resolve it, you must cause the macro processor to scan the text twice. Begin the text inside the %DO loop with a double ampersand, as shown here:

```
%macro num2;
   %*second try--correct;
   %do i=1 %to 5;
      &&d&i
      %end;
   %mend num2;
```

When you call NUM2, the macro processor first resolves the double ampersand into a single ampersand; then it scans and holds D as constant text; and then it resolves &I into its current value. The result is &D1, for example, as before. However, the macro processor makes an additional scan of all text changed in the preceding scan. Thus, in the second scan, the macro processor encounters the reference &D1 and resolves it. Calling macro NUM2 in your program

```
data dec;
   set %num2;
run;
```

produces the correct names, as follows:

```
DATA DEC;
   SET JAN FEB MAR APR MAY JUN JUL AUG SEP OCT NOV;
RUN;
```

Using a Triple Ampersand

You can read a reference beginning with three ampersands as a double ampersand followed by another macro variable reference. For example, consider these statements:

```
%let d=data;
%let data=datayr90;
data &&&d;
```

The macro processor first resolves the initial && into &; then it resolves &D into **DATA**. The result is the reference &DATA. The macro processor then rescans all text generated in the preceding scan and resolves &DATA into **DATAYR90**. The DATA statement becomes the following:

```
DATA DATAYR90;
```

Using a triple ampersand increases the efficiency of the macro processor in some cases, as described below.

Storing Only One Copy of a Long Macro Variable Value

Because macro variables can have very long values, the way you store macro variables can affect the efficiency of a program. Indirect references using three ampersands enable you to store fewer copies of a long value.

For example, suppose your program contains long macro variable values that represent sections of SAS programs, as shown here:

```
%let pgm=%str(data flights;
             set schedule;
             totmiles=sum(of miles1-miles20);
          proc print;
             var flightid totmiles;);
```

Because you want the SAS program to end with a RUN statement, you write macro CHECK:

```
%macro check(val);
   %*first version;
   &val
   %if %index(&val,%str(run;))=0 %then %str(run;);
%mend check;
```

First, macro CHECK generates the program statements in the value of parameter VAL (a macro variable defined in the %MACRO statement). Then the %INDEX function searches the value of VAL for the characters **run;**. (The %STR function treats the semicolon as text.) If the characters are not present, the %INDEX function returns a 0. The %IF condition becomes true, and the macro processor generates a RUN statement. To use macro CHECK with variable PGM, assign parameter VAL the value of PGM as follows:

```
%check(&pgm)
```

As a result, the SAS System sees these statements:

```
DATA FLIGHTS;
   SET SCHEDULE;
   TOTMILES=SUM(OF MILES1-MILES20);
PROC PRINT;
   VAR FLIGHTID TOTMILES;
RUN;
```

Macro CHECK works properly. However, the macro processor assigns the value of PGM as the value of VAL during the execution of CHECK. Thus, the macro processor must store two long values (the value of PGM and the value of VAL) while CHECK is executing. To make the program more efficient, write the macro so that it uses the value of PGM rather than copying the value into VAL, as shown here:

```
%macro check2(val);
   %*second version;
   &&&val
   %if %index(&&&val,%str(run;))=0 %then %str(run;);
%mend check2;
```

You call CHECK2:

```
%check2(pgm)
```

The result is the same as with CHECK; the program becomes the following:

```
DATA FLIGHTS;
   SET SCHEDULE;
   TOTMILES=SUM(OF MILES1-MILES20);
PROC PRINT;
   VAR FLIGHTID TOTMILES;
RUN;
```

However, the value you assign to VAL is simply the name **PGM**, not the value of PGM. The macro processor resolves &&&VAL into &PGM and then into the value of PGM (the SAS statements). Thus, the long value is stored only once.

Using More Than Three Ampersands

You can use any number of ampersands in a macro variable reference, although using more than three is rare. If you need more than three, just remember that the macro processor resolves two ampersands into one ampersand and rescans all text generated in the preceding scan.

Scanning Macro Variable References

When you use macro variable references as part of longer strings, you need to understand how the macro processor decides when to stop scanning a reference and when to rescan the result. The macro processor uses a technique called *forward scan*.

Consider the reference &&D&I from the preceding section:

```
%let d1=jan feb mar;
%let d2=apr may jun;
%let d3=jul aug sep;
%let d4=oct;
%let d5=nov;
%macro num2;
    %do i=1 %to 5;
        &&d&i
        %end;
    %mend num2;
```

In each iteration of the %DO loop, the macro processor reads && and generates &; reads and generates the constant text D; and reads and generates the current value of I, for example, **1**.

Once the macro processor encounters the pattern &*name* (or the special case &&), it continues scanning and resolving references as far as possible (generally to a special character such as a blank or a semicolon). When the macro processor reaches the end, it makes a new scan, beginning with the first item resolved in the previous scan and continuing to the end. If it resolves references during the second scan, it makes a third scan, beginning with the first item resolved in the second scan, and so forth. When a scan does not produce any changes, the resolution is complete. **Figure 2.1** illustrates this process.

Scan	Text	Result
1	&&d&i	&d1
2	&d1	jan feb mar
3	jan feb mar	no change; complete

Figure 2.1   Scanning Process

Although the most common characters that end the macro processor's forward scan are the blank and semicolon, any character that cannot be part of a SAS name (or that cannot resolve into part of a SAS name) stops the scan.* For example, consider these statements:

```
%let x=jan;
%let y=1990;
data &x&y(keep=score);
```

* The end of a macro's execution also stops forward scan.

The macro processor resolves &X into **JAN** and continues scanning with &Y. Although an ampersand cannot be part of a SAS name, it can indicate a reference that resolves into a SAS name; thus, the macro processor continues to scan and resolves &Y into **1990**. However, a parenthesis cannot be part of a SAS name; thus, the forward scan ends at the parenthesis. The DATA statement becomes the following:

```
DATA JAN1990(KEEP=SCORE);
```

REFERENCING ENVIRONMENTS

Every SAS program has one or more referencing environments. A *referencing environment* is the area in which a macro variable is available for use. Referencing environments are important because they determine when macro variables are available, and thus whether the macro processor can locate a macro variable that your program references.

Types of Referencing Environments

You can think of referencing environments as large areas completely surrounding progressively smaller areas. The largest, outermost referencing environment is the *global referencing environment*, that is, the entire SAS job or session. The global environment contains macro variables created outside of any macro, macro variables created in %GLOBAL statements, automatic macro variables (discussed in **AUTOMATIC MACRO VARIABLES** later in this chapter), and most macro variables created by the DATA step SYMPUT routine (discussed in **Creating a Variable with the SYMPUT Routine** later in this chapter and in Chapter 6). The global environment and the macro variables in it exist for the duration of the SAS job or session.

Each macro you invoke creates its own *local referencing environment*. The local referencing environment is empty until the macro creates a macro variable (except with a %GLOBAL statement). Likewise, each macro invocation nested within that macro creates a local environment that is empty until that macro creates a macro variable (except with a %GLOBAL statement). Because any number of macro invocations can be nested, a program can contain any number of levels of nested referencing environments. A local environment and the macro variables within it last only as long as the macro executes; when the macro stops executing, that environment ceases to exist.

The environment in which macro activity is currently occurring is the *current referencing environment*.

How the Macro Processor Uses Referencing Environments

The macro processor uses referencing environments according to the following rules:

- When executing macro program statements that can create macro variables, the macro processor attempts to change the value of an existing macro variable, regardless of environment, rather than creating a new macro variable. The %GLOBAL and %LOCAL statements are exceptions.
- When executing macro program statements that can create macro variables, the macro processor creates the variable in the current environment if no macro variable with the same name is available to it.
- The %GLOBAL statement creates a variable in the global environment if a variable with the same name does not already exist there, regardless of which environment is current.

- The %LOCAL statement and macro parameters create macro variables in the current local environment if no variables with the same names already exist there, even if variables with those names exist in other environments.
- The SYMPUT routine in the DATA step and certain types of %GOTO destinations are special cases.

The following sections discuss each of these rules in detail.

Using an Existing Variable

When the macro processor executes a macro program statement that can create a macro variable (such as a %LET statement), it searches the current referencing environment first and then all other existing environments for a macro variable of that name. If it finds one, it changes the value of that variable rather than creating a new variable.

The macro processor first searches the current environment; then the next most recently created environment; then the next most recently created one; and so on. For example, suppose you have two %LET statements that assign values to macro variable NEW:

```
%let new=inventry;
%macro name1;
   %let new=report;
%mend name1;
```

The program

```
%name1
```

```
data &new;
```

causes the SAS System to see the following:

```
DATA REPORT ;
```

When the macro processor encounters the %LET statement during the execution of NAME1, it searches the current environment (the local environment of NAME1) without finding a variable named NEW. Then it searches the next most recently created environment (in this case the global environment). Because NEW exists in the global environment, the macro processor changes the value of that variable rather than creating a new one. Macro NAME1's local environment remains empty. **Figure 2.2** illustrates the environments that exist before, during, and after NAME1's execution.

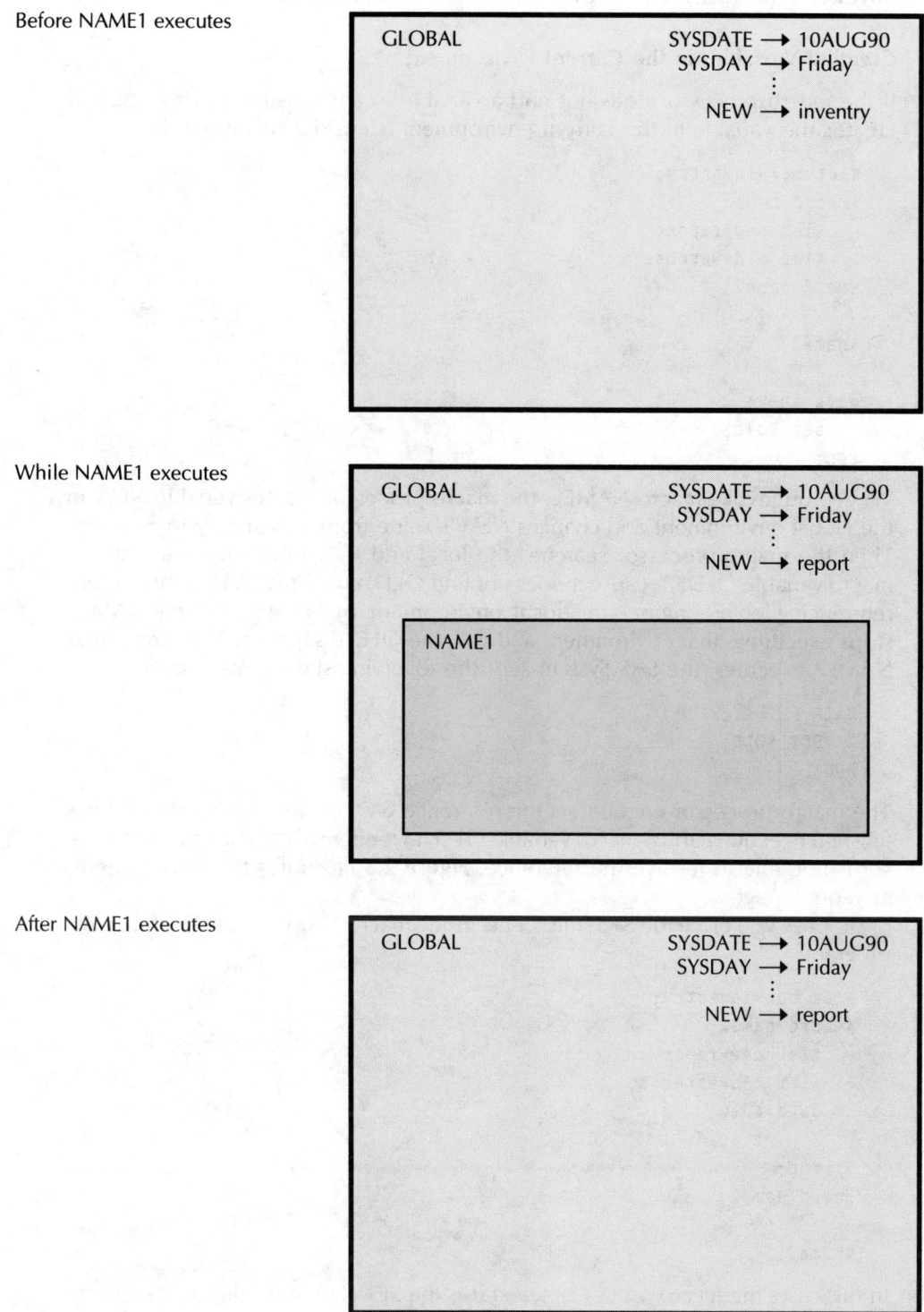

Figure 2.2 Snapshots of Referencing Environments

SYSDATE and SYSDAY are automatic macro variables; see **AUTOMATIC MACRO VARIABLES** later in this chapter for information on them.

Creating Variables in the Current Environment

If the macro processor does not find a variable in any existing environment, it creates the variable in the current environment. Consider this example:

```
%let new=inventry;
%macro name2;
    %let new=report;
    %let old=warehse;
%mend name2;

%name2

data &new;
    set &old;
run;
```

When you invoke macro NAME2, the macro processor locates variable NEW in the global environment and changes NEW's value from **inventry** to **report**. Then the macro processor searches the local and the global environments for macro variable OLD. Because it does not find OLD, it creates OLD in the current referencing environment—the local environment of NAME2. When NAME2 stops executing, that environment and variable OLD disappear. Therefore, after NAME2 executes, the SAS System sees the following statements:

```
DATA REPORT;
    SET &OLD;
RUN;
```

The macro processor encounters the reference &OLD after macro NAME2 has finished executing; thus, macro variable OLD no longer exists. The macro processor is not able to resolve the reference. **Figure 2.3** illustrates the environments at various stages.

Suppose you place the SAS statements inside macro NAME2, as in the following program:

```
%let new=inventry;
%macro name2;
    %let new=report;
    %let old=warehse;
    data &new;
        set &old;
    run;
%mend name2;

%name2
```

In this case, the macro processor generates the SET statement during the execution of NAME2, and it locates OLD in NAME2's local environment. Therefore, macro execution causes the SAS System to see the following:

```
DATA REPORT;
    SET WAREHSE;
RUN;
```

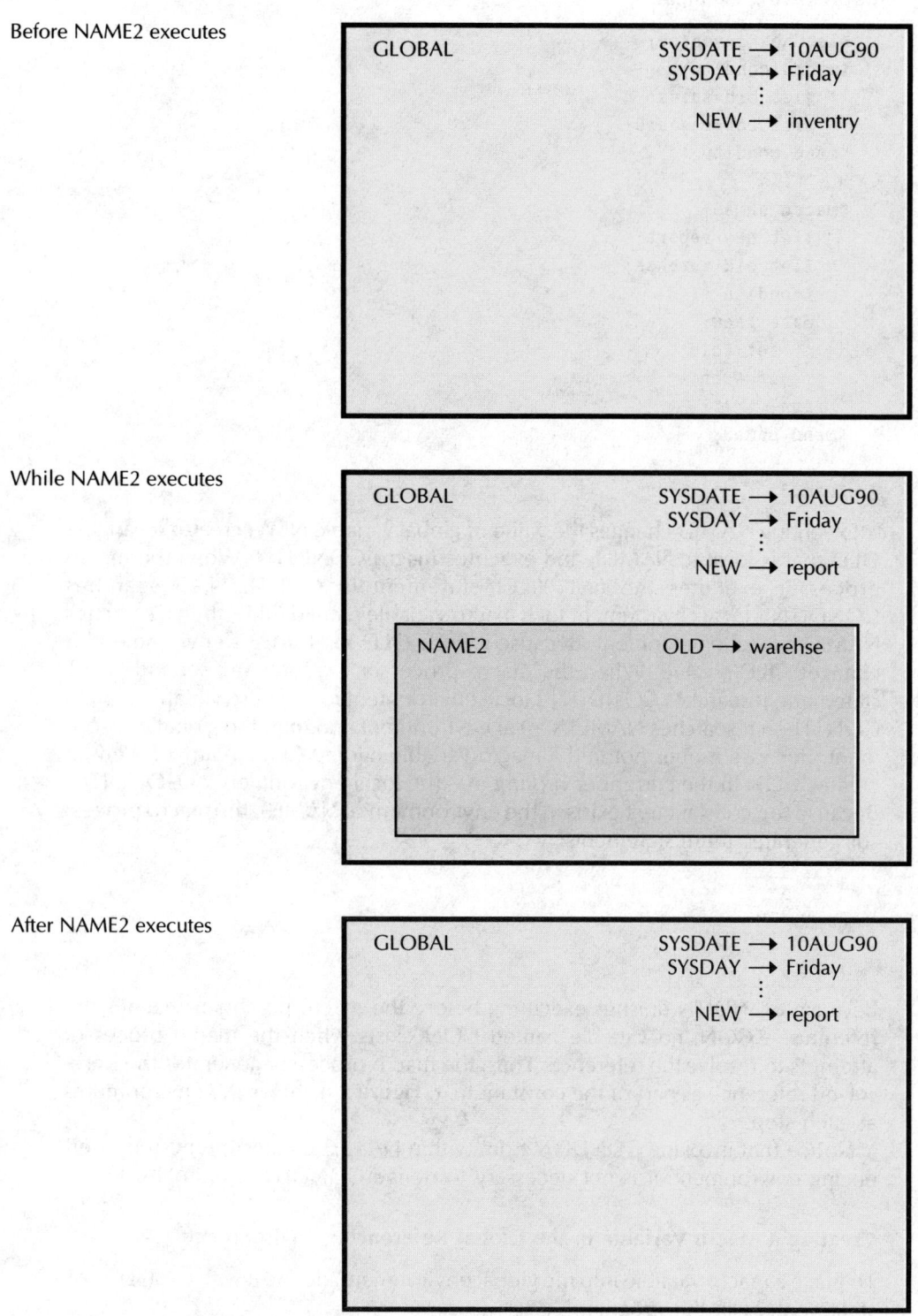

Figure 2.3 Referencing Environments at Various Stages

The same rule applies regardless of how many levels of nesting exist. Consider the following example:

```
%let new=inventry;
%macro conditn;
   %let old=sales;
   %let con=cases>0;
%mend conditn;

%macro name3;
   %let new=report;
   %let old=warehse;
   %conditn
   data &new;
      set &old;
      if &con;
   run;
%mend name3;

%name3
```

Executing NAME3 changes the value of global variable NEW, creates a variable OLD that is local to NAME3, and executes macro CONDITN. When the macro processor executes the first %LET statement in CONDITN, it searches CONDITN's local environment for a macro variable named OLD; then it searches NAME3's local environment. Because it finds OLD in NAME3's environment, it changes OLD's value. When the macro processor executes the second %LET statement, it searches CONDITN's local environment for a macro variable named CON. Then it searches NAME3's local environment and then the global environment. Because it does not find a macro variable named CON in any of them, it creates CON in the current environment—the local environment of CONDITN. Because the constant text exists in the environment of NAME3, the macro processor generates these statements:

```
DATA REPORT;
   SET SALES;
   IF &CON;
RUN;
```

Because CONDITN finishes executing before the macro processor reaches the reference &CON, no variable named CON exists when the macro processor attempts to resolve the reference. Thus, the macro processor generates the unresolved reference as part of the constant text. **Figure 2.4** shows the environments at each step.

Notice that invoking CONDITN from within NAME3 creates the nested referencing environment; it is not necessary to define CONDITN within NAME3.

Creating a Macro Variable in the Global Referencing Environment

To place a macro variable into the global environment, define it with a %GLOBAL statement, as in this program:

```
%macro conditn;
   %global con;
   %let old=sales;
   %let con=cases>0;
%mend conditn;
```

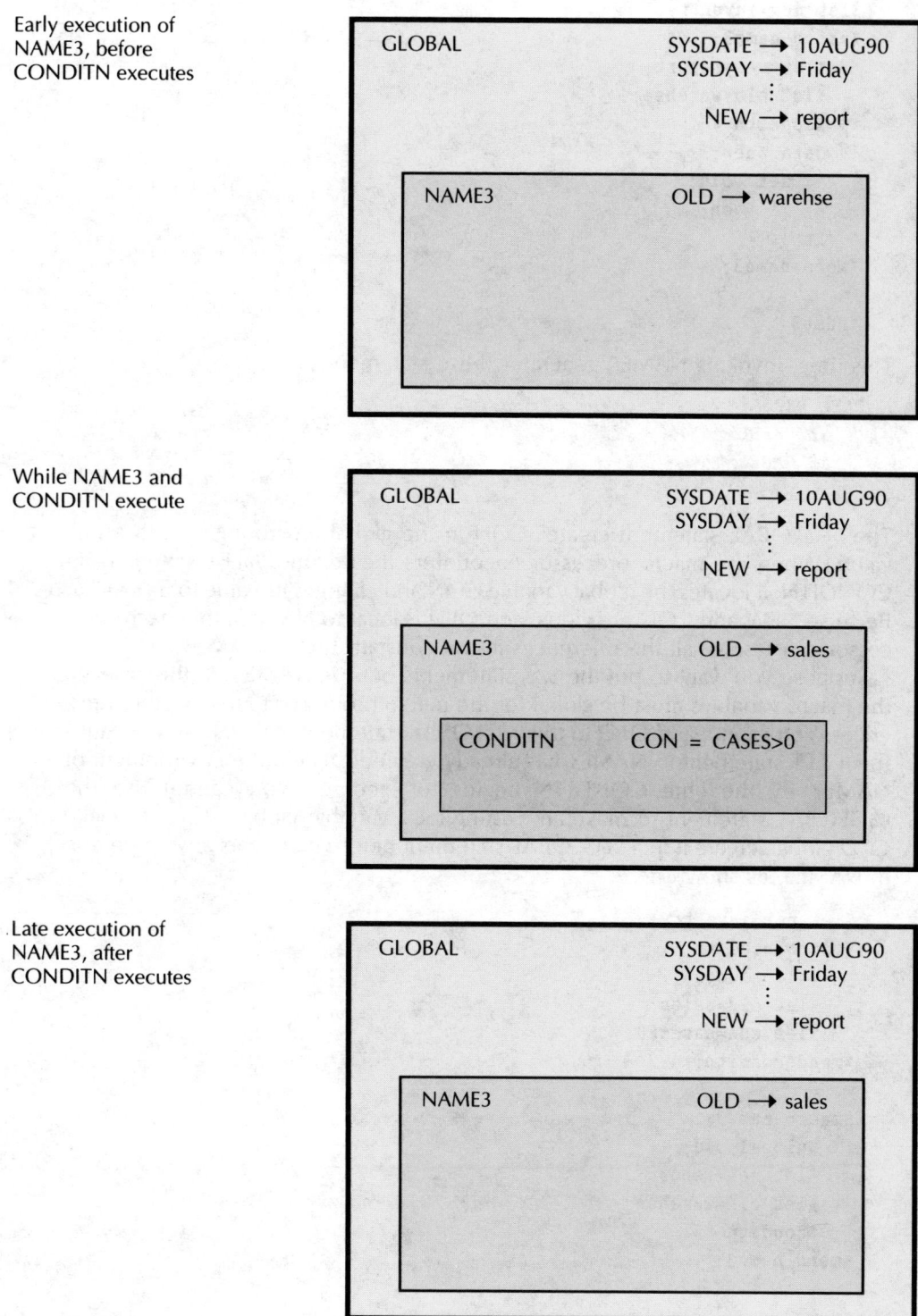

Figure 2.4   Referencing Environments Showing Two Levels of Nesting

The rest of the program remains the same:

```
%let new=inventry;
%macro name3;
   %let new=report;
   %let old=warehse;
   %conditn
   data &new;
      set &old;
      if &con;
   run;
%mend name3;

%name3
```

This time, invoking NAME3 generates these statements:

```
DATA REPORT;
   SET SALES;
   IF CASES>0;
RUN;
```

The %GLOBAL statement creates CON in the global environment with a null value. When the macro processor encounters the second %LET statement in CONDITN, it locates the global variable CON and changes its value to **cases>0**. Because NEW and CON are global and OLD is local to NAME3, the macro processor can resolve all the references in the constant text in NAME3.

Suppose you want to put the SAS statements outside NAME3. In this case, all the macro variables must be global for the macro processor to resolve the references. You cannot add OLD to the %GLOBAL statement in CONDITN because the %LET statement in NAME3 has already created OLD in the environment of NAME3 by the time CONDITN begins to execute. (You cannot use the %GLOBAL statement to make an existing local variable global.) Thus, to make OLD global, create it in a %GLOBAL statement before it appears anywhere else in NAME3, as shown here:

```
%let new=inventry;
%macro conditn;
   %global con;
   %let old=sales;
   %let con=cases>0;
%mend conditn;

%macro name3;
   %global old;
   %let new=report;
   %let old=warehse;
   %conditn
%mend name3;

%name3

data &new;
   set &old;
   if &con;
run;
```

Now the %LET statement in NAME3 changes the value of the existing global variable OLD rather than creating OLD in the current environment. The SAS System sees the following statements:

```
DATA REPORT;
   SET SALES;
   IF CASES>0;
RUN;
```

Creating a Variable in the Current Local Environment

At times you need to ensure that the macro processor creates a macro variable in the current local environment rather than changing the value of an existing macro variable. For example, suppose you want to use macro NAMELST to create a list of names for a VAR statement, as shown here:

```
%macro namelst(name,number);
    %do n=1 %to &number;
        &name&n
    %end;
%mend namelst;
```

You invoke NAMELST in this program:

```
%let n=North State Industries;
proc print;
    var %namelst(dept,5);
    title "Quarterly Report for &n";
run;
```

After macro execution, the SAS System sees the following:

```
PROC PRINT;
    VAR DEPT1 DEPT2 DEPT3 DEPT4 DEPT5;
    TITLE "Quarterly Report for 6";
RUN;
```

The macro processor changes the value of the global variable N each time it executes the iterative %DO loop. (After the loop stops executing, the value of N is 6, as described in **Iterative %DO Statement** in Chapter 3). To avoid inadvertent conflicts like this one, use a %LOCAL statement to create a variable N in the local environment, as shown here:

```
%macro namels2(name,number);
    %local n;
    %do n=1 %to &number;
        &name&n
    %end;
%mend namels2;
```

Now executing the same program

```
%let n=North State Industries;
proc print;
    var %namels2(dept,5);
    title "Quarterly Report for &n";
run;
```

causes the SAS System to see the following:

```
PROC PRINT;
    VAR DEPT1 DEPT2 DEPT3 DEPT4 DEPT5;
    TITLE "Quarterly Report for North State Industries";
RUN;
```

Figure 2.5 shows the environments before NAMELS2 executes, while NAMELS2 is executing, and when the macro processor encounters the reference &N in the TITLE statement.

Before NAMELS2 executes

While NAMELS2 executes
(at end of last iteration
of %DO loop)

After NAMELS2 executes

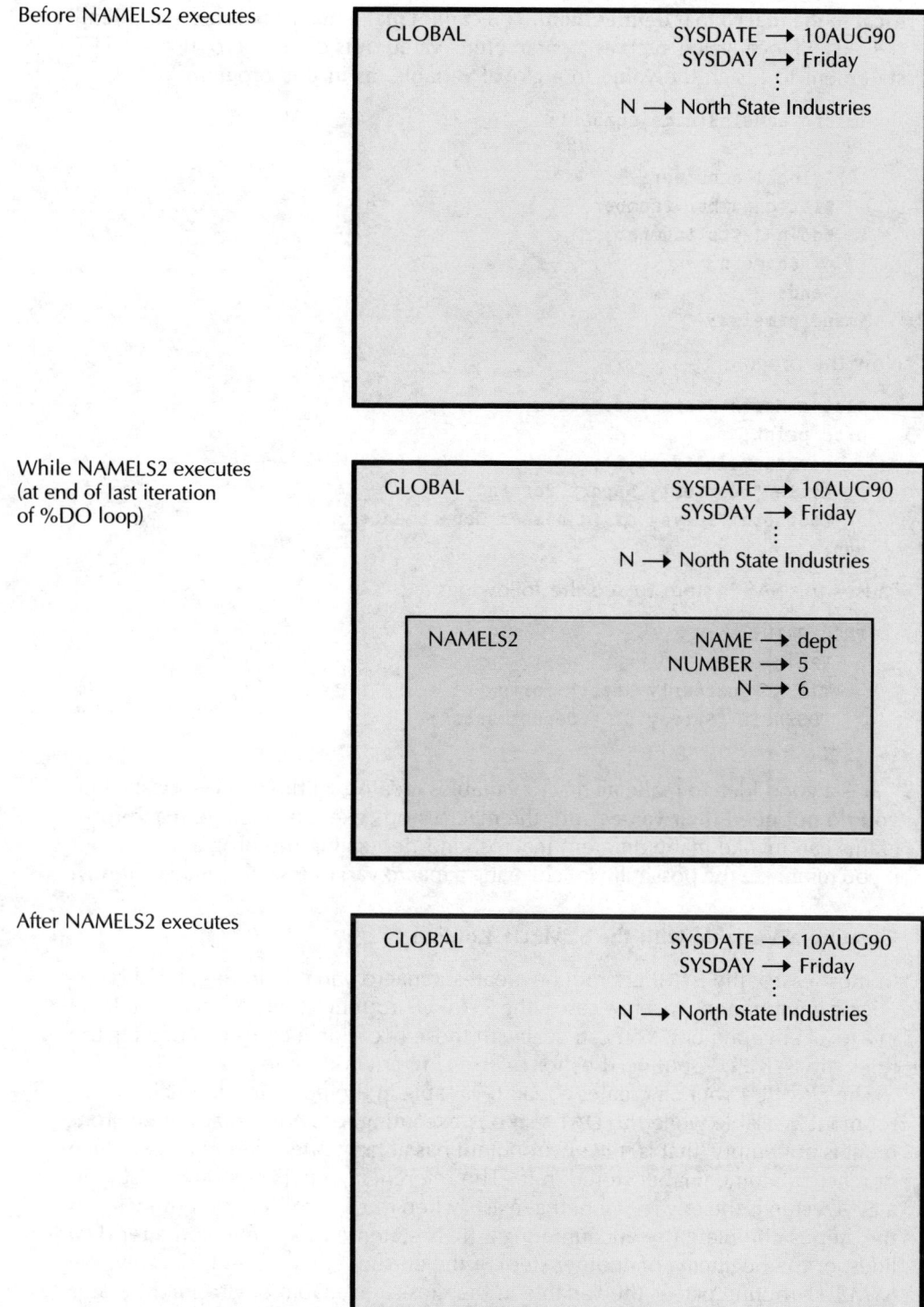

Figure 2.5   Global and Local Variables with the Same Name

Note that in **Figure 2.5** NAME and NUMBER are local to NAMELS2 even though you do not define them in the %LOCAL statement. **Macro parameters are always local to the macro that defines them. You cannot make macro parameters global.**

To use a local value such as a parameter's value outside a macro, use a %LET statement to assign the value to a global variable, as in this program:

```
%macro namels3(name,number);
    %local n;
    %global g_number;
    %let g_number=&number;
    %do n=1 %to &number;
        &name&n
    %end;
%mend namels3;
```

Now the program

```
%let n=North State Industries;
proc print;
    var %namels3(dept,5);
    title "Quarterly Report for &n";
    footnote "Survey of &g_number Departments";
run;
```

causes the SAS System to see the following:

```
PROC PRINT;
    VAR DEPT1 DEPT2 DEPT3 DEPT4 DEPT5;
    TITLE "Quarterly Report for North State Industries";
    FOOTNOTE "Survey of 5 Departments";
RUN;
```

It is a good idea to make all macro variables created within macros local when you do not need their values after the macro stops executing. Large macro programs can invoke many different macros, and debugging the programs is easier if you minimize the possibility of changing a macro variable's value inadvertently.

Creating a Variable with the SYMPUT Routine

In most cases, the SYMPUT routine creates a macro variable in the global referencing environment. In a few cases, the SYMPUT routine creates a macro variable in a local environment. You can deal with those occasional cases by knowing the rules the SYMPUT routine uses for referencing environments.

The SYMPUT routine creates a macro variable in the current referencing environment available while the DATA step is executing, provided that the environment is not empty (that is, the environment has at least one other macro variable or macro statement label stored in it). The referencing environment available to a DATA step is the environment that exists when the SAS System determines that the step is complete (by encountering a RUN statement, a semicolon after data lines, or the beginning of another step). If the current environment is empty, the SYMPUT routine places the variable in the closest available environment that is not empty.

For example, macro ENV1, shown here, contains a complete DATA step with a CALL SYMPUT statement:

```
%macro env1(dsn);
   data &dsn;
      set warehse end=last;
      if last then call symput('datein1',left(put(recdate,date7.)));
   run;
%mend env1;
```

If you invoke ENV1 in the program

```
%env1(inventry)
```

```
proc print;
   title "Last Receive Date Is &datein1";
run;
```

the SAS System sees the following:

```
DATA INVENTRY;
   SET WAREHSE END=LAST;
   IF LAST THEN CALL SYMPUT('DATEIN1',LEFT(PUT(RECDATE,DATE7.)));
RUN;
```

```
PROC PRINT;
   TITLE "Last Receive Date is &datein1";
RUN;
```

Because the DATA step is complete within the environment of ENV1 and because the local environment of ENV1 is not empty (it contains parameter DSN), the SYMPUT routine creates DATEIN1 in the local environment of ENV1. Therefore, the value is not available to the TITLE statement. **Figure 2.6** shows all of the referencing environments in this example, including when SAS statements execute and when macro variables are available.

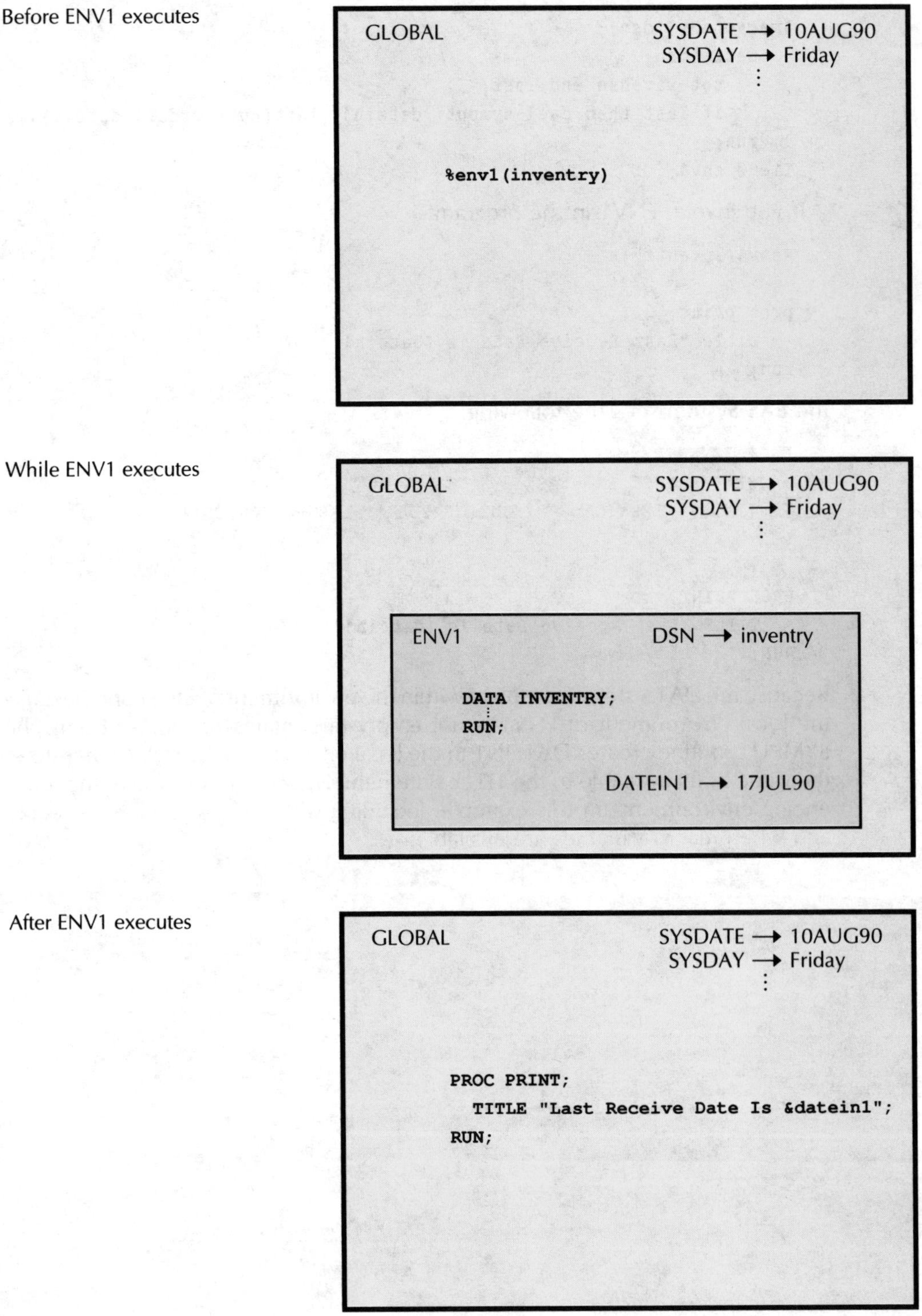

Before ENV1 executes

```
GLOBAL                    SYSDATE ──▶ 10AUG90
                          SYSDAY ──▶ Friday
                                ⋮



        %env1(inventry)
```

While ENV1 executes

```
GLOBAL                    SYSDATE ──▶ 10AUG90
                          SYSDAY ──▶ Friday
                                ⋮


    ┌─────────────────────────────────────────┐
    │ ENV1                  DSN ──▶ inventry   │
    │                                          │
    │    DATA INVENTRY;                        │
    │     ⋮                                    │
    │    RUN;                                  │
    │                                          │
    │                    DATEIN1 ──▶ 17JUL90   │
    │                                          │
    └─────────────────────────────────────────┘
```

After ENV1 executes

```
GLOBAL                    SYSDATE ──▶ 10AUG90
                          SYSDAY ──▶ Friday
                                ⋮



    PROC PRINT;
       TITLE "Last Receive Date Is &datein1";
    RUN;
```

Figure 2.6 The SYMPUT Routine in a Macro Generating a Complete
DATA Step

In macro ENV2, shown here, the DATA step is not complete within the macro because there is no RUN statement:

```
%macro env2(dsn);
   data &dsn;
      set warehse end=last;
      if last then call symput('datein2',left(put(recdate,date7.)));
%mend env2;
```

Invoking ENV2 in the program

```
%env2(inventry)

run;
proc print;
   title "Last Receive Date Is &datein2";
run;
```

causes the SAS System to see the following:

```
DATA INVENTRY;
   SET WAREHSE END=LAST;
   IF LAST THEN CALL SYMPUT('DATEIN2',LEFT(PUT(RECDATE,DATE7.)));
RUN;

PROC PRINT;
   TITLE "Last Receive Date Is 17JUL90";
RUN;
```

The DATA step is complete only when SAS encounters the RUN statement in open code; thus, the current environment of the DATA step is the global environment. The SYMPUT routine creates DATEIN2 as a global macro variable, and the value is available to the TITLE statement. **Figure 2.7** shows all of the referencing environments in this example, including when SAS statements execute and when macro variables are available.

Before ENV2 executes

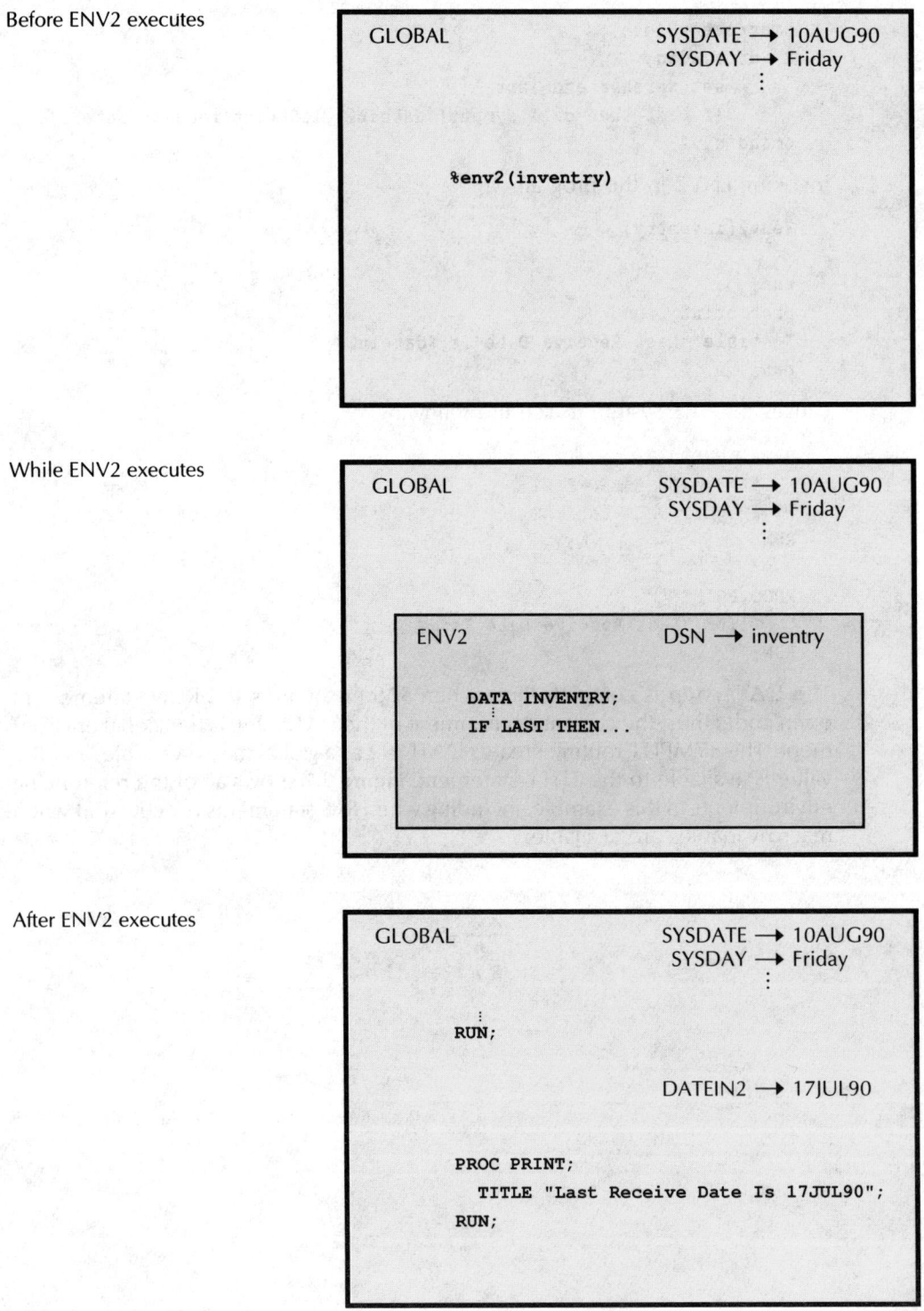

While ENV2 executes

After ENV2 executes

Figure 2.7   The SYMPUT Routine in a Macro Generating an Incomplete
DATA Step

In the following example, macro ENV3 contains a complete DATA step and has an empty environment:

```
%macro env3;
   data &dsn;
      set warehse end=last;
      if last then call symput('datein3',left(put(recdate,date7.)));
   run;
%mend env3;
```

Suppose you invoke ENV3 within another macro, for example, QUICK:

```
%macro quick(dsn);
   %env3
   proc print data=&dsn(keep=month1-month10);
      title "Items Through Date=&datein3";
   run;
   title;
%mend quick;
```

Invoking QUICK in the program

```
%quick(inventry)
```

```
proc means;
   footnote "Items End with &datein3";
run;
```

causes the SAS System to see the following:

```
DATA INVENTRY;
   SET WAREHSE END=LAST;
   IF LAST THEN CALL SYMPUT('DATEIN3',LEFT(PUT(RECDATE,DATE7.)));
RUN;
PROC PRINT DATA=INVENTRY(KEEP=MONTH1-MONTH10);
   TITLE "Observations Through Date=17JUL90";
RUN;
TITLE;


PROC MEANS;
   FOOTNOTE "Items End with &datein3";
RUN;
```

The SYMPUT routine stores the value of DATEIN3 in the environment of QUICK because that is the first nonempty environment it encounters. Thus, the value of DATEIN3 is available to the TITLE statement generated by QUICK but not to the FOOTNOTE statement in open code. **Figure 2.8** shows all of the referencing environments in this example, including when SAS statements execute and when macro variables are available.

While ENV3 executes
within QUICK

After ENV3 executes

After QUICK executes

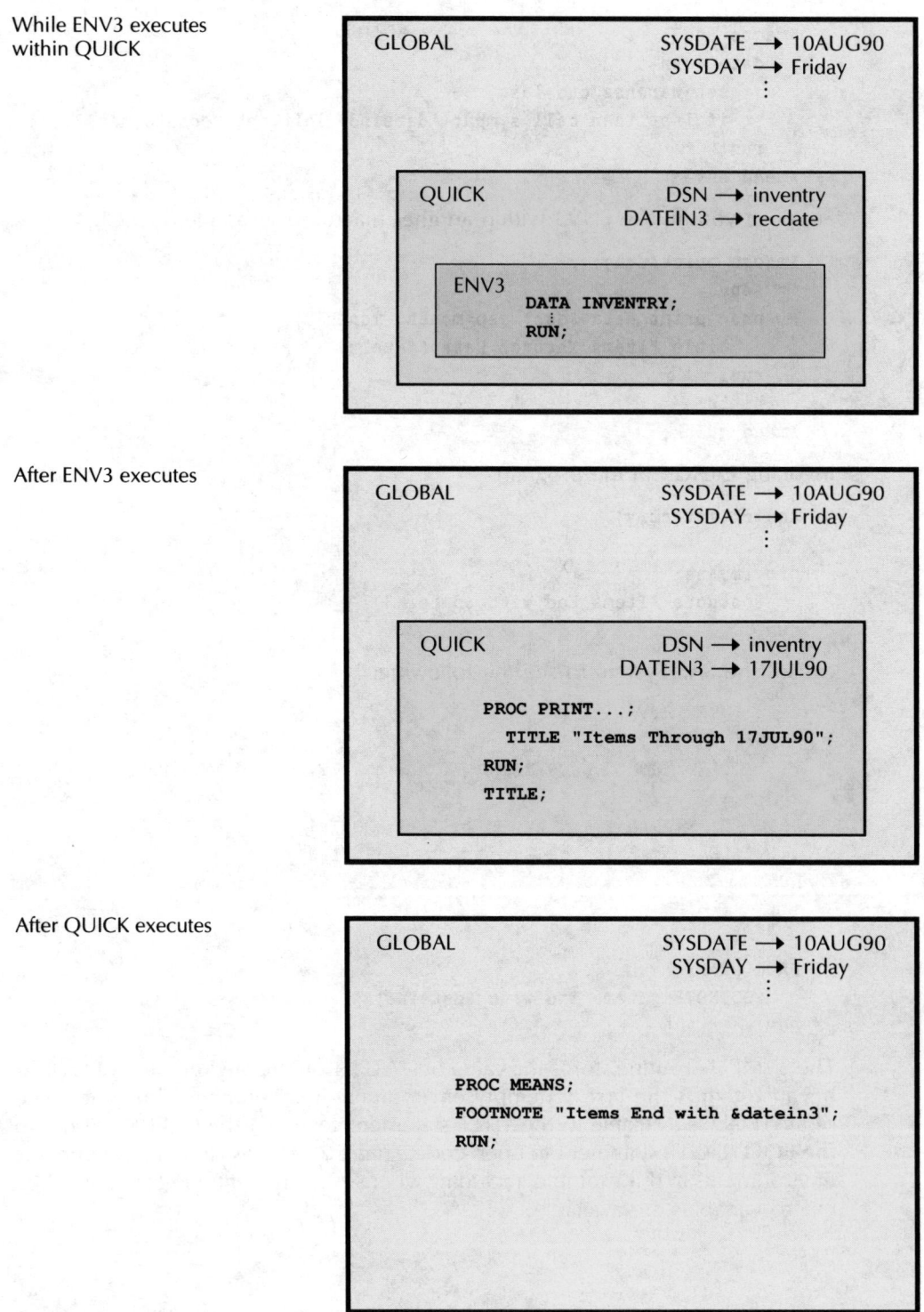

Figure 2.8   The SYMPUT Routine in a Nested Macro

AUTOMATIC MACRO VARIABLES

When you invoke the SAS System, the macro processor creates automatic macro variables that supply a variety of information. Reference automatic macro variables exactly as you do macro variables that you create.

Caution: The three-letter prefix SYS is reserved for use by the SAS System for automatic macro variables. Do not use names that begin with the prefix SYS for your own macro variables. See Appendix 2, "Reserved Words in the Macro Facility," for a complete list of reserved words in the macro language.

Note: Some other products in the SAS System also provide automatic macro variables; those variables are described in the documentation for the product that uses them.

For example, suppose you want to include today's day and date in a FOOTNOTE statement. Write the statement to reference the automatic macro variables SYSDAY and SYSDATE, as shown here:

```
footnote "Report for &sysday, &sysdate";
```

If you run the program on June 14, 1990, macro variable resolution causes the SAS System to see this statement:

```
FOOTNOTE "Report for Thursday , 14JUN90 ";
```

All automatic variables except for SYSPBUFF are global. **Table 2.1** lists the automatic macro variables and describes their read/write status. Then each macro variable is described in alphabetical order. You can assign values to automatic macro variables listed as having read/write status. You cannot assign values to automatic macro variables listed as having read only status.

Table 2.1   Automatic Macro Variables

Variable	Read/Write Status
SYSBUFFR	read/write
SYSCMD	read only
SYSDATE	read only
SYSDAY	read only
SYSDEVIC	read/write
SYSDSN	read/write
SYSENV	read only
SYSERR	read only
SYSINDEX	read only
SYSINFO	read only
SYSJOBID	read only
SYSLAST	read/write
SYSLIBRC	read/write
SYSMENV	read only
SYSMSG	read/write
SYSPARM	read/write
SYSPBUFF	read/write
SYSRC	read/write
SYSSCP	read only
SYSTIME	read only
SYSVER	read only

Each macro variable is described in alphabetical order below:

SYSBUFFR   receives text entered in response to a %INPUT
statement that the macro processor cannot match with
any variable in the statement. For example, if the
%INPUT statement has the form

```
%input name city;
```

and you enter

```
alvarez cary nc
```

the characters `alvarez` become the value of NAME,
the characters `cary` become the value of CITY, and the
characters `nc`, including a leading blank, become the
value of SYSBUFFR. Until the first execution of a
%INPUT statement, SYSBUFFR has a null value.
SYSBUFFR receives a new value during each execution
of a %INPUT statement: either the excess characters
entered in response to the %INPUT statement or a null
value if there are no excess characters. If the %INPUT
statement contains no macro variable names, all
characters entered are assigned to SYSBUFFR.

SYSCMD   contains the last command from the command line of a
macro window that was not recognized by the SAS
Display Manager System. SYSCMD receives either a null
value or the last unrecognized command during each
execution of a %DISPLAY statement. You cannot change
the value of this variable. See **%WINDOW Statement** in
Chapter 3 for an example that uses SYSCMD.

SYSDATE   gives the date when your SAS job began executing, or
when your SAS session began, in DATE6. or DATE7.
format. For example, in a job that started executing on
October 12, 1990, the value of SYSDATE would be
`12OCT90`. Chapter 11, "Writing Utility Macros," shows a
macro that creates a variable containing the formatted
value of SYSDATE. You cannot change the value of this
variable.

SYSDAY   gives the day of the week the SAS job or session started
execution, such as `Monday`. You cannot change the
value of this variable.

SYSDEVIC   gives the name of the current graphics device, the value
of the SAS system option DEVICE=. Assigning a value to
SYSDEVIC is the same as specifying a value for the
DEVICE= system option.

SYSDSN   gives the name of the most recently created SAS data set
as two left-aligned words in eight-character fields.
Automatic macro variable SYSLAST is generally more
useful since it contains the same information in a more
easily recognizable format. Some examples of values in
SYSDSN include the following:

```
WORK    QCDATA
```

```
FIRSTLIBSALESRPT
```

If no SAS data set has been created in the current program, the value of SYSDSN is eight blanks followed by _NULL_ and two more blanks, as in

   ƀƀƀƀƀƀƀƀ_NULL_ƀƀ

where the character ƀ represents a blank space. You can change the value of SYSDSN directly. Assigning a value to SYSDSN is the same as specifying a value for the _LAST_= system option.

SYSENV   contains the value **FORE** if the input stream comes from the terminal or if the SAS log file or the SAS procedure output file goes to the terminal. SYSENV contains the value **BACK** if neither the SAS log file nor the SAS output file uses the terminal, and the input stream comes from an external file, such as when you submit a SAS job in batch mode or when you invoke the SAS System with the name of a file that contains SAS code. You cannot change the value of this variable.

SYSERR   contains the return code set by SAS procedures. Values for SYSERR are as follows:

    0   Execution completed successfully and without warning messages.

    1   Execution was canceled by the user with a RUN CANCEL statement.

    2   Execution was canceled by the user with an ATTN or BREAK command.

    4   Execution completed successfully but with warning messages.

Value greater than 4
      An error occurred. Future versions of the SAS System will specify values for particular kinds of errors.

You cannot change the value of this variable.

SYSINDEX   gives the number of macros that have started execution so far in the current SAS job or session. Use SYSINDEX in your macros when you need a unique number that changes after each macro invocation. You cannot change the value of this variable.

SYSINFO   contains return code information provided by some SAS procedures. Values of SYSINFO are described with the procedures that use it. You cannot change the value of this variable.

SYSJOBID   gives the name of the currently executing batch job or the userid that invoked the current SAS session. The value SYSJOBID contains depends on the operating system you use to run the SAS System. Refer to the SAS documentation for your operating system for more detailed information. You cannot change the value of this variable.

SYSLAST   gives the name of the most recently created SAS data set in the form *libref.SASdata-set*. Unlike the value of

SYSDSN, the value of SYSLAST is left-aligned and contains a period, as shown here:

```
WORK.QCDATA
```

You can insert a reference to SYSLAST directly into SAS code in place of a data set name. If no SAS data set has been created in the current program, the value of SYSLAST is _NULL_. Assigning a value to SYSLAST is the same as specifying a value for the _LAST_= system option.

SYSLIBRC   contains the return code set by the last LIBNAME statement. SYSLIBRC contains a 0 if the last LIBNAME statement successfully executed or some other nonzero value if the last LIBNAME statement did not successfully execute.

SYSMENV   gives the currently active macro execution environment. Values for SYSMENV can be

    S   indicates that the macro was part of the SAS program.

    D   indicates that the macro was invoked from a display manager or windowing procedure command line.

You cannot change the value of this variable.

SYSMSG   contains a message you specify for display in the message area of a macro window. The value of SYSMSG is set to null after each execution of a %DISPLAY statement. See **%WINDOW Statement** in Chapter 3 for an example that uses SYSMSG.

SYSPARM   contains the same value you specify with the SYSPARM= system option, which is the same value returned by the DATA step function SYSPARM. The default value of SYSPARM is null. Assigning a value to SYSPARM is the same as specifying a value for the SYSPARM= system option.

SYSPBUFF   receives all text supplied as macro parameter values in a macro invocation for macros defined with the PARMBUFF option of the %MACRO statement. This includes the parentheses and commas for name-style invocations. Using the PARMBUFF option and SYSPBUFF, you can define a macro that accepts a varying number of parameters at each invocation. SYSPBUFF is local to the macro being invoked. See **%MACRO Statement** in Chapter 3 for an example that uses SYSPBUFF.

SYSRC   gives the last return code generated by your operating system based on commands you execute using the X statement in open code, the X command in display manager, or the %SYSEXEC, %TSO or %CMS macro statements. Return codes are integers. The default value of SYSRC is 0. Refer to the SAS documentation for your operating system for return code examples.

SYSSCP   returns the abbreviation for the operating system you are using. You cannot change the value of this variable.

SYSTIME   gives the time the SAS program started execution in TIME5. format, as in **15:25**. You cannot change the value of this variable.

SYSVER   gives the release of SAS software you are using, as in **6.06**. You cannot change the value of this variable.

Chapter 3
Macro Program Statements

This chapter describes the program statements available in the macro language. For reference purposes, it includes discussions of macro invocations and macro statement labels with the statements.

You can use any macro program statement inside of a macro definition. You can use several macro program statements anywhere in a SAS session or job, either inside or outside macro definitions. The area outside of macro definitions is sometimes called *open code*.

For convenience, the following lists identify macro program statements based on where you can use them.

Table 3.1 Macro Program Statements and Where to Use Them

Statements Used Anywhere		Statements Used Only in Macro Definitions	
%*comment	Macro invocations	%DO	%IF-%THEN
%DISPLAY	%MACRO	%DO %UNTIL	Iterative %DO
%GLOBAL	%MEND	%DO %WHILE	%label:
%INPUT	%PUT	%END	%LOCAL
%KEYDEF	%SYSEXEC	%GOTO	
%LET	%WINDOW		

Contents

%*comment Statement

The macro comment statement enables you to place comments in a macro. Invoking a macro does not produce text from macro comment statements (as it does from SAS comment statements, which the macro language treats as constant text). Macro comment statements can appear only inside a macro.

The form of the macro comment statement is

%*comment*;

where *comment* can be any message.

For example, the following macro produces code to check for errors in the data:

```
%macro verdata(in);
   %*                               ;
   %*****macro for quick data checking****;
   %*                               ;
   data check;
      infile &in;
      input x y z;
      if x<0 or y<0 or z<0 then list;
      *checks first three variables in file &in;
   run;
%mend verdata;
```

Invoking macro VERDATA with

```
%verdata(ina)
```

generates this SAS program:

```
DATA CHECK;
   INFILE INA;
   INPUT X Y Z;
   IF X<0 OR Y<0 OR Z<0 THEN LIST;
   *CHECKS FIRST THREE VARIABLES IN FILE &IN;
RUN;
```

Note that in the SAS comment statement, the macro variable reference &IN is not resolved.

In addition, the SAS System treats the comment symbols /* and */ as comments both in SAS statements and in the macro facility. When these symbols appear in a macro program statement, the macro processor ignores text within the comment.

%DISPLAY Statement

The %DISPLAY statement displays a macro window. You can display one group of fields in each execution of a %DISPLAY statement. If you display a window containing any unprotected fields, you must enter values into any required fields and press ENTER to remove the display. If a window contains only protected fields, pressing ENTER removes the display. While a window is being displayed, you can use commands and function keys to view other windows, change the size of the current window, and so on. The form of the %DISPLAY statement is

%DISPLAY *window*<.*group*> <NOINPUT> <BLANK> <BELL>;

where

window <.*group*>	names the window and group of fields to be displayed. If the window has more than one group of fields, give the complete *window.group* specification; if a window contains a single unnamed group, specify only *window*.
NOINPUT	specifies that you cannot input values into fields displayed in the window. If you do not specify the NOINPUT option, you can input values into unprotected fields displayed in the window. Use the NOINPUT option when the %DISPLAY statement is inside a macro definition and you want to merge more than one group of fields into a single display. Using NOINPUT in a particular %DISPLAY statement causes the group displayed to remain visible when later groups are displayed.
BLANK	clears the display. Use the BLANK option to prevent fields from a previous display from appearing in the current display. This option is useful only when the %DISPLAY statement is inside a macro definition; when the %DISPLAY statement is outside a macro definition, the display is cleared automatically after the execution of each %DISPLAY statement.
BELL	rings the terminal's bell when the window is displayed.

Chapter 5, "Macro Windows," discusses displaying windows.

%DO Statement

The simple %DO statement works in the macro language the same way the simple DO statement works in the DATA step. Text and program statements following the %DO statement are treated as a unit until a matching %END statement appears. You can use the %DO statement only inside a macro definition.

The form of the %DO statement is

%DO;
> *text and macro program statements*

%END;

You usually use the %DO statement with the %IF-%THEN statement to execute a block of code conditionally. For example, the following macro uses %DO groups to issue one of two PROC steps:

```
%macro do1(request);
   %if %upcase(&request)=STAT %then
      %do;
         proc means;
            title "Summary of All Numeric Variables";
         run;
      %end;
   %else
      %do;
         proc print;
            title "Listing of Data";
         run;
      %end;
   title;
%mend do1;
```

(The %UPCASE function, which converts lowercase characters to uppercase, is described in Chapter 4, "Macro Functions.")

Invoking macro DO1 with

```
%do1(stat)
```

generates these statements:

```
PROC MEANS;
    TITLE "Summary of All Numeric Variables";
RUN;
TITLE;
```

However, the invocation

```
%do1(none)
```

generates these statements:

```
PROC PRINT;
    TITLE "Listing of Data";
RUN;
TITLE;
```

Iterative %DO Statement

The iterative %DO statement executes a portion of a macro repetitively; the number of times the section is executed depends on the value of a macro variable used as an index variable.

The form of the iterative %DO statement is

%DO *macro-variable=start* **%TO** *stop* <**%BY** *increment*>;
    text and macro program statements
%END;

where the following terms can appear:

macro-variable   names a macro variable or a macro expression that generates a macro variable name whose value governs execution of the iterative %DO loop. If the macro variable used as the index does not exist, the macro processor creates it in the current referencing environment.

start   specify integers or macro expressions that yield integers
stop   to control the number of times the portion of the macro between the iterative %DO and %END statements is executed. You cannot replace *start* and *stop* with a list of values as you can in the DATA step iterative DO statement.

The %DO group is executed first with *macro-variable* equal to *start*. Execution continues with the value of the macro variable changing by the value of *increment*, discussed below, until the value of *macro-variable* is greater than *stop*.

Values of *start* and *stop* are calculated before the first execution of the loop; you cannot change them during the execution of the loop.

If you need to calculate the value of the index variable after the last iteration of the %DO loop, use this formula:

%EVAL(*start* + *increment* * ((*stop-start*) / *increment* + 1))

(See Chapter 4, "Macro Functions," for a discussion of the %EVAL function.)

increment   specifies an integer (other than 0) or a macro expression that yields an integer to be added to the value of the index variable in each execution of the loop. If you omit *increment*, the macro processor uses 1. *Increment* is evaluated before the first execution of the loop.

When *increment* is positive, *start* should be less than *stop*; when *increment* is negative, *start* should be greater than *stop*. Otherwise, the loop is not executed.

You cannot add a %WHILE or %UNTIL clause to an iterative %DO statement (as you can add a WHILE or UNTIL clause in the DATA step).

Examples

The following examples illustrate the iterative %DO statement.

Example 1:   Generating a Series of DATA Steps

Macro CREATE, shown here, generates three DATA steps:

```
%macro create;
   %do i=1 %to 3;
      data month&i;
         infile in&i;
         input product cost date;
      run;
   %end;
%mend create;
```

Invoking CREATE, as in

```
%create
```

generates these statements:

```
DATA MONTH1;
   INFILE IN1;
   INPUT PRODUCT COST DATE;
RUN;
DATA MONTH2;
   INFILE IN2;
   INPUT PRODUCT COST DATE;
RUN;
DATA MONTH3;
   INFILE IN3;
   INPUT PRODUCT COST DATE;
RUN;
```

Each time the iterative %DO loop executes, the macro processor replaces the reference &I with the value of macro variable I in that iteration. Because the value of I ranges from 1 to 3, the loop executes three times and produces three DATA steps.

Example 2:   Nested loops

When you nest iterative %DO loops, the inner loop goes through all its iterations during each iteration of the outer loop. You can cause execution to leave the loop with a %GOTO statement, described later in this chapter.

For example, suppose you need to generate a set of data set names for days in the month of August. You want the names to contain the number of the week and number of the day, as in W1D1, W1D2, W1D3, and so on. Because August has 31 days, the last data set name is W5D3. Macro DAYDATA, shown below, produces the names. Match the circled numbers to the explanations that follow.

```
%macro daydata;
   %do week=1 %to 5;  ❶
      %do day=1 %to 7;  ❷
         w&week.d&day  ❸
         %if &week=5 and &day=3 %then %goto out;  ❹
      %end;
   %end;
%out: %mend daydata;
```

1. The first iterative %DO statement generates WEEK values from **1** to **5**.
2. The second iterative %DO statement generates DAY values from **1** to **7**.
3. The constant text combines the prefix W, the macro variable reference &WEEK., the prefix D, and the reference &DAY to produce the names.
4. When the value of WEEK is **5** and the value of DAY is **3**, the %IF statement in the inner loop becomes true, and the %GOTO statement causes execution to leave the loop.

Invoking macro DAYDATA in the DATA statement

```
data %daydata;
```

causes the SAS System to see this statement:

```
DATA W1D1 W1D2 W1D3 W1D4 W1D5 W1D6 W1D7 W2D1 W2D2 W2D3 W2D4
     W2D5 W2D6 W2D7 W3D1 W3D2 W3D3 W3D4 W3D5 W3D6 W3D7 W4D1 W4D2
     W4D3 W4D4 W4D5 W4D6 W4D7 W5D1 W5D2 W5D3;
```

%DO %UNTIL Statement

The %DO %UNTIL statement executes the statements in a loop repetitively until a condition becomes true. The %DO %UNTIL statement checks the value of the condition at the bottom of the loop; thus, a %DO %UNTIL loop is always executed at least once. The form of the %DO %UNTIL statement is

%DO %UNTIL(*expression*);
   text and macro program statements
%END;

where

> *expression*   can be any macro expression. The macro processor evaluates the expression, substituting macro variable values or the result of a macro call.

The following examples illustrate %DO %UNTIL statements:

```
%do %until(&hold=no);
%do %until(%index(&target,&source)=0);
```

Macro DU, shown here, illustrates the %DO %UNTIL statement:

```
%macro du(num);
   %put beginning macro du: num is &num;
   %do %until(&num>3);
      %put ***&num***;
      %let num=%eval(&num+1);
   %end;
   %put ending macro du: num is &num;
%mend du;
```

The following invocation writes the lines shown:

```
%du(2)

beginning macro du: num is 2
***2***
***3***
ending macro du: num is 4
```

In each execution of the loop, the %PUT statement executes; then the %LET statement assigns NUM a new value (using the %EVAL function, described in Chapter 4, "Macro Functions"); and then the macro processor evaluates the condition of the %DO %UNTIL loop. During the second execution, the value of NUM becomes 4, and the loop ceases execution.

Suppose the initial condition of the %DO %UNTIL loop is false, as in the following:

```
%du(5)
```

The preceding invocation writes these lines:

```
beginning macro du: num is 5
***5***
ending macro du: num is 6
```

In the first iteration of the loop, the %PUT statement writes the line ***5***; then the %LET statement assigns NUM the value 6; and then the %DO %UNTIL statement checks its condition and ceases to execute the loop. This invocation shows that a %DO %UNTIL loop is always executed at least once.

%DO %WHILE Statement

The %DO %WHILE statement executes a group of statements repetitively while a condition remains true. The %DO %WHILE statement tests the condition at the top of the loop. If the condition is false the first time the macro processor tests it, the %DO %WHILE loop is not executed. The form of the %DO %WHILE statement is

%DO %WHILE(*expression*);
    text and macro program statements
%END;

where

> *expression* can be any macro expression. The macro processor evaluates the expression, substituting macro variable values or the result of a macro call.

These examples illustrate %DO %WHILE statements:

```
%do %while(&a<&b);
%do %while(%length(&name)>20 and &city ne);
```

Macro DW, shown here, illustrates the %DO %WHILE statement:

```
%macro dw(num);
   %put beginning macro dw: value of num is &num;
   %do %while(&num>5 and &num <=10);
      %put ***&num***;
      %let num=%eval(&num+1);
   %end;
   %put ending macro dw: value of num is &num;
%mend dw;
```

The following invocation writes the lines shown:

```
%dw(8)

beginning macro dw: value of num is 8
***8***
***9***
***10***
ending macro dw: value of num is 11
```

The %DO %WHILE loop executes three times, when the value of NUM is **8**, **9**, and **10**. During the third execution, the %EVAL function increments the value of NUM to **11**; when the macro processor evaluates the %DO %WHILE expression in preparation for the fourth execution, the expression is no longer true. Thus, the loop ceases execution, and the final %PUT statement in macro DW writes its message.

When the condition is false the first time it is evaluated, as given by the following invocation, macro DW writes the lines shown:

```
%dw(1)

beginning macro dw: value of num is 1
ending macro dw: value of num is 1
```

The macro processor evaluates the %DO %WHILE expression before the first execution of the loop; because the expression is not true, the macro processor does not execute the loop.

%END Statement

The %END statement ends a %DO group. The form of the %END statement is

%END;

A %END statement must end every %DO group in the macro, as in this example:

```
%macro test(finish);
   %let i=1;
   %do %while (&i<&finish);
      %put the value of i is &i;
      %let i=%eval(&i+1);
   %end;
%mend test;
```

%GLOBAL Statement

The %GLOBAL statement creates global macro variables, that is, macro variables that are available to all referencing environments of a job (except where blocked by local macro variables of the same names). See Chapter 2, "Macro Variables," for a discussion of referencing environments. The %GLOBAL statement can appear either inside or outside a macro definition.

The form of the %GLOBAL statement is

%GLOBAL *macro-variable-1* <. . . *macro-variable-n*>;

where

macro-variable   can be the name of a global macro variable or a macro expression that generates one or more macro variable names. For example, this %GLOBAL statement creates three global macro variables:

```
%global datavar keep1 keep2;
```

Note that you cannot use a SAS variable list or a macro expression that generates a SAS variable list in a %GLOBAL statement.

Once you have defined a macro variable as local, you cannot use a %GLOBAL statement while that macro is executing to make that variable global. (Thus, you cannot use a %GLOBAL statement to make a macro parameter global.) If you want to create a global macro variable within a macro, specify it in a %GLOBAL statement before you use it in any other macro program statements in the macro.

Macro variables created with a %GLOBAL statement have null values until you assign them other values. If you have already created a global macro variable and assigned it another value, including that variable in a %GLOBAL statement does not remove the value.

Suppose you have a large SAS data set containing variables named TEST1 through TEST100. Because you analyze different groups of variables at different times, you write macro VARS, which creates a VAR statement you can use with procedures, such as the following statement:

```
var test1-test20;
```

You give the first and last variables in the list as parameter values. You want to use the same numbers in titles outside the macro, but parameters are available only inside the macro. Therefore, you create global macro variables and assign the parameter values to them, as follows:

```
%macro vars(first=1,last=);
   %global gfirst glast;
   %let gfirst=&first;
   %let glast=&last;
   var test&first-test&last;
%mend vars;
```

You can invoke VARS in a program and also use the values of FIRST and LAST in a TITLE statement after macro VARS ceases execution, as shown here:

```
proc print;
   %vars(last=50)
   title "Analysis of Tests &gfirst-&glast";
run;
```

The SAS System sees the following program:

```
PROC PRINT;
   VAR TEST1-TEST50;
   TITLE "Analysis of Tests 1-50";
RUN;
```

If you omit the %GLOBAL statement, GFIRST and GLAST are created in the local environment of VARS. In that case the macro processor cannot resolve the references in the TITLE statement. The TITLE statement contains the references &GFIRST and &GLAST, and the macro processor issues a warning message.

%GOTO or %GO TO Statement

The %GOTO or %GO TO statement causes the macro processor to branch to the label specified in the %GOTO or %GO TO statement. The statements work the same way as the GOTO and GO TO statements in the DATA step.

The form of the %GOTO statement is

%GOTO | %GO TO *label*;

where

> *label* is either the name of the label in the macro to which you want execution to branch or a macro expression that generates the label. See **%*label*: Statement** later in this chapter for information on statement labels in the macro language. The %GOTO statement and the statement label must be in the same referencing environment. Do not put a percent sign in front of the label in a %GOTO statement unless you are calling a macro of that name to generate the label.
>
> A macro expression that produces the label in a %GOTO statement is called a *computed %GOTO destination*. The computed %GOTO destination becomes an entry in the current local referencing environment.

A %GOTO statement cannot cause execution to branch to a point inside an iterative %DO, %DO %UNTIL, or %DO %WHILE loop that is not currently executing.

Here are examples of %GOTO statements:

```
%goto xxx;
%go to name1;
%goto &where;
%go to %find;
```

The following example uses a %GOTO statement to jump out of an iterative %DO loop:

```
%macro dseries;
   %local units fracs;
   %do units=1 %to 2;
      %do fracs=0 %to 8 %by 2;
         &units..&fracs
         %if &units=2 %then %goto out;
      %end;
   %end;
%out: %mend dseries;
```

Macro DSERIES generates constant text containing decimal values by concatenating the value of UNITS, a decimal point, and the value of FRACS. (The first period after &UNITS is a delimiter; the second period produces the decimal point in constant text.) The %IF condition in the inner %DO loop becomes true the first time that UNITS=2 (when FRACS=0); the %GOTO statement causes execution to leave the loop. Thus, the last value generated is 2.0.

This program invokes macro DSERIES in a PROC PLOT step:

```
proc plot;
   plot y*x / vref=%dseries
              href=%dseries;
run;
```

As the macro executes, the SAS System sees this program:

```
PROC PLOT;
   PLOT Y*X / VREF=1.0  1.2  1.4  1.6  1.8  2.0
              HREF=1.0  1.2  1.4  1.6  1.8  2.0;
RUN;
```

The following program illustrates a computed %GOTO destination and how it affects the referencing environments in a program. Match the circled numbers to the explanations that follow.

```
%macro days;  ❶
   %if &sysday=Friday or &sysday=Saturday %then
      %goto %substr(&sysday,1,3);  ❷
   data daily;
      infile inx;
      input dept1-dept3;
   run;
   %fri: data _null_;  ❸
   call symput('day6','day 6');
   run;
   %sat: data _null_;
   call symput('day7','day 7');
   run;
   %put first time--day6 is &day6 and day7 is &day7;  ❹
%mend days;


%days
%put second time--day6 is &day6 and day7 is &day7;  ❺
```

1. Macro DAYS creates no macro variables; thus, its local environment appears to be empty.
2. The macro processor constructs the destination label from the first three letters of SYSDAY (an automatic macro variable) during macro execution. The computed (constructed) destination becomes an entry in the local referencing environment.
3. Both DATA _NULL_ steps are complete within macro DAYS; the CALL SYMPUT statements create macro variables DAY6 and DAY7 in the current referencing environment of DAYS, provided that the environment is not empty. (Chapter 6, "DATA Step Interfaces," discusses the rules the SYMPUT routine uses for storing variables in referencing environments.) Because the computed %GOTO destination is stored in the local environment of DAYS, that environment is not empty, and the SYMPUT routines store variables DAY6 and DAY7 in it.

4. The %PUT statement within macro DAYS writes this line:

```
FIRST TIME--DAY6 IS DAY 6 AND DAY7 IS DAY 7
```

5. The %PUT statement outside macro DAYS writes this line:

```
SECOND TIME--DAY6 IS &DAY6 AND DAY7 IS &DAY7
```

In addition, if the SERROR option is in effect, the macro processor issues a warning message. Because DAY6 and DAY7 are local variables, they disappear when macro DAYS ceases execution.

%IF-%THEN / %ELSE Statements

The %IF-%THEN and %ELSE statements work like the corresponding statements IF-THEN and ELSE in the DATA step.

The form of the %IF-%THEN and %ELSE statements is

%IF *expression* **%THEN** *macro-expression;*
<**%ELSE** *macro-expression;*>

where

expression	is any macro expression that yields a logical expression. The macro processor evaluates the expression, substituting macro variable values or the result of a macro call. If the expression is true (has a nonzero numeric value), the %THEN clause is processed. If the expression is false (zero), the %ELSE statement, if one is present, is processed. If the expression resolves to a null value or a value containing nonnumeric characters, the macro processor issues an error message. See Chapter 9, "Macro Compilation and Execution," for a discussion of macro expressions.
macro-expression	is any macro expression, including constant text, or a macro program statement. If constant text contains semicolons, enclose it in the %STR function (described in Chapter 4, "Macro Functions").

The macro language does not use a subsetting %IF statement; thus, you cannot use %IF without %THEN.

The following examples illustrate valid %IF-%THEN statements:

- `%if &name=GEORGE %then %let lastname=smith;`
  `%if %upcase(&name)=GEORGE %then %let lastname=smith;`

In the first statement, if the value of macro variable NAME is the uppercase string **GEORGE**, the expression is true, and the %LET statement is executed. Any other value for NAME, such as **George**, does not make the expression true. In the second %IF statement, the %UPCASE function converts lowercase characters to uppercase so that the values **George** and **george**, for example, also make the expression true. (The %UPCASE function is discussed in Chapter 4.)

- `%if &i=10 and &j>5 %then %put check the index variables;`

This %IF statement contains a compound expression.

- `%if &city ne %then %str(keep citypop statepop;);`
  `%else %str(keep statepop;);`

If the value of macro variable CITY is not null, the %THEN statement generates the first KEEP statement. The %STR function, which treats semicolons as text, prevents the semicolon at the end of the constant text from ending the %THEN clause. (If that semicolon ended the %THEN clause, the macro processor would treat the second semicolon as text. Because the macro processor does not allow constant text between a %THEN and a %ELSE clause, the macro processor would issue an error message.) If the value of CITY is null, the %ELSE statement generates a different KEEP statement.

Macro FISCAL, shown here, generates one of two groups of PROC steps:

```
%macro fiscal;
   %if "&sysdate"="15APR90" %then
      %do;
         proc means data=total;
         run;
         proc chart data=total;
            hbar revenue / type=mean;
         run;
      %end;
   %else
      %do;
         proc means data=monthly;
         run;
         proc print data=monthly;
         run;
      %end;
%mend fiscal;
```

If the value of the automatic macro variable SYSDATE is **15APR90**, the expression is true, and macro FISCAL processes the %DO statement in the %THEN clause. If the value of SYSDATE is not **15APR90**, the %ELSE statement is executed.

Enclosing both &SYSDATE and the comparison string in double quotes avoids problems that can occasionally arise when a string beginning with a number **0** through **9** followed by a letter **A** through **F** is interpreted as a hexadecimal number instead of as a character string.

%INPUT Statement

The %INPUT statement enables you to supply values to macro variables during macro execution; it permits the construction of conversational macros. When the macro processor reaches a %INPUT statement during macro execution, it waits for you to enter values at the keyboard for the macro variables named in the statement. You can use the %INPUT statement inside or outside a macro and in display manager or interactive line mode.

The form of the %INPUT statement is

%INPUT <*name-1* <. . . *name-n*>>;

where

> *name* can be a macro variable name or a macro expression that produces a macro variable name. The %INPUT statement can contain any number of names separated by blanks.

If a %INPUT statement does not contain any macro variable names, all text entered is assigned to the automatic macro variable SYSBUFFR. (See **AUTOMATIC MACRO VARIABLES** in Chapter 2, "Macro Variables," for more information about SYSBUFFR.)

The value for each macro variable named in the %INPUT statement must be a single word or a quoted string, and values must be separated by blanks. The macro processor matches macro variable values with macro variable names in order. (Therefore, if you supply more than one word as the value of a macro variable, the second word becomes the value of the next macro variable; the macro variables and values become mismatched.) After all values have been matched with macro variable names, excess text becomes the value of the automatic macro variable SYSBUFFR.

The macro processor interprets the line submitted after a %INPUT statement as the value of the macro variable or variables named or as the value of SYSBUFFR. If you submit a %INPUT statement in open code as part of a longer program in the display manager PROGRAM EDITOR window, the line following the %INPUT statement must contain a response. Likewise, if you invoke a macro containing a %INPUT statement as part of a longer program, the line following the macro invocation must contain a response. Otherwise, the macro processor interprets the next line in the program as the response to the %INPUT statement.

Examples

The following examples illustrate the %INPUT statement.

Example 1: Assigning Values to Variables Named in a %INPUT Statement

Macro PLACES, shown here, uses macro variables CITY and STATE to show how the macro processor assigns values with the %INPUT statement:

```
%macro places;
   %put Enter values for city and state.;
   %input city state;
   %put *&city* **&state** ***&sysbuffr***;
%mend places;
```

Each time you invoke macro PLACES, the first %PUT statement writes the following:

```
Enter values for city and state.
```

If you respond

```
Reno Nevada
```

Reno is the value of CITY, **Nevada** is the value of STATE, and SYSBUFFR has a null value (0 characters). The second %PUT statement writes the following:

```
*Reno* **Nevada** ******
```

If you respond

```
San Francisco California
```

San is the value of CITY, **Francisco** is the value of STATE, and **California** (beginning with the blank following **Francisco**) is the value of SYSBUFFR. Therefore, the second %PUT statement writes the following:

```
*San* **Francisco** *** California***
```

If you respond

```
'San Francisco' California
```

'San Francisco' is the value of CITY, **California** is the value of STATE, and SYSBUFFR has a null value. The second %PUT statement writes the following:

```
*'San Francisco'* **California** ******
```

Note that the quotes around **'San Francisco'** are part of the value of CITY; to remove the quotes, add a %LET statement containing the %SUBSTR function to the macro, as shown here:

```
%macro places2;
    %put Enter values for city and state.;
    %input city state;
    %put *&city* **&state** ***&sysbuffr***;
    %let city2=%substr(&city,2,%length(&city)-2);
    %put ****&city2****;
%mend places2;
```

Invoking PLACES2 causes the last %PUT statement to write the following:

```
****San Francisco****
```

Example 2:   Assigning a Response to SYSBUFFR

Macro CITIES, shown here, assigns the entire response to SYSBUFFR and then assigns the value of SYSBUFFR to another macro variable. This is the simplest way to input a value containing blanks.

```
%macro cities;
    %put Enter a value for city.;
    %input;
    %let city=&sysbuffr;
    %put *&city*;
%mend cities;
```

The first %PUT statement prompts you for a value, as follows:

```
Enter a value for city.
```

If you respond

```
Baton Rouge
```

the second %PUT statement writes the following:

```
*Baton Rouge*
```

Example 3:   Responding with a Value Containing an Unmatched Quote

You can use the %INPUT statement to assign a value containing an unmatched quote or parenthesis; however, you must use the %BQUOTE function to use that value later. The following example illustrates a response with an unmatched quote and the use of the %BQUOTE function:

```
%put Enter a name:;
%input;
```

The macro processor displays

```
Enter a name:
```

and you respond with the following:

```
O'Neal
```

The name **O'Neal** becomes the value of SYSBUFFR. To write the value of SYSBUFFR with the %PUT statement, quote the value of SYSBUFFR with the %BQUOTE function, as in

```
%put %bquote(&sysbuffr);
```

which writes the following:

```
O'Neal
```

Chapter 4, "Macro Functions," introduces the %BQUOTE function, and Chapter 10, "Macro Quoting," describes it in detail.

%KEYDEF Statement

The %KEYDEF statement enables you to define a function key or to find out the definition of a function key on your terminal. You can use the %KEYDEF statement within a macro definition or in open code.

You can only use the %KEYDEF statement in a SAS display manager session. Function key definitions you assign with the %KEYDEF statement only remain in effect for the duration of your current SAS session or until you change them again during the session. You can save function key definitions in the KEYS display manager window using the SAVE display manager command.

The form of the %KEYDEF statement is

%KEYDEF *key-name* | *'key-name'* | *"key-name"* <*text*>;

where

key-name | *'key-name'* | *"key-name"*
    is the name of any function key on your terminal, for example, F1. If you use only the *key-name* argument, the SAS System issues a message identifying the definition of the function key you specify. To specify a *key-name* containing a special character, or one with more than one word (for example, 'SHF F1' for a shift F1), enclose the entire *key-name* in either single or double quotes. You can specify only one *key-name* in any %KEYDEF statement. The maximum length for *key-name* is eight characters.

    Note: The names of function keys vary by operating system and terminal. Here are some examples of function key names:

        • f1
        • ^a
        • 'SHF F6'
        • pf12

    Function key names do not always contain numbers, as the second example shows. See your SAS Software Consultant or refer to the SAS documentation for your operating system for details.

<*text*>
    is any text you want to assign to a function key. Omitting *text* causes the macro processor to display the current definition for *key-name* in the SAS log.

    The maximum amount of text in a function key definition is 80 characters. Typical function key definitions include display manager commands. By using the SUBMIT display manager command, you can assign DATA or PROC step statements to a function key.

    You can assign macro invocations or macro variable references that generate display manager commands to a function key. If you assign a macro or a macro variable reference that generates more than 80 characters of text using double quotes or no quotes, the SAS System truncates the value assigned to the key to 80 characters without providing a warning or an error message.

    You can specify *text* in three different ways:

        text
        (unquoted string)
            assigns everything between *key-name* and the first semicolon to a function key. The SAS System automatically uppercases text you assign as an unquoted string.

~*text*

(string following a tilde)

assigns to a function key characters you want to insert after your current cursor position. When you press a function key after you assign it *text* with a tilde, the SAS System does not treat *text* as a display manager command, but instead it inserts the text after the current cursor position in any field of any window that accepts input. The tilde does not become part of the text you insert. The first semicolon in *text* ends the %KEYDEF statement. The SAS System automatically uppercases text you assign following a tilde. The tilde works the same way in the %KEYDEF statement as it does in the KEYDEF display manager command, documented in Chapter 18, "SAS Display Manager Commands," in *SAS Language: Reference, Version 6, First Edition.*

'*text*' | "*text*"

(as a quoted string)

includes semicolons and lowercase text in values you assign to function keys. Including semicolons allows you to specify more than one display manager command in a key definition. You can also assign display manager SUBMIT commands that contain SAS statements to function keys.

How the %KEYDEF Statement Treats Quoted Key Names and Text

The SAS System interprets a quoted key name by removing leading and trailing blanks, reducing multiple embedded blanks to one blank for each series, and truncating anything over eight characters. The SAS System interprets quoted *text* by inserting a leading and trailing blank, concatenating all individually quoted portions of *text* into a single string, reducing multiple embedded blanks between each quoted portion to one blank for each portion, and truncating anything over 80 characters.

Assigning a Macro to a Function Key

You can assign either a macro invocation or the text generated by a macro to a function key. If you use double quotes or no quotes around a macro invocation in a %KEYDEF statement, you assign the text the macro generates because macro execution occurs during the execution of the %KEYDEF statement. If you use single quotes, you assign the invocation itself because the macro reference does not resolve when the %KEYDEF statement executes, so macro invocation and execution occurs whenever you use the function key.

Using single quotes when you assign a macro or a macro variable reference to a function key is one way to circumvent the 80-character limit. It prevents macro invocation or macro variable resolution until you press the function key.

Consider the following examples:

- using single quotes. After you submit the statement

```
%keydef f1 '%erase';
```

function key f1 invokes the macro ERASE, which executes each time you press the function key.

- using double quotes. After you submit the statement

```
%keydef f2 "%findr";
```

function key f2 contains whatever text the macro %FINDR generates enclosed in quotes because the macro executes when you submit the %KEYDEF statement.

- using no quotes. After you submit the statement

```
%keydef f3 %ckclear;
```

function key f3 contains whatever text macro CKCLEAR generates when you submit the %KEYDEF statement, but the result is not enclosed in quotes. (However, the macro CKCLEAR can generate quotes as part of its text.)

Assigning SUBMIT Commands to a Function Key

You can use the %KEYDEF statement to assign SAS code to a function key by using the display manager SUBMIT command, as in the following example:

```
%keydef f1 'submit "proc print data=hotdog;";
           submit "run;"';
```

In this example, the first semicolon ends the PROC PRINT statement you want to submit, the second semicolon marks the end of the first SUBMIT display manager command, the third semicolon marks the end of the RUN statement, and the last semicolon marks the end of the %KEYDEF statement itself. Notice how single quotes in this statement enclose the entire key definition, which includes other quoted strings.

Using Comments in a %KEYDEF Statement

You can include comments in key definitions to clarify the functions you assign to keys, as in the following examples:

```
%keydef f1 "%app /* Appends transaction file to master */";
%keydef f2 '%printit /* Prints selected variables */';
```

Using a Macro to Assign Many Function Keys

The following macro, MYKEYS, uses the %KEYDEF statement to set a series of key definitions:

```
%macro mykeys;
   %keydef f1 zoom;
   %keydef f2 "clear log;clear output";
   %keydef f4 rfind;
%mend mykeys;
```

See Also

KEYDEF display manager command in Chapter 18 in *SAS Language: Reference, Version 6, First Edition*

%*label*: Statement

Statement labels in the macro language work like statement labels in the DATA step, and the rules for naming labels in the macro language are also the same. Macro statement labels begin with a percent sign.

The form of macro statement labels is

%*label*: *macro-text*

where

> *label*   is any SAS name.
>
> *macro-text*   is a macro program statement or macro expression. Here are some examples of statement labels in the macro language:

```
%one: %let book=elementary;
%final: data _null_;
%out: %mend;
```

When you label a statement in the macro language, put a percent sign in front of the label. When you use the label in a %GOTO statement, do not use a percent sign. A percent sign in front of a label name in a %GOTO statement tells the macro processor to call a macro of that name. If the macro processor cannot find the macro called, it issues an error message.

In macro INFO, shown here, the %GOTO statement causes execution to jump to label QUICK when the uppercase value of parameter TYPE is SHORT:

```
%macro info(type);
   %if %upcase(&type)=SHORT %then %goto quick;
   proc contents;
   run;
   proc freq;
      tables _numeric_;
   run;
   %quick: proc print data=_last_(obs=10);
   run;
%mend info;
```

The call

```
%info(short)
```

causes the macro processor to generate these statements:

```
PROC PRINT DATA=_LAST_(OBS=10);
RUN;
```

Invoking the macro with a different parameter value, such as

```
%info(long)
```

generates these statements:

```
PROC CONTENTS;
RUN;
PROC FREQ;
   TABLES _NUMERIC_;
RUN;
PROC PRINT DATA=_LAST_(OBS=10);
RUN;
```

An alternative to using the %GOTO statement and statement label, as in macro INFO, is to use a %IF-%THEN statement with a %DO group:

```
%macro info2(type);
   %if %upcase(&type) ne SHORT %then
      %do;
          proc contents;
          run;
          proc freq;
             tables _numeric_;
          run;
      %end;
   proc print data=_last_(obs=10);
   run;
%mend info2;
```

%LET Statement

The %LET statement, used either inside or outside a macro, creates a macro variable and assigns it a value, or changes the value of an existing macro variable. A %LET statement can define only one macro variable at a time.

The form of the %LET statement is

%LET *macro-variable*=<*value*>;

where

    macro-variable   is either the name of a macro variable or a macro expression that produces a macro variable name. The name can refer to a new or existing macro variable.

    value   is a string or a macro expression that yields a string. Omitting *value* produces a value of null (0 characters). Leading and trailing blanks in *value* are ignored; to make them significant, enclose *value* in the %STR function (described in Chapter 4, "Macro Functions").

This example uses %LET to create a macro variable named STATE with a value of **NC**:

```
%let state=NC;
```

Macro LISTING, shown here, references STATE:

```
%macro listing;
   proc print data=&state;
      title "Listing of &state Residents";
   run;
%mend listing;
```

You can supply values with a %LET statement before calling the macro, as in these examples:

```
%let state=NC;
%listing


%let state=SC;
%listing
```

The preceding %LET statements and macro invocations generate these statements:

```
PROC PRINT DATA=NC;
   TITLE "Listing of NC Residents";
RUN;

PROC PRINT DATA=SC;
   TITLE "Listing of SC Residents";
RUN;
```

Macro CREATE, shown here, creates a series of global macro variables and assigns each of them a value with the %LET statement. CREATE illustrates using a macro expression to create a macro variable name in a %LET statement.

```
%macro create(num);
   %do i=1 %to &num;
      %global x&i;
      %let x&i=&i;
   %end;
%mend create;
```

The following invocation causes the iterative %DO loop to execute three times:

```
%create(3)
```

Each execution produces a %GLOBAL statement and a %LET statement, as follows:

```
%GLOBAL X1;
%LET X1=1;
%GLOBAL X2;
%LET X2=2;
%GLOBAL X3;
%LET X3=3;
```

The macro variable reference &I produces part of the macro variable name in the %GLOBAL and %LET statements, as well as the value of each macro variable.

%LOCAL Statement

The %LOCAL statement specifies macro variables that are to be local to the macro. The statement is useful for ensuring that values of macro variables created earlier in a program are not inadvertently affected by values assigned in the current macro. You can use the %LOCAL statement only inside a macro.

The form of the %LOCAL statement is

%LOCAL *macro-variable-1* <. . . *macro-variable-n*>;

where

> *macro-variable*   can be the name of a local macro variable or a macro expression that generates one or more macro variable names. For example, this %LOCAL statement defines two local macro variables:
>
> ```
> %local total1 total2;
> ```
>
> Note that you cannot use a SAS variable list or a macro expression that generates a SAS variable list in a %LOCAL statement.

Variables created with a %LOCAL statement have null values until you assign them other values. However, if a previously defined local macro variable is included in a %LOCAL statement, the macro variable retains its previously assigned value.

In the following example, macro PRINTIT defines a local macro variable named COUNT:

```
%macro printit(stop);
   %local count;
   %let count=1;
   %do %while (&count<=&stop);
      proc print data=d&count;
         title "Daily Data for Day &count";
      run;
      %let count=%eval(&count+1);
   %end;
%mend printit;
```

If COUNT is also defined as a macro variable outside macro PRINTIT, the previously defined value is not influenced by the values assigned within PRINTIT. The %EVAL function, which increments COUNT's value, is described in Chapter 4, "Macro Functions."

Suppose you invoke macro PRINTIT in the following program:

```
%let count=Accounting Department;
proc means data=current;
   title "Summary of Numeric Variables for &count";
run;

%printit(2)

proc print data=current;
   title "General Information for &count";
run;
```

After macro execution and macro variable resolution, the SAS System sees these statements:

```
PROC MEANS DATA=CURRENT;
    TITLE "Summary of Numeric Variables for Accounting Department";
RUN;

PROC PRINT DATA=D1;
    TITLE "Daily Data for Day 1";
RUN;
PROC PRINT DATA=D2;
    TITLE "Daily Data for Day 2";
RUN;

PROC PRINT DATA=CURRENT;
    TITLE "General Information for Accounting Department";
RUN;
```

Macro DSNAME, shown here, executes %LOCAL statements conditionally:

```
%macro dsname(sasdsn);
    %if %scan(&sasdsn,2) ne %then
        %do;
            %local name1 name2;
            %let name1=%scan(&sasdsn,1);
            %let name2=%scan(&sasdsn,2);
            %put name1 is &name1 and name2 is &name2;
        %end;
    %else
        %do;
            %local fullname;
            %let fullname=work.&sasdsn;
            %put fullname is &fullname;
        %end;
%mend dsname;
```

Macro DSNAME first checks to see whether the value of SASDSN is one word or two words separated by a period. (The %SCAN function is discussed in Chapter 4). If the value contains two words, DSNAME creates the local macro variables NAME1 and NAME2; if the name contains a single word, DSNAME creates the local macro variable FULLNAME instead. The invocations

```
%dsname(in.clinic)
%dsname(visits)
```

write these messages:

```
name1 is in and name2 is clinic
fullname is work.visits
```

Macro Invocations

A *macro invocation*, or *macro call*, causes the macro processor to begin executing a macro. The macro processor resolves all macro expressions in a macro invocation before beginning to execute the macro. In Release 6.06, there are two kinds of macro invocations:

- name-style. You can use a name-style invocation for any macro.
- statement-style. You can use a statement-style invocation to make a macro invocation look like a SAS statement. To use a statement-style invocation, make sure the macro definition contains the STMT option in the %MACRO statement and the system option IMPLMAC is in effect.

Name-Style Invocations

You can use a name-style invocation with any macro; it is the most common kind of macro invocation. You must use a name-style invocation for a macro defined without the STMT option in the %MACRO statement. If a macro is defined with the STMT option and the NOIMPLMAC system option is in effect when you invoke it, you can invoke it with a name-style invocation.

The form of a name-style invocation is

%*macro-name* <(<*parameter-value-list* >)>

The following terms can appear in the invocation:

macro-name	is the name of the macro you are invoking or a macro expression that produces the name of the macro you are invoking.
parameter-value-list	

contains a series of values you specify at the time you invoke the macro, which the macro uses when it executes. How you specify the values in *parameter-value-list* depends on whether it contains *positional-values*, *keyword-parameters*, or both. The syntax for each follows:

positional-value-1 <. . . ,*positional-value-n*>
specifies values for one or more positional parameters. The macro processor matches the first positional parameter value with the first positional parameter in the %MACRO statement, the second with the second, and so on. Thus, the order in which you give positional parameter values in the macro call is important. To omit a positional parameter value at the end of a value list, simply omit it; to omit a positional value that is not the last in the list, mark its place with a comma. Omitting a positional parameter value in a macro invocation assigns the parameter a null value.

If an invocation contains both *positional-values* and *keyword-parameters*, the *positional-values* must come first.

keyword-parameter-1=<*value*>
<. . . ,*keyword-parameter-n*=<*value*>>
specifies the names of one or more *keyword-parameters* followed by a *value*. You can

specify *keyword-parameters* and *values* in any order after the last *positional-value*. Using the parameter name and an equal sign without a value assigns a value of null; omitting the parameter name and value causes the parameter to retain the value assigned in the macro definition, including a null value if no default was specified. To omit a keyword parameter in the macro call, simply omit it.

You can omit the entire *parameter-value-list* in the macro call; in that case, all the parameters retain their default values. In a display manager or interactive line mode session, you need to indicate to the macro processor that you do not want to specify any parameter values by entering either an empty set of parentheses or more code. In an interactive SAS session, a macro invocation without a *parameter-value-list* is not complete until you submit an empty set of parentheses or more code. In a noninteractive or batch program, you don't need to do anything special to indicate the absence of a *parameter-value-list*.

Macro CREATE, shown here, has two positional parameters, NEW and OLD:

```
%macro create(new,old);
   data &new;
      set &old;
      if profit>0;
   run;
%mend create;
```

To invoke CREATE, supply values for NEW and OLD in the same order they were defined:

```
%create(revenue,year90)
```

Macro execution generates these statements:

```
DATA REVENUE;
   SET YEAR90;
   IF PROFIT>0;
RUN;
```

Holding the place of a positional parameter with a comma, as in the invocation

```
%create(,year91)
```

produces these statements:

```
DATA ;
   SET YEAR91;
   IF PROFIT>0;
RUN;
```

The blank after DATA is the blank that separated DATA and &NEW in the macro definition.

When you invoke a macro with positional parameters, use commas to delimit your parameters. You can use the fact that blanks do not delimit parameters to your advantage. For example, the invocation

```
%create(revenue backup,year91)
```

produces these statements:

```
DATA REVENUE BACKUP;
   SET YEAR91;
   IF PROFIT>0;
RUN;
```

In the macro invocation, all text up to the comma, including the blank, is the value of parameter NEW. Thus, you can use macro CREATE to create several data sets instead of just one.

Macro CHOOSE, shown here, has two keyword parameters. Parameter P is given the default value `print`; T by default has a null value.

```
%macro choose(p=print,t=);
   proc &p;
      title "&t";
   run;
%mend choose;
```

Select the title you want when you invoke the macro

```
%choose(t=printout of data)
```

to generate these statements:

```
PROC PRINT;
   TITLE "PRINTOUT OF DATA";
RUN;
```

The invocation

```
%choose()
```

uses the default parameter values and generates these statements:

```
PROC PRINT;
   TITLE "";
RUN;
```

The order for keyword variables in the invocation is not important. The invocation

```
%choose(t=average values,p=means)
```

yields these statements:

```
PROC MEANS;
   TITLE "AVERAGE VALUES";
RUN;
```

In the following example, macro BUILD contains both a positional and a keyword parameter. Positional parameter NEW contains the name of the SAS data set; keyword parameter IN contains the fileref of the external file of raw data. The default value for IN is `inone`.

```
%macro build(new,in=inone);
   data &new;
      infile &in;
      input a b c;
   run;
   proc print;
   run;
%mend build;
```

The name-style invocation

```
%build(april90,in=ina)
```

assigns NEW the value `april90`, changes the value of IN to `ina`, and generates these statements:

```
DATA APRIL90;
    INFILE INA;
    INPUT A B C;
RUN;
PROC PRINT;
RUN;
```

You must give the value for NEW, a positional parameter, before the value for the keyword parameter IN.

Statement-Style Invocations

Statement-style macro invocations enable you to make macro calls that look like SAS statements. The call begins with a keyword (the macro name) and ends with a semicolon, and parameter values are separated by blanks. You must use a statement-style macro call as a complete statement; the call cannot appear within a SAS statement. In order to use statement-style invocations, the %MACRO statement defining the macro must contain the STMT option, and the system option IMPLMAC must be in effect. If a macro is defined with the STMT option and the NOIMPLMAC system option is in effect when you invoke it, you can invoke it with a name-style invocation.

The form of a statement-style macro invocation is

macro-name <parameter-value-list>;

These terms can appear in a statement-style invocation:

macro-name   specifies the name of the macro. Do not put a percent sign in front of the name.

parameter-value-list

contains a series of values you specify at the time you invoke the macro, which the macro uses when it executes. How you specify the values in *parameter-value-list* depends on whether it contains *positional-values*, *keyword-parameters*, or both. The syntax for each follows:

positional-value-1 <. . . ,positional-value-n>
specifies values for one or more positional parameters. The macro processor matches the first positional parameter value in the call with the first positional parameter in the macro definition, the second with the second, and so on.

In a statement-style invocation, you cannot allow positional parameters to retain their null values by omitting them in the macro call unless the parameters omitted are the last in the list. (Commas are treated as characters in the values instead of as delimiters, and a blank cannot hold a place. Thus, omitting a value in the call causes the parameters and values to become mismatched.) To allow a positional parameter to receive a null value, use a

%IF statement in the macro definition to conditionally assign the null value:

```
%macro test(name,id) / stmt;
    %if &name=skip %then %let name=;
    %put &name &id;
%mend test;
```

The call

```
test skip 12345;
```

assigns NAME a value of null within the macro, and the %PUT statement writes only the ID number. (To supply a value containing blanks, as in the name **MARY WHITE**, enclose the value in quotes; the quotes become part of the value.)

If a statement-style invocation contains both *positional-values* and *keyword-parameters*, the *positional-values* must come first.

keyword-parameter-1 = <*value*>
<. . . ,*keyword-parameter-n* = <*value*>>
specifies the names of one or more *keyword-parameters* followed by a *value*. You can specify *keyword-parameters* and *values* in any order after the last *positional-value*. Using the parameter name and an equal sign without a value assigns a value of null; omitting a keyword parameter and value in the macro call causes the parameter to retain the value assigned in the macro definition.

Specifying only the name of a *keyword-parameter* without an equal sign in a statement-style invocation assigns the parameter a value of 1. Assigning a value to a keyword parameter by specifying only its name is most useful when the default value of the parameter is 0, since 1 has a value of true and 0 has a value of false, as in the DATA step. Thus, you can write %IF statements such as the following:

```
%if &macro-variable %then statement;
```

By assigning a default value of 0 to keyword parameters, you can turn parameters "on" in an invocation by just specifying the name of the parameter without the equals sign. Omitting the name of the parameter in an invocation turns it "off."

Macro CHART, shown here, is a statement-style macro that generates a PROC CHART step:

```
%macro chart(type,var) / stmt;
    proc chart;
        &type &var / discrete;
    run;
%mend chart;
```

Invoking macro CHART in the program

```
*correct usage;
data new;
   set in.old;
run;

chart hbar sales;
```

causes the SAS System to see these statements:

```
*CORRECT USAGE;
DATA NEW;
   SET IN.OLD;
RUN;

PROC CHART;
   HBAR SALES / DISCRETE;
RUN;
```

Macro VLIST is another statement-style macro. However, the following SAS program invokes it in the wrong place:

```
%macro vlist / stmt;
   age height weight
%mend vlist;

data new;
   set old;
   *note incorrect invocation;
   keep vlist;
run;
```

The SAS System sees this DATA step:

```
DATA NEW;
   SET OLD;
   *NOTE INCORRECT INVOCATION;
   KEEP VLIST;
RUN;
```

Because the word VLIST is not the first word in a statement, the macro processor does not scan the name VLIST, so you never invoke it. The text VLIST is passed to the DATA step without change; therefore, the SAS System interprets VLIST as a variable name and produces an error message if it cannot find that variable.

Macro SHOW, shown here, illustrates ways to assign keyword parameter values:

```
%macro show(obs=500,stay=0) / stmt;
   %if &stay %then
   %put the value of obs is &obs and the value of stay is &stay..;
   %else
   %put the value of obs is &obs and the value of stay remains &stay..;
%mend show;
```

Referring to STAY by its name only, as in the call

```
show stay;
```

produces the following message:

```
THE VALUE OF OBS IS 500 AND THE VALUE OF STAY IS 1.
```

Because the name of the keyword parameter STAY appears in the macro call, STAY receives a value of 1, and the %IF statement is true. Macro parameter OBS, which was not mentioned in the call, retains its default value.

Some other calls and the messages they write are shown here:

```
show obs;
```
THE VALUE OF OBS IS 1 AND THE VALUE OF STAY REMAINS 0.

```
show obs=250;
```
THE VALUE OF OBS IS 250 AND THE VALUE OF STAY REMAINS 0.

```
show obs stay;
```
THE VALUE OF OBS IS 1 AND THE VALUE OF STAY IS 1.

Usage Notes

Combining Different Styles of Invocations

Do not combine elements of name-style and statement-style macro invocations in the same call since unexpected results can occur. For example, the following program contains a percent sign in front of a statement-style macro call:

```
%macro new(start=0,list=) / stmt;
   %if &start %then %str(keep &list;);
   %else %str(keep month;);
%mend new;

data thisweek;
   set lastweek;
   *note mixed style of invocation;
   %new start list=week;
run;
```

In this program, the macro processor reads %NEW as a name-style macro invocation and does not interpret START or LIST as macro parameters. Therefore, the parameters retain their default values. The SAS System reads the program

```
DATA THISWEEK;
   SET LASTWEEK;
   *NOTE MIXED STYLE OF INVOCATION;
   KEEP MONTH;
   START LIST=WEEK;
RUN;
```

and produces an error message because of the following invalid SAS statement:

```
START LIST=WEEK;
```

Placing a Semicolon after a Name-Style Invocation

Placing a semicolon after a name-style macro invocation introduces a semicolon into your SAS program. If the semicolon is not needed in the program, it either becomes a null statement or causes an error. For example, macros LIST1 and LIST2, shown here, each produce part of a variable list:

```
%macro list1;
   name age sex
%mend list1;
```

```
%macro list2;
   height weight
%mend list2;
```

If you invoke these macros in the SAS program

```
proc print;
   var %list1; %list2;
run;
```

the following SAS statements result:

```
PROC PRINT;
   VAR NAME AGE SEX; HEIGHT WEIGHT;
RUN;
```

The VAR statement ends prematurely because of the semicolon following the text generated by LIST1, and the text generated by LIST2 becomes an invalid SAS statement.

Conflict of Names

When you define a statement-style macro, be careful that the macro name does not appear at the beginning of other SAS statements in your program as a variable name or other SAS name. For example, consider the following program:

```
%macro a / stmt;
   data one;
      a=1;
   run;
%mend a;

a;
```

The macro processor interprets the following statement as an invalid statement-style invocation of macro A, not as constant text:

```
A=1;
```

%MACRO Statement

The %MACRO statement begins the definition of a macro, assigns the macro a name, and may optionally include a parameter list of macro variables, a list of options, or both. The %MACRO statement can appear anywhere in a SAS program, except within data lines; however, a macro must be defined before it can be invoked. If two macros are defined with the same name, the second one replaces the first. A macro definition cannot contain a CARDS statement, a PARMCARDS statement, or data lines.

Once defined, a macro is an entry in a SAS catalog in the WORK library; however, the SAS System does not currently support copying or renaming macros as it does other types of SAS catalog entries.

The form of the %MACRO statement is

%MACRO *name*<(*parameter-list*)> < / <STMT> <PARMBUFF>>;

These terms can appear in the %MACRO statement:

name   names the macro. *Name* must be a SAS name that you supply; you cannot use a macro expression to generate a macro name in a %MACRO statement. In addition, certain names are reserved for current or possible future use by the macro processor; you cannot use a reserved word as a macro name. See Appendix 2, "Reserved Words in the Macro Facility," for a list of reserved words.

parameter-list   names one or more local macro variables whose values you can specify when you invoke the macro. Variables you use as parameters are always local to the macro that uses them, even if variables with the same names exist in the global referencing environment. You must supply each parameter name; you cannot use a macro expression to generate it. A %MACRO statement *parameter-list* can contain any number of macro parameters separated by commas. The macro variables in the parameter list are usually referenced in the macro.

The parameters in the list can be positional or keyword. The syntax for each follows:

positional-parameter-1 <. . . ,*positional-parameter-n*>
defines one or more *positional-parameters* by giving only the name of the parameter in the *parameter-list*. You can define a list of positional parameters in any order, but in the macro invocation, their values must appear in the same order in which the parameter names appear in the %MACRO statement. Positional parameters have null values when the macro is defined.

If both positional and keyword parameters appear in a macro definition, positional parameters must come first.

keyword-parameter-1 = <*value*>
<. . . ,*keyword-parameter-n* = <*value*>>
defines one or more *keyword-parameters* by giving the name of the parameter and an equal sign. You can optionally give a default value after the equal

sign; *keyword-parameters* without a value after the equal sign have a default value of null.

If both positional and keyword parameters appear in a macro definition, positional parameters must come first.

STMT   specifies that the macro can accept either a name-style invocation or a statement-style invocation. Macros defined with the STMT option are sometimes called *statement-style macros*. See **Macro Invocations** earlier in this chapter for a description of statement-style invocations.

The IMPLMAC system option must be in effect to use statement-style macro invocations; however, you can use a name-style invocation for a macro defined with the STMT option even if the IMPLMAC option is not in effect. Note that if the IMPLMAC option is in effect and you have defined a statement-style macro in your program, the macro processor scans the first word of every SAS statement to see whether it is a statement-style macro invocation; when the NOIMPLMAC option is in effect, the macro processor only treats words following the % symbols as potential macro invocations.

PARMBUFF   assigns the entire list of parameter values in a macro call, including the parentheses in a name-style invocation, as the value of the automatic local macro variable SYSPBUFF. (See Chapter 2, "Macro Variables," for a description of SYSPBUFF.) You can specify PARMBUFF or use the alias PBUFF. Using the PARMBUFF option, you can define a macro that accepts any number of parameter values.

You can specify the PARMBUFF option in a macro definition regardless of whether the definition contains a parameter list. If the macro definition includes both a set of parameters and the PARMBUFF option, the macro invocation causes the parameters to receive values and the entire invocation list of values to be assigned to the SYSPBUFF macro variable as well. To invoke a macro defined with the PARMBUFF option in a display manager or interactive line mode session without supplying a value list, you must enter an empty set of parentheses or more code after the invocation to indicate the absence of a value list, even if the macro definition contains no parameters.

You can nest macro definitions, but doing so is rarely needed. In most cases, nesting a macro invocation inside another macro definition is sufficient. Chapter 9, "Macro Compilation and Execution," describes the effect of nesting macro definitions compared with that of nesting macro invocations.

In the example below, macro P generates a PROC PRINT step in which you specify a list of variables to print and a list of variables to total. Parameter VAR contains the variables to appear in the VAR statement; parameter SUM contains those to appear in the SUM statement.

```
%macro p(var,sum);
   proc print;
        var &var;
        sum &sum;
   run;
%mend p;
```

The invocation

```
%p(school district enrollmt, enrollmt)
```

generates these statements:

```
PROC PRINT;
   VAR SCHOOL DISTRICT ENROLLMT;
   SUM ENROLLMT;
RUN;
```

In the macro invocation, all text up to the comma is the value of parameter VAR; text following the comma is the value of parameter SUM.

In the following example, macro PRINTZ uses the PARMBUFF option to allow you to input a different number of arguments each time you invoke it, as long as you specify at least one parameter:

```
%macro printz(x)/parmbuff;
   %let stop=%length(&syspbuff);
   %do i=1 %to &stop;
      %let dsname=%scan(&syspbuff,&i);
      %if &dsname ne %then
         %do;
             proc print data=&dsname;
         %end;
      %else %let i=&stop;
   %end;
   run;
%mend printz;
```

The %SCAN function treats the commas separating the parameter values in a name-style invocation as delimiters. The %DO loop stops when the %SCAN function returns a null result, indicating that there are no more parameters. When you invoke the macro like this

```
%printz(purple,red,blue,teal)
```

the SAS System sees these statements:

```
PROC PRINT DATA=PURPLE;
PROC PRINT DATA=RED;
PROC PRINT DATA=BLUE;
PROC PRINT DATA=TEAL;
RUN;
```

Thus, you can use the PARMBUFF option to write macros that accept a varying list of parameter values. You specify how the macro is to use the values by the way you use the value of SYSPBUFF.

%MEND Statement

The %MEND statement ends a macro definition. The form of the %MEND statement is

%MEND <*macro-name*>;

where

macro-name   optionally names the macro being closed. Repeating the name of the macro is useful for clarity. If you specify *macro-name*, the name in the %MEND statement must match the name in the %MACRO statement.

The following example illustrates the %MEND statement:

```
%macro d(dsn);
   data &dsn;
      set perm.dataset;
      if month="&dsn";
   run;
%mend d;
```

%PUT Statement

The %PUT statement writes text to the SAS log. It can be used inside or outside a macro.

The form of the %PUT statement is

%PUT *text*;

where

> *text*   is any text. If *text* is longer than the current line size, the additional characters appear on the next line.

The %PUT statement removes leading and trailing blanks unless you use a macro language quoting function. (See Chapter 10, "Macro Quoting," for details.)

Macro TESTPUT, shown here, illustrates several %PUT statements. Match the circled numbers to the descriptions that follow the invocation.

```
%macro testput;
    %put Macro TESTPUT has begun execution.;      ❶
    %put Macro TESTPUT was invoked on &sysday..;  ❷
    %put %str(Use a semicolon(;) to end a SAS statement.);  ❸
    %put %str( );  ❹
    %put %str(Enter the student%'s address.);  ❺
%mend testput;
```

Invoking macro TESTPUT with

```
%testput
```

writes these lines:

```
Macro TESTPUT has begun execution.
Macro TESTPUT was invoked on Monday.
Use a semicolon(;) to end a SAS statement.

Enter the student's address.
```

1. The first %PUT statement writes a simple line of text.
2. The macro variable reference in the second %PUT statement resolves before the statement executes. Because a period after a macro variable reference is a delimiter, the second period in the text is the period that ends the sentence. (See Chapter 2, "Macro Variables," for more information.)
3. To write a semicolon, enclose the text in the %STR function, which treats special characters as text. (The %STR function is discussed in Chapter 4, "Macro Functions.")
4. Enclosing the blank in the %STR function makes the blank significant, and writing only a blank produces a blank line.
5. This %PUT statement writes an unmatched quote.

%SYSEXEC Statement

The %SYSEXEC statement enables you to issue an operating system command in open code, or within a macro, in a display manager or interactive line mode SAS session. The %SYSEXEC statement causes the operating system to immediately execute the command you specify and assigns any return code from the operating system to the automatic macro variable SYSRC. The %SYSEXEC statement is analogous to the X statement, or the X display manager command. You can use the %SYSEXEC statement to write portable macros that run on multiple operating systems.

The form of the %SYSEXEC statement is

%SYSEXEC <*command*>;

where

 no argument   puts you into operating system mode, where you can issue operating system commands and return to your SAS session.

 command   is any operating system command.

Note: The %SYSEXEC statement is operating system dependent. See the SAS documentation for your operating system to determine whether it is a valid statement on your system. The following items related to the use of the %SYSEXEC statement are operating system specific:

- the availability of the %SYSEXEC statement in batch processing or noninteractive mode
- the way you return from operating system mode to your SAS session after executing the %SYSEXEC statement with no argument
- the commands you can use with the %SYSEXEC statement
- the return codes you get in the automatic macro variable SYSRC.

In the following macro, ACLIB, the %SYSEXEC statement executes one of two operating system utility programs based on the value of automatic macro variable SYSSCP. If the value of SYSSCP is anything other than **OS** or **VMS**, ACLIB writes a message in the SAS log indicating that there are no utilities available. Notice the two periods after the last reference to automatic macro variable SYSSCP; the first period is a delimiter for the reference, and the second period is part of the output you want the %PUT statement to generate. See **AUTOMATIC MACRO VARIABLES** in Chapter 2, "Macro Variables," for more information about SYSSCP.

```
%macro aclib;
    %if %upcase(&sysscp)=OS %then
        %sysexec ex 'bigboy.tools.clist(tiefiles)';
    %else %if %upcase(&sysscp)=VMS %then
        %sysexec @tiefiles;
    %else %put NO UTILITIES AVAILABLE ON &sysscp..;
%mend aclib;
```

%WINDOW Statement

The %WINDOW statement creates customized windows controlled by the macro processor. Macro windows can display text and accept input. They have command and message lines, and the name of the window appears at the top of the window. You can use command-line commands and function keys with macro windows. You can also replace the command line with an action bar generated by the PMENU facility. You can use the %WINDOW statement either inside or outside a macro definition and in a display manager, interactive line mode, or noninteractive session.

You must define a window before you display it. Once defined, a macro window exists until the end of the SAS session, and you can display a window or redefine it at any point. Use the %DISPLAY statement (described earlier in this chapter) to display macro windows.

Defining a macro window within a macro definition causes the macro processor to redefine the window each time the macro executes. If you repeatedly display a window whose definition does not change, it is more efficient to define the window outside a macro or in a macro that you execute once rather than in the macro in which you display it.

If a %WINDOW statement contains the name of a new macro variable, the macro processor creates that variable in the current referencing environment.

This statement description gives reference information for macro windows and shows some examples. Chapter 5, "Macro Windows," discusses creating and displaying macro windows in detail.

The forms of the %WINDOW statement are

%WINDOW *window <window-options> field-definition-1*
        <. . . field-definition-n>;
%WINDOW *window <window-options> group-definition-1*
        <. . . group-definition-n>;
where

window names the window. *Window* is required and must be a valid SAS name.

window-options specify characteristics of the window as a whole. Specify all *window-options* before any field or group definitions. The following *window-options* are available:

COLOR=*color*
    specifies the color of the window background. The default color is black. *Color* can be one of the following:

BLACK	GRAY (or GREY)	PINK
BLUE	GREEN	RED
BROWN	MAGENTA	WHITE
CYAN	ORANGE	YELLOW

The representation of colors may vary, depending on the monitor you use. In addition, on some terminals the background color affects the entire window; on other terminals, it affects only the window border.

COLUMNS=*columns*
    specifies the number of columns in the window, *including borders*. A window can contain any number of columns and can extend beyond the border of the

display (useful mainly when a window will be displayed on a device larger than the one on which it is developed). If you do not specify a number, the window fills all remaining columns in the display; the number of columns depends on the type of monitor being used.*

ICOLUMN=*column*

specifies the initial column within the display at which the window is displayed. If you do not specify a number, the macro processor displays the window at column 1 of the display.

IROW=*row*

specifies the initial row (line) within the display at which the window is displayed. If you do not specify a number, the macro processor displays the window at row 1 of the display.

KEYS=<<*libref.>catalog.>keys-entry*

specifies the name of a KEYS entry that contains the function key definitions for the window. If you specify just *keys-entry*, the SAS System looks in the SASUSER.PROFILE catalog for a KEYS entry of that name. To use a different catalog, specify the three-level name. If you omit the KEYS= option, the SAS System uses the current function key settings defined in the display manager KEYS window.

You can create function key definitions with the display manager KEYS window, the display manager KEYDEF command, or the %KEYDEF statement.

MENU=<<*libref.>catalog.>pmenu-entry*

specifies the name of a pmenu you have built with the PMENU procedure. If you specify just *pmenu-entry*, the SAS System looks in the SASUSER.PROFILE catalog for a PMENU entry of that name. To use a different catalog, specify the three-level name. The PMENU procedure is documented in the *SAS Procedures Guide, Version 6, Third Edition.*

ROWS=*rows*

specifies the number of rows in the window, *including borders.*** A window can contain any number of rows and can extend beyond the border of the display (useful mainly when a window will be displayed on a device larger than the one on which it is developed). If you do not specify a number, the window fills all remaining rows in the display; the number of rows depends on the type of monitor being used.

---

* Depending on the monitor, the left and right borders each absorb 0-3 columns on the display. If you create windows for display on different types of monitors, make sure all fields can be displayed in the narrowest window. Also, if you have worked with windows in Release 6.03, note that the definition of the COLUMNS= option is different in Release 6.06. In Release 6.03, the COLUMNS= value excludes the borders.

** If you have worked with windows in Release 6.03, note that the definition of the ROWS= option is different in Release 6.06. In Release 6.03, the ROWS= value excludes the borders.

field-definition   identifies and describes a macro variable or string to be displayed in the window. A window can contain any number of fields. The form of a field is given in **Defining Fields** later in this section.

group-definition   names a group and defines all fields within a group. A *group-definition* consists of the GROUP= option, described here, and one or more *field-definitions*.

GROUP=*group*

names a group of fields that you want to display in the window at the same time. A window can contain any number of groups of fields; if you omit the GROUP= option, the window contains one unnamed group of fields. *Group* must be a valid SAS name. When you refer to a group in a %DISPLAY statement, write the name as *window.group*.

Organizing fields into groups allows you to create a single window with several possible contents. You choose the group to be displayed in a particular execution of the %DISPLAY statement by specifying *window.group*.

field-definition

identifies and describes a macro variable or string to be displayed in the window. A window can contain any number of fields. The form of a field is given in **Defining Fields** below.

Defining Fields

Use a field to identify a macro variable value or piece of constant text to be displayed, its position within the window, and its attributes. Enclose constant text in quotes. The position of an item is its beginning row and column; attributes include color, whether you can enter a value into the field, and characteristics such as highlighting.

Caution: Do not allow a field to overlap another field displayed at the same time. Serious complications, including the incorrect assignment of values to macro variables, may result. The SAS System writes a warning in the SAS log if fields overlap.*

The form of a field definition containing a macro variable is

<*row column*> *macro-variable* <*field-length*> <*options*>

The form of a field definition containing constant text is

<*row column*> '*text*' | "*text*" <*options*>

The elements of a field definition are defined as follows:

row
column

identify the position of the macro variable or constant text. Each *row* and *column* specification consists of a pointer control and, usually, a *macro-expression* that generates a number. The pointer controls available are described below. The macro processor evaluates the *macro-expression* when it defines the window, not when it displays the window. Thus, the row and column position of a field are fixed when the field is being displayed.

---

* Some terminals treat adjacent fields with no intervening blanks as overlapping fields.

If you omit *row* in the first field of a group, the macro processor uses the first line of the window; if you omit *row* in a later field specification, the macro processor continues on the line from the previous field. The macro processor treats the first usable line of the window as row 1 (that is, it excludes the border, command line or action bar, and message line). The macro processor treats the column after the left border as column 1. If you omit *column*, the macro processor uses column 1. Although you can specify either *row* or *column* first, the examples in this book show the row first.

The following row pointer controls are available:

#*macro-expression*
  specifies the row within the window given by the value of *macro-expression*. The *macro-expression* must either be a positive integer or generate a positive integer.

/
  moves the pointer to column 1 of the next line.

The following column pointer controls are available:

@*macro-expression*
  specifies the column within the window given by the value of *macro-expression*. The *macro-expression* must either be a positive integer or generate a positive integer.

+*macro-expression*
  moves the pointer the number of columns given by the value of *macro-expression*. The *macro-expression* must either be a positive integer or generate a positive integer.

macro-variable
  names a macro variable to be displayed or to receive the value you enter at that position. *Macro-variable* must be a macro variable name (not a macro variable reference) or a macro expression that resolves to a macro variable name. By default, you can enter or change a macro variable value displayed in a field. To display the value without allowing changes, use the PROTECT= option (described later in this section). On some terminals a field containing a macro variable must have at least one blank space at each end of the field. Otherwise, the macro processor treats the fields as overlapping.

field-length
  is an integer specifying how many positions in the current row are available for displaying the macro variable's value or for accepting input. The maximum value of *field-length* is the number of positions remaining in the row; you cannot extend a field beyond one row. Note that *field-length* does not affect the length stored for the macro variable; it affects only the number of characters displayed or accepted for input in a particular field.

  If you omit *field-length* when the field contains an existing macro variable, the macro processor uses a field equal to the current length of the macro variable value, up to the number of positions remaining in the row or remaining until the next field begins. (If the current value of the macro variable is null, as in a macro variable defined in a %GLOBAL or %LOCAL statement, the macro processor uses a field length of 0; you cannot input any characters into the field.) If you omit *field-length* when the macro variable is created in that field, the macro processor uses a field of eight positions. To be safe, specify a *field-length* whenever a field contains a macro variable.

'text' | "text"
>   contains constant text to be displayed. The text must be enclosed in
    either single or double quotes. You cannot enter a value into a field
    containing constant text.

options
>   can include the following:

>   ATTR=attribute | (attribute-1 <. . . ,attribute-n>)
>   controls several attributes of the field. The attributes and
        combinations of attributes available depend on the type of monitor
        you use. The abbreviation for this option is A=.

>   BLINK
>   causes the field to blink.
>   HIGHLIGHT
>   displays the field at high intensity.
>   REV_VIDEO
>   displays the field in reverse video.
>   UNDERLINE
>   underlines the field.

>   AUTOSKIP=YES | NO
>   controls whether the cursor moves to the next unprotected field of
        the current window or group when you have entered data in all
        positions of a field. If you specify AUTOSKIP=YES, the cursor
        moves automatically to the next unprotected field; if you specify
        AUTOSKIP=NO, the cursor does not move automatically. (The
        availability of the AUTOSKIP= option depends on your operating
        system and monitor.) The abbreviation for this option is AUTO=.

>   COLOR=color
>   specifies a color for the field. The default color is white. Color can
        be one of the following:

BLACK	GRAY (or GREY)	PINK
BLUE	GREEN	RED
BROWN	MAGENTA	WHITE
CYAN	ORANGE	YELLOW

>   The representation of colors may vary, depending on the monitor
        you use. The abbreviation for this option is C=.

>   DISPLAY=YES | NO
>   determines whether the macro processor displays the characters
        you are entering into a macro variable value as you enter them. If
        you specify DISPLAY=YES (the default value), the macro processor
        displays the characters as you enter them. If you specify
        DISPLAY=NO, the macro processor does not display the
        characters as you enter them. Use the DISPLAY= option only with
        fields containing macro variables; constant text is displayed
        automatically.

>   PROTECT=YES | NO
>   controls whether information can be entered into a field containing
        a macro variable. If you specify PROTECT=NO (the default value),
        you can enter information. If you specify PROTECT=YES, you
        cannot enter information into a field. Use the PROTECT= option
        only for fields containing macro variables; fields containing text are
        automatically protected. The abbreviation for this option is P=.

REQUIRED=YES | NO

determines whether the user must enter a value for the macro variable in that field. If you specify REQUIRED=YES, the user must enter a value into that field in order to remove the display. You cannot enter a null value into a required field. If you specify REQUIRED=NO (the default value), the user does not have to enter a value in that field in order to remove the display. Entering a command on the command line of the window removes the effect of REQUIRED=YES.

Automatic Variables

The %WINDOW statement creates two automatic macro variables:

SYSCMD

contains the last command from the window's command line that was not recognized by display manager. Its value is set to null before each execution of a %DISPLAY statement. Entering a word or phrase on the command line that display manager does not recognize assigns that word or phrase as the value of SYSCMD. This is the only way to change the value of SYSCMD; otherwise, the value is read only. You can use SYSCMD to enter values on the command line that work like user-created display manager commands. Chapter 5 shows an example.

SYSMSG

contains text you specify (for example, with a %LET statement) to be displayed on the message line of the window. The value of SYSMSG is set to null after each execution of a %DISPLAY statement. Chapter 5 contains an example.

Display Manager Commands Available to Macro Windows

You can use the following categories of display manager commands in macro windows:

color commands
window call commands
window management commands
window size and position commands.

Commands in these categories are listed in Table 7.2 in *SAS Language: Reference, Version 6, First Edition*. File management, scrolling, searching, and editing commands are not available.

Examples

The following examples briefly illustrate the %WINDOW and %DISPLAY statements. For more extensive examples, see Chapter 5.

Example 1:   Simple %WINDOW Statement

The following %WINDOW statement creates a window with a single group of fields:

```
%window welcome color=blue
        #5 @28 'Welcome to the SAS System.' attr=highlight
           color=yellow
        #7 @15
           "You are executing Release &sysver on &sysday, &sysdate.."
        #12 @29 'Press ENTER to continue.';
```

The WELCOME window fills the entire display. The window is blue, the first line of text is high-intensity yellow, and the other two lines are white at normal intensity. The second line of text references the automatic macro variables SYSVER, SYSDAY, and SYSDATE. (Two periods are needed after the reference &SYSDATE because the first one is treated as a delimiter for the reference.) The WELCOME window does not require you to input any values. However, you must press ENTER to remove the display.

To display window WELCOME, submit this statement:

```
%display welcome;
```

Display 3.1 shows the window. (The highlighted field appears in italics.)

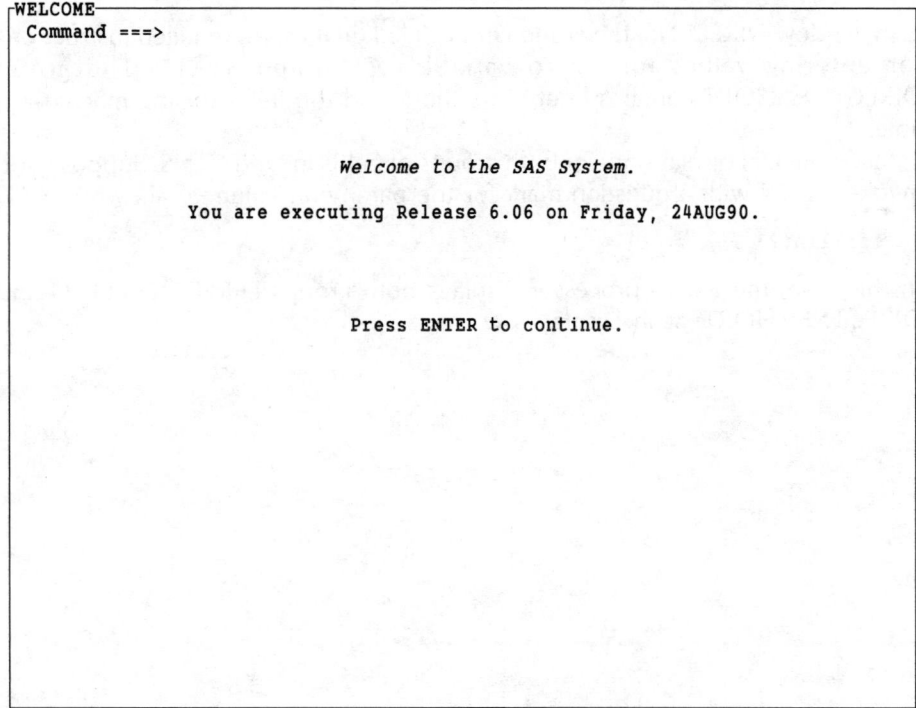

Display 3.1   Simple Window with One Group of Fields

Example 2:   Displaying Different Groups of Text within a Window

The following example illustrates defining two groups of fields within a window and displaying one or both groups:

```
%window directns
       group=long
       #3 @5 "The value for CITY can contain"
          +1 "up to twenty characters."
       #4 @5 "Do not use apostrophes."
       #6 @5 "If necessary, abbreviate the city name"
          +1 "to fit the field."
       #8 @5 "The value for STATE must be a"
          +1 "two-character abbreviation."
       #10 @5 "Both CITY and STATE are required."

       group=short
       #13 @15 "City:" @22 city 20 attr=underline required=yes
       #15 @14 "State:" @22 state 2 attr=underline required=yes;


%macro fillin(type);
    %if &type=? %then %display directns.long noinput;
    %display directns.short;
    %mend fillin;
```

In window DIRECTNS, the group DIRECTNS.LONG gives detailed instructions for entering values for macro variables CITY and STATE. The group DIRECTNS.SHORT contains brief instructions and the fields for the macro variables.

Macro FILLIN displays one or both groups of fields in DIRECTNS. Suppose you invoke FILLIN with a question mark for the parameter value, as shown:

```
%fillin(?)
```

In this case, the macro processor displays both groups DIRECTNS.LONG and DIRECTNS.SHORT, as in **Display 3.2**.

```
┌DIRECTNS─────────────────────────────────────────────────────────────
│ Command ===>
│
│
│      The value for CITY can contain up to twenty characters.
│      Do not use apostrophes.
│
│      If necessary, abbreviate the city name to fit the field.
│
│      The value for STATE must be a two-character abbreviation.
│
│      Both CITY and STATE are required.
│
│
│              City:   _____
│
│              State:  __
│
│
│
│
│
│
│
│
│
```

Display 3.2   Displaying Two Groups of Fields at Once

If you enter any other parameter value, as in

```
%fillin(short)
```

the macro processor displays only DIRECTNS.SHORT, as in **Display 3.3**.

```
┌DIRECTNS─────────────────────────────────────────────────────────────
│ Command ===>
│
│
│
│
│
│
│
│
│
│
│
│                  City:   _____
│
│                  State:  __
│
│
│
│
│
│
│
```

Display 3.3   Displaying One Group of Fields

Chapter 4
Macro Functions

Macro functions process one or more macro expressions, called *arguments*, to produce a new character string, the result or *returned value*. You can use all macro functions either inside or outside a macro. This chapter describes the types of macro functions and then describes each function in alphabetical order.

Contents

MACRO FUNCTION CATEGORIES

Macro functions can be divided into three categories: character functions, the evaluation function, and quoting functions.

Macro Character Functions

Macro character functions either change or provide information about the string that is their argument. Macro character functions have names corresponding to DATA step character functions (such as %SUBSTR and SUBSTR); the two perform similar tasks. However, macro functions work on strings (for example, macro variable values). DATA step functions work on DATA step variables and character strings.

Note that some macro character functions come in pairs, such as %SCAN and %QSCAN. The two work alike except that the plain function (without the Q) returns an unquoted value, whereas the function beginning with Q returns a quoted result. In general, you should use the function beginning with a Q when the argument has been previously quoted or when you want the result to be quoted (for example, when the result may contain an unmatched quote or parenthesis). See Chapter 10, "Macro Quoting," for details on quoting functions.

The macro character functions are as follows:

%INDEX   finds the first occurrence of a string.

%LENGTH   finds the length of an argument.

%QSCAN   scans for words and quotes the result, including % and &.

%QSUBSTR   produces a substring of a character string and quotes the result, including % and &.

%QUPCASE   translates characters to uppercase and quotes the result, including % and &.

%SCAN   scans for words and returns an unquoted result.

%SUBSTR   produces a substring of a character string and returns an unquoted result.

%UPCASE   translates characters to uppercase and returns an unquoted result.

Macro Evaluation Function

The evaluation function is %EVAL. Because the macro processor is a string-handling facility, digits in macro expressions are treated as strings. The %EVAL function assigns numeric properties to integers in macro expressions and performs calculations using integer arithmetic only. The %EVAL function also evaluates logical expressions such as &A>&B.

Macro Quoting Functions

The quoting functions in the macro language perform the activity equivalent to enclosing a portion of a SAS statement in single or double quotes. That is, the macro facility treats the text within the function as a unit and does not perform any evaluation or interpretation of the text. For example, you can use a quoting function to cause the macro processor to treat semicolons as text (in other words, as part of a string). Using quoting functions rather than enclosing text in single or double quotes is necessary because the macro processor treats the

SAS language characters single quote (') and double quote (") as text rather than as macro language symbols.

Note the following points about using macro quoting functions:

- Most macro quoting functions occur in pairs, such as %STR and %NRSTR (listed later in this section). The plain function (without the letters NR) affects text in a particular category, except for the ampersand and percent sign. The function beginning with NR affects the same category but includes the ampersand and percent sign.

- The %STR, %NRSTR, %QUOTE, and %NRQUOTE functions (described later in this section) require unmatched quotes and parentheses to be marked with a percent sign, (for example, %'). Within these functions, if a textual percent sign happens to precede a quote or parenthesis, code two percent signs (%%) to indicate that the percent sign does not mark the quote or parenthesis. The %BQUOTE, %NRBQUOTE, and %SUPERQ functions do not require unmatched quotes and parentheses in the resolved value of their arguments to be marked.

- A value that has been quoted remains quoted until you enclose it in the %UNQUOTE function (described later in this section) or, if the value is part of generated SAS statements, until the SAS compiler receives the text while a DATA step, a PROC step, or a global statement is being constructed. In addition, using the %SCAN, %SUBSTR, or %UPCASE function on a quoted value returns an unquoted result; to return a quoted value, use the %QSCAN, %QSUBSTR, or %QUPCASE function.

This chapter describes each quoting function briefly and in alphabetical order. Chapter 10 provides detailed information on macro quoting functions, their relationships to each other, and examples of their use.

The macro quoting functions are as follows:

%BQUOTE	quotes a resolved value, including unanticipated special characters.
%NRBQUOTE	quotes a resolved value, including unanticipated special characters, %, and &.
%NRQUOTE	quotes a resolved value, including % and &.
%NRSTR	quotes constant text, including % and &.
%QUOTE	quotes a resolved value.
%STR	quotes constant text.
%SUPERQ	prevents any resolution of the value of the macro variable named in its argument.
%UNQUOTE	undoes quoting.

MACRO FUNCTION DESCRIPTIONS

%BQUOTE: quotes a resolved value, including unanticipated special characters

%BQUOTE(*argument*)

Argument can be any macro expression. The %BQUOTE function removes the meaning from items, including unmatched quotes and parentheses, that are produced by resolving *argument*. The %BQUOTE function does not remove the meaning from the ampersand or the percent sign; to do that, use the %NRBQUOTE function. It is most useful when the resolved value may contain unmatched quotes or parentheses that have not been marked with a percent sign. For example, suppose you create the following macro:

```
%macro bq;
   %global place;
   %put Enter the location of the meeting.;
   %input;
   %let place=%bquote(&sysbuffr);
%mend bq;
```

Next you invoke macro BQ and respond to the %INPUT statement as shown in the following program:

```
%bq
Enter the location of the meeting.
Rick's office
```

This response assigns a value to macro variable SYSBUFFR that contains an unmatched single quote. When the macro processor resolves the quoted reference &SYSBUFFR, the unmatched single quote does not cause problems, and the value is assigned to PLACE.

Note: In Version 6 the %BQUOTE function quotes mnemonic operators such as LE and AND in addition to special characters; in Version 5 it does not quote mnemonic operators.

Chapter 10, "Macro Quoting," discusses the %BQUOTE function in more detail and includes an example of the difference in the %BQUOTE function between Version 5 and Version 6.

%EVAL: evaluates arithmetic and logical expressions

%EVAL(*expression*)

The %EVAL function evaluates arithmetic and logical expressions in the macro language. The %EVAL function performs integer arithmetic. That is, calculations on fractions are not allowed, and if a division operation results in a fraction, the fraction is truncated to an integer. All features in the macro language that evaluate expressions contain an implied %EVAL that evaluates the condition and returns a value of 1 if the condition is true and 0 if it is false. See Chapter 9, "Macro Compilation and Execution," for more information on macro expressions and how the %EVAL function evaluates them, including a list of features that use an implicit %EVAL.

Suppose the following statement appears in a SAS program:

```
%let x=100;
```

Then the following statement assigns Y the value **300**:

```
%let y=%eval(&x+200);
```

Without the %EVAL function, as in the following, the value of Y is the seven-character string **100+200**:

```
%let y=&x+200;
```

%INDEX: finds the first occurrence of a string

%INDEX(*source,excerpt*)

The %INDEX function searches *source* for the first occurrence of the string identified in *excerpt*, where *source* and *excerpt* can be any strings or macro expressions that yield strings. If the string is not found, the function returns a 0. This example uses the %INDEX function to calculate the value of B:

```
%let a=a very long value;
%let b=%index(&a,v);
%put V appears at position &b..;
```

The %PUT statement writes this line:

```
V appears at position 3.
```

This example uses the %INDEX function to determine whether a parameter value represents a one-level or a two-level SAS data set name:

```
%macro check(dsn);
   %global name;
   %if %index(&dsn,.)=0 %then %let name=work.&dsn;
   %else %let name=&dsn;
   %put The data set name is &name..;
%mend check;
```

If the value of parameter DSN does not contain a period, the %INDEX function returns the value 0, and the %IF condition becomes true. The first %LET statement attaches the string **work.** to the value of DSN before assigning the value to the global macro variable NAME. Thus, the invocation

```
%check(report)
```

writes this line:

```
The data set name is work.report.
```

(Two periods are necessary in the %PUT statement because the first period becomes a delimiter for the reference &NAME; the second period becomes the period written by the %PUT statement.) In this invocation, the value of DSN contains a period:

```
%check(in.sales)
```

The %INDEX function returns the value 3. The %IF condition is not true, and the %ELSE statement is executed. The second %LET statement simply assigns the value of DSN to NAME, and the %PUT statement writes this line:

```
The data set name is in.sales.
```

%LENGTH: finds the length of an argument

%LENGTH(*argument*)

Argument can be any macro expression. The %LENGTH function returns the length of the resolved value of *argument* (or the length of *argument* if *argument* does not require resolution). If *argument* has a null value, %LENGTH returns a value of 0. For example, the statements

```
%let a=happy;
%let b=new year;
%put *%length(&a)* **%length(&b)** ***%length(&a &b)***;
```

write this line:

```
*5* **8** ***14***
```

The following example uses the %LENGTH function and the DATA step LENGTH function to illustrate the difference between using a macro function and a DATA step function.

Suppose you regularly create a SAS data set named DAILY and you often need to check the length of character values for different variables in it. (The CONTENTS procedure shows the maximum length of a value, but the data values themselves may have much shorter lengths.) A DATA _NULL_ step with the LENGTH function can check the length of the values. In addition, you want to verify that the variable name you enter has a valid length, to reduce the chances of your having entered an invalid name. Macro CKLEN shows the program:

```
%macro cklen(name,len);
    %if %length(&name)>=1 and %length(&name)<=8 %then
        %do;
            data _null_;
                set daily;
                if length(&name)>&len then put
                    "Warning: &name over &len characters: " &name _n_=;
            run;
        %end;
    %else %put Variable name &name has invalid length.;
%mend cklen;
```

Suppose you invoke CKLEN in the following program:

```
data daily;
    input ncfirms $30.;
    cards;
Best & Worst, Inc.
McGillicuddy and Sirkin
J. Rodriguez Assoc.
;


%cklen(ncfirms,20)
```

The SAS System sees these statements:

```
DATA DAILY;
    INPUT NCFIRMS $30.;
    CARDS;
Best & Worst, Inc.
McGillicuddy and Sirkin
J. Rodriguez Assoc.
;

DATA _NULL_;
    SET DAILY;
    IF LENGTH(NCFIRMS)>20 THEN PUT
        "Warning: ncfirms over 20 characters: " NCFIRMS _N_=;
RUN;
```

The %LENGTH function determines that the length of the string NCFIRMS is within the range specified; therefore, the %IF condition is true and the %THEN statement generates the DATA _NULL_ step. The DATA _NULL_step executes to check the values of variable NCFIRMS. Because one value is longer than 20 characters, the DATA step PUT statement writes the following message in the SAS log:

```
Warning: ncfirms over 20 characters: McGillicuddy & Sirkin _N_=2
```

%NRBQUOTE: quotes a resolved value, including unanticipated special characters, %, and &

%NRBQUOTE(*argument*)

Argument can be any macro expression. The %NRBQUOTE function is most useful when the argument contains a macro variable reference or a macro invocation that may generate an unmatched quote or parenthesis.

The %NRBQUOTE function quotes the result of resolving a macro variable reference or executing a macro. The %NRBQUOTE function quotes the same items as the %BQUOTE function and also removes the meaning of any ampersands and percent signs in the resolved value. It is most useful when the resolved value may contain unmatched quotes or parentheses that have not been marked with a percent sign or strings that look like macro variable references or macro invocations that you do not want the macro processor to attempt to resolve.

Note: In Version 6 the %NRBQUOTE function quotes mnemonic operators such as LE and AND in addition to special characters; in Version 5 it does not quote mnemonic operators. Chapter 10, "Macro Quoting," illustrates this change using the %BQUOTE function.

The following example demonstrates quoting a macro variable reference and an unmatched single quote in the resolved value of SYSBUFFR:

```
%macro nrbq;
    %global place;
    %put Enter the location of the meeting.;
    %input;
    %let place=%nrbquote(&sysbuffr);
%mend nrbq;
```

Suppose you invoke macro NRBQ and respond to the %INPUT statement as shown in the following program:

```
%nrbq
Enter the location of the meeting.
R&D lab in Building C's annex
WARNING: Apparent symbolic reference D not resolved.
```

In assigning the value of SYSBUFFR to macro variable PLACE, the macro processor attempts to resolve all macro expressions in the value of SYSBUFFR and then quotes the result. It cannot resolve the reference &D (because you have not defined a macro variable named D). Therefore, the macro processor issues a warning message.

The macro processor never again attempts to resolve the reference &D, as the following example shows:

```
%put 1) &place;
%let D=Development;
%put 2) &place;
```

The %PUT statements write the following:

```
1) R&D lab in Building C's annex
2) R&D lab in Building C's annex
```

The macro processor does not issue a warning message for an unresolved reference in the first %PUT statement or resolve the reference &D in the second %PUT statement after a value becomes available.

See Chapter 10 for more information on the %NRBQUOTE function.

%NRQUOTE: quotes a resolved value including % and &

%NRQUOTE(*argument*)

Argument can be any macro expression. The %NRQUOTE function quotes the same items as the %QUOTE function and also the ampersand and percent sign. The %NRQUOTE function is most useful when *argument* contains a macro variable reference or a macro invocation.

This example uses the %NRQUOTE function to quote an ampersand in the resolved value of SYSBUFFR:

```
%macro nrq;
   %global place;
   %put Enter the location of the meeting.;
   %input;
   %let place=%nrquote(&sysbuffr);
%mend nrq;
```

Suppose you invoke macro NRQ and respond to the %INPUT statement as shown in the following program:

```
%nrq
Enter the location of the meeting.
R&D lab
WARNING: Apparent symbolic reference D not resolved.
```

In the %LET statement, the macro processor attempts to resolve all macro expressions in the value of SYSBUFFR and then quotes the result. It cannot resolve the reference &D (because you have not defined a macro variable called D), but it quotes the ampersand. Therefore, the macro processor does not attempt to resolve the reference &D again. The following example shows how the macro processor treats references to PLACE:

```
%put First: &place;
%let d=development;
%put Second: &place;
```

The macro processor writes the following:

```
First: R&D lab
Second: R&D lab
```

The macro processor does not issue a warning message for an unresolved reference in the first %PUT statement or resolve the reference &D in the second %PUT statement after a value becomes available.

See Chapter 10, "Macro Quoting," for more information on the %NRQUOTE function.

%NRSTR: quotes constant text, including % and &

%NRSTR(*argument*)

Argument can be any character string. The %NRSTR function quotes the same items as the %STR function and also the ampersand and percent sign. Thus, macro invocations in the argument of the %NRSTR function are not executed, macro variable references are not resolved, and macro function arguments are not evaluated.

For example, suppose you have a SAS program containing two macros named DAILY and WEEKLY. The statement

```
%put %nrstr(Enter %daily or %weekly:);
```

results in this message:

```
Enter %daily or %weekly:
```

If you do not use the %NRSTR function, the %PUT statement writes the text generated by the macros:

```
Enter text produced by macro daily or text produced by macro weekly:
```

See Chapter 10, "Macro Quoting," for more information on the %NRSTR function.

%QSCAN: scans for words and quotes the result, including % and &

%QSCAN(*argument,n*<*,delimiters*>)

Argument can be a string or a macro expression that yields a string; *n* can be a number or a macro expression that yields a number; and *delimiters* can be a list of characters or a macro expression that yields a list of characters. The %QSCAN function is identical to the %SCAN function except that the result is quoted, whereas %SCAN returns an unquoted result. The %QSCAN function quotes its result in the same way the %NRBQUOTE function quotes its argument. The significance of all special characters and mnemonic operators returned by the function is removed. For example, suppose a program contains three macros named A, B, and C. The statements

```
%let x=%nrstr(%a*%b*%c);
%put !&x! !!%scan(&x,3,*)!! !!!%qscan(&x,3,*)!!!;
```

write this line:

```
!%a*%b*%c! !!text produced by macro c!! !!!%c!!!
```

See Chapter 10, "Macro Quoting," for more information on the %QSCAN function.

%QSUBSTR: produces a substring of a character string and quotes the result, including % and &

%QSUBSTR(*argument,position*<*,length*>)

Argument, position, and *length* can be any macro expression. *Position* and *length* must be numbers or must resolve to numbers. The %QSUBSTR function is identical to the %SUBSTR function except that the result is quoted, whereas %SUBSTR returns an unquoted result. The %QSUBSTR function quotes its result in the same way the %NRBQUOTE function quotes its argument. The significance of all special characters and mnemonic operators returned by the function is removed. The statements

```
%let a=1;
%let abc=5;
%let def=%nrstr(&abc);
%put *&def* *%qsubstr(&def,1,2)* *%substr(&def,1,2)*;
```

write this line:

```
*&abc* *&a* *1*
```

See Chapter 10, "Macro Quoting," for more information on the %QSUBSTR function.

%QUOTE: quotes a resolved value

%QUOTE(*argument*)

The %QUOTE function quotes the result of resolving *argument* , where *argument* can be any macro expression. Its effect occurs during macro execution. The %QUOTE function does not remove the meaning from the percent sign or the ampersand; to do that, use the %NRQUOTE function. If the resolved value contains unmatched quotes or parentheses, either precede them with a percent sign or use the %BQUOTE function.

For example, consider the following program. Possible values for parameter STATE include **nc** (for North Carolina) and **or** (for Oregon).

```
%macro dept1(state);
    %*without %quote function--incorrect;
    %if &state=nc %then
        %put North Carolina Department of Revenue;
    %else %put Department of Revenue;
%mend dept1;


%dept1(or)
```

When macro DEPT1 executes, the implicit %EVAL function in the %IF condition evaluates **or** as a logical operator in the following expression:

```
or=nc
```

The macro processor produces an error message for an invalid operand in the expression.

To treat characters that result from resolving &STATE as text, enclose the reference in the %QUOTE function, as shown here:

```
%macro dept2(state);
    %*with %quote function--correct;
    %if %quote(&state)=nc %then
        %put North Carolina Department of Revenue;
    %else %put Department of Revenue;
%mend dept2;


%dept2(or)
```

The %IF condition now compares the strings **or** and **nc**, and the %PUT statement writes the following:

```
Department of Revenue
```

The following example uses both the %QUOTE and %STR functions:

```
%macro keepit(klist);
    %if %quote(&klist) ne %then %str(keep &klist;);
    %else
        %do;
            %put no keep list given;
            run cancel;
        %end;
%mend keepit;


%keepit(year1-year10)
```

The %QUOTE function encloses the reference &KLIST so that when &KLIST resolves into **year1-year10**, the hyphen is interpreted as text. The implicit

%EVAL function in the %IF condition then compares the string `year1-year10` to a null string. If you omit the %QUOTE function, the macro processor treats the hyphen as a subtraction operator and issues a message for an invalid operator.

The %STR function encloses the KEEP statement in order to treat its semicolon as text rather than as the end of the %THEN clause. If you omit the %STR function, the first semicolon ends the %THEN clause, and the second semicolon is text. Because the macro language does not allow text between a %THEN clause and a %ELSE clause, the macro processor issues an error message.

See Chapter 10, "Macro Quoting," for more information on the %QUOTE function.

%QUPCASE: translates characters to uppercase and quotes the result, including % and &

%QUPCASE(*argument*)

Argument can be any string, including macro variable references and macro calls. The %QUPCASE function is identical to the %UPCASE function except that the result is quoted, whereas %UPCASE returns an unquoted result. The %QUPCASE function quotes its result in the same way the %NRBQUOTE function quotes its argument. The significance of all special characters and mnemonic operators returned by the function is removed. The statements

```
%let x=%nrstr(%eval(5+3));
%put *&x* *%qupcase(&x)* *%upcase(&x)*;
```

write this line:

```
*%eval(5+3)* *%EVAL(5+3)* *8*
```

See Chapter 10, "Macro Quoting," for more information on the %QUPCASE function.

%SCAN: scans for words and returns an unquoted result

%SCAN(*argument,n*<*,delimiters*>)

Argument can be a string or a macro expression that yields a string; *n* can be a number or a macro expression that yields a number; and *delimiters* can be a list of characters or a macro expression that yields a list of characters. An implied %EVAL gives *n* numeric properties.

The %SCAN function returns the *n*th word of *argument*, where words are strings of characters separated by one or more delimiters. On ASCII systems, if you specify no delimiters, the SAS System treats all of the following characters as delimiters:

blank . < (+ & ! $ *) ; ^ — / , % ¦

On ASCII systems without the ^ character, the %SCAN function uses the ~ character instead.

On EBCDIC systems, if you specify no delimiters, the SAS System treats all of the following characters as delimiters:

blank . < (+ | & ! $ *) ; ¬ — / , % ¦ ¢

These lists are the same ones used by the DATA step SCAN function. Note that both the ampersand and percent sign are delimiters on both ASCII and EBCDIC systems. If the number of words in *argument* is less than *n*, the result of the function is a null string. The %SCAN function returns an unquoted result, even if the argument was quoted. To return a quoted result, use the %QSCAN function. See Chapter 10, "Macro Quoting," for more information on macro quoting.

For example, the following statements assign B a value of `ledger`, the third word in the value of macro variable A:

```
%let a=payroll+payables+ledger+receive+inventry;
%let b=%scan(&a,3);
```

The following statements assign Q a value of `qtr.third`, the third word in P (delimited by the dollar sign character):

```
%let p=qtr.first$qtr.second$qtr.third$qtr.fourth;
%let q=%scan(&p,3,$);
```

The statements

```
%let x=test;
%let y=value;
%let z=%nrstr(&x &y);
%put *%scan(&z,1,%str( ))* **%qscan(&z,1,%str( ))**;
```

write this line:

```
*test* **&x**
```

In order to specify a blank as a delimiter, you must use the %STR function, described later in this chapter, to make the blank significant. The %SCAN function returns the unquoted value &X, which resolves into `test`. The %QSCAN function retains the quoting applied by the %NRSTR function and returns a quoted macro variable reference. To treat the ampersand as part of the word to be retrieved, specify the delimiter to be used (a blank in this case). If you use the default list of delimiters, the macro processor treats the ampersand as a delimiter.

%STR: quotes constant text

%STR(*argument*)

Argument can be any string. Use the %STR function when *argument* contains constant text. The %STR function removes the meaning from items that are known when the macro processor is compiling (constructing) a macro or a macro program statement. If the items are produced by resolving a macro expression, use the %QUOTE function instead. The %STR function does not remove the meaning of the ampersand or percent sign. To remove the meaning of those characters also, use the %NRSTR function.

When you use an unmatched quote or parenthesis in the argument of the %STR function, place a percent sign before the character, as shown:

```
%let place=%str(Len%'s office);
```

The percent sign indicates that the character is an unmatched item to be quoted. If a percent sign in text precedes a quote or parenthesis, write the textual percent sign as two percent signs (%%). **Table 10.1** in Chapter 10, "Macro Quoting," illustrates marking unmatched quotes and parentheses with a percent sign.

Do not enclose other macro functions or macro invocations with a list of parameter values in the %STR function. %STR quotes the parentheses; therefore, the macro processor does not recognize the arguments of the function or the parameter values.

To quote the comment symbols /* and */, quote each character separately, as shown:

```
%str(/)%str(*)
```

Nesting the same argument within the %STR and %QUOTE functions is redundant. For example, in the combination

```
%quote(%str(argument))
```

the items quoted at macro compilation by the %STR function remain quoted at macro execution; thus, the %QUOTE function has no effect.

The most common uses of the %STR function are to

- treat a semicolon as text rather than as part of a macro program statement
- make blanks significant that otherwise would be ignored
- read or write an unmatched quote or parenthesis that has been marked with a percent sign.

The following examples show those uses.

Suppose you want to use a %LET statement to create a macro variable named P whose value represents the following SAS statements:

```
proc print;
run;
```

Because the %LET statement ends in a semicolon, the semicolons after PRINT and RUN must not signal the end of the %LET statement. To prevent the textual semicolons from ending the %LET statement, enclose the semicolons in the %STR function; the macro processor then treats them as part of the string. The %LET statement becomes

```
%let p=%str(proc print; run;);
```

The semicolon not enclosed in %STR ends the %LET statement. You can also enclose just the semicolons in the %STR function, as shown:

```
%let p=proc print%str(;) run%str(;);
```

However, enclosing the entire value makes the statement easier to read.

The following statement makes the leading blanks in the value of TIME significant:

```
%let time=%str(   now);
```

This statement assigns a value containing leading blanks and an unmatched right parenthesis:

```
%let order=%str(   1%) first item:);
```

The percent sign marks the unmatched parenthesis.

See Chapter 10 for more information on the %STR function.

%SUBSTR: produces a substring of a character string and returns an unquoted result

%SUBSTR(*argument,position*<*,length*>)

Argument, position, and *length* can be any macro expression. *Position* and *length* must be numbers or must resolve to numbers. The %SUBSTR function produces a substring of *argument* beginning at *position* for a length of *length* characters. If you omit *length*, the %SUBSTR function produces a string containing the characters from *position* to the end of *argument*. If you attempt to produce a substring extending past the end of *argument*, %SUBSTR issues a warning message and returns a substring to the end of *argument*. If you attempt to begin a substring after the end of *argument*, %SUBSTR issues a warning message and returns a null value. The %SUBSTR function returns an unquoted result, even if the argument was quoted. To return a quoted result, use the %QSUBSTR function. (See Chapter 10, "Macro Quoting," for more information on macro quoting.)

For example, the following statements assign SECOND the value **book** by selecting a string from the value of FIRST, beginning at position 6 for a length of 4:

```
%let first=this book;
%let second=%substr(&first,6,4);
```

The following statements compare the %SUBSTR and %QSUBSTR functions:

```
%let a=one;
%let b=two;
%let c=%nrstr(&a &b);
%put *%substr(&c,1,2)* **%qsubstr(&c,1,2)**;
```

The %PUT statement writes this line:

```
*one* **&a**
```

The %SUBSTR function yields the unquoted macro variable reference &A, which resolves into **one**. The %QSUBSTR function retains the quoting produced by the %NRSTR function and yields a quoted macro variable reference.

The following example illustrates using a macro variable reference whose resolved value contains commas as the first argument of the %SUBSTR function. You must quote the resolved value with a quoting function. The following statements generate error messages since the %SUBSTR function treats the commas in the resolved value of X as delimiters for arguments:

```
%let x=arrive,depart,latearrs,latedeps;
%let y=%substr(&x,8,6);                /* INCORRECT */
```

As a result, the SAS System reports that there are too many arguments to the %SUBSTR function. The following statement uses the %QUOTE function to quote the value of X when the reference resolves so that the %SUBSTR function works as you expect and assigns the value **depart** to macro variable Y:

```
%let y=%substr(%quote(&x),8,6);        /* CORRECT  */
```

%SUPERQ: prevents resolution of a macro variable

%SUPERQ(*macro-variable*)

The %SUPERQ function prevents the beginning of resolution in *macro-variable*. Thus, any items in the value of *macro-variable* that could require quoting are quoted. *Macro-variable* must be either the name of a macro variable with no leading ampersand or a macro expression that produces the name of a macro variable with no leading ampersand. The %SUPERQ function is particularly useful when you want to examine a value assigned with the %INPUT statement, %WINDOW statement, or SYMPUT routine that might contain an ampersand or a percent sign. Consider the following example:

```
data _null_;
   call symput('mv1','Smith&Jones');
   call symput('mv2','%macro abc;');
run;

%let testmv1=%superq(mv1);   /* No ampersand before name */
%let testmv2=%superq(mv2);   /* No ampersand before name */

%put TESTMV1 is &testmv1 and TESTMV2 is &testmv2..;
```

The %PUT statement writes this line:

```
TESTMV1 is Smith&Jones and TESTMV2 is %macro abc;.
```

In the DATA _NULL_ step, the SYMPUT routine assigns a value to each macro variable. In the %LET statements, the %SUPERQ function prevents the macro processor from beginning to resolve the values of MV1 and MV2 before assigning the values to TESTMV1 and TESTMV2. You can think of the values of TESTMV1 and TESTMV2 as "pictures" of the original values of MV1 and MV2. The %PUT statement then writes the pictures in its text. Because the macro processor does not attempt resolution, it does not issue a warning message for the unresolved reference &JONES or an error message for beginning a macro definition inside a %LET statement.

For comparison, consider this example using the %NRBQUOTE function:

```
data _null_;
   call symput('mv3','Smith&Jones');
   call symput('mv4','%macro abc;');
run;

%let testmv3=%nrbquote(&mv3);    /* Note addition of ampersand */
%let testmv4=%nrbquote(&mv4);    /* Note addition of ampersand */

%put TESTMV3 is &testmv3 and TESTMV4 is &testmv4..;
```

The DATA _NULL_ step assigns values to the macro variables as before. In the %LET statements, the %NRBQUOTE function resolves the values of MV3 and MV4 as far as possible and then assigns the result to TESTMV3 and TESTMV4. (Note that you must include an ampersand in the argument of the %NRBQUOTE function because the %NRBQUOTE function works on macro variable references.) The first %LET statement causes a warning message to be issued for the unresolvable reference &JONES. The second %LET statement produces an error message indicating that open code statement recursion has been detected. The error occurs because the macro processor, while resolving the value of MV4 in order to quote the result, detects the beginning of another macro program statement inside the %LET statement. The %PUT statement writes this line:

```
TESTMV3 is Smith&Jones and TESTMV4 is .
```

See Chapter 10, "Macro Quoting," for detailed information on the %SUPERQ function.

%UNQUOTE: undoes quoting

%UNQUOTE(*argument*)

Argument can be any macro expression. The %UNQUOTE function undoes the effect of all macro quoting functions. That is, it restores the special meaning that was removed from characters by a quoting function. It takes effect during macro execution.

You can also use the %UNQUOTE function to restore normal tokenization of text when the tokenization has been altered by a quoting function. Chapter 8, "How the SAS System Processes a Program," describes tokenization, and Chapter 10, "Macro Quoting," describes the use of %UNQUOTE for restoring tokenization.

Consider the following pair of macros:

```
%macro code(codepw);
   %if %upcase(&codepw)=PASSWORD %then %put The code is 984629.;
%mend code;
```

```
%macro start(startpw);
  %let info=%nrstr(Confidential. %code(&startpw));
  %if %upcase(&startpw)=PASSWORD %then %put %unquote(&info);
  %else %put &info;
%mend start;
```

Macro CODE contains a security code, and macro START is a driver macro that stores a quoted invocation of CODE as the value of macro variable INFO. The user invokes macro START and gives a password as the value of parameter STARTPW. If the password is correct, macro START writes the unquoted value of INFO (which includes an invocation of CODE with the correct value of parameter CODEPW). If the password is not correct, macro START writes the quoted value of INFO. The following invocations show the responses produced by incorrect and correct passwords:

```
%start(wrongword)
Confidential. %code(&startpw)
```

```
%start(password)
The code is 984629.
Confidential.
```

The correct invocation produces the sentence **The code is 984629.** before **Confidential.** because macro CODE, which contains a %PUT statement, executes before the %PUT statement in macro START completes its execution.

See Chapter 10 for more detailed information on the %UNQUOTE function.

%UPCASE: translates characters to uppercase and returns an unquoted result

%UPCASE(*argument*)

Argument can be any string, including macro variable references and macro calls. The %UPCASE function translates lowercase characters in *argument* into uppercase. The %UPCASE function returns an unquoted result, even if the argument was quoted. To return a quoted result, use the %QUPCASE function. (See Chapter 10, "Macro Quoting," for more information on macro quoting.)

The %UPCASE function is useful in comparisons because the macro facility does not automatically translate lowercase characters to uppercase before performing a comparison. For example, macro SHORT, shown here, compares a value you input to the string DEC:

```
%macro short;
    %put enter a three-character month name;
    %input month;
    %if %upcase(&month)=DEC %then %str(proc print data=endyr; run;);
    %else %str(proc contents; run;);
%mend short;
```

The %UPCASE function causes all of these responses to satisfy the %IF condition:

```
DEC
Dec
dec
```

The following statements compare the %UPCASE and %QUPCASE functions:

```
%let a=begin;
%let b=%nrstr(&a);
%put *%upcase(&b)* **%qupcase(&b)**;
```

The %PUT statement writes this line:

```
*begin* **&A**
```

The %UPCASE function converts the resolved value of B into uppercase and produces the unquoted uppercase value &A, which resolves into its value (in this case, the lowercase value **begin**). The %QUPCASE function converts the value of macro variable B into uppercase while retaining the quoting applied by the %NRSTR function; thus, the result is the quoted uppercase value &A.

Chapter 5

Macro Windows

Macro windows allow you to create displays with text that users can read and with input fields into which they can enter values. You can perform simple branching from one window to another. For many applications, macro windows are sufficient. For more complex applications, such as those requiring the software to recognize a particular cursor position or to perform automatic field validation, you must use SAS/AF software.

This chapter discusses the tasks involved in creating and displaying macro windows and provides some background information on how the SAS System creates, stores, and displays macro windows.

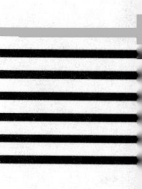

Contents

HOW TO CREATE WINDOWS

This section discusses how to create windows and control their appearance.

Creating a Simple Window

This %WINDOW statement defines a simple macro window:

```
%window first #8 @30 'First Window';
```

The following %DISPLAY statement displays the macro window FIRST, as shown in **Display 5.1**:

```
%display first;
```

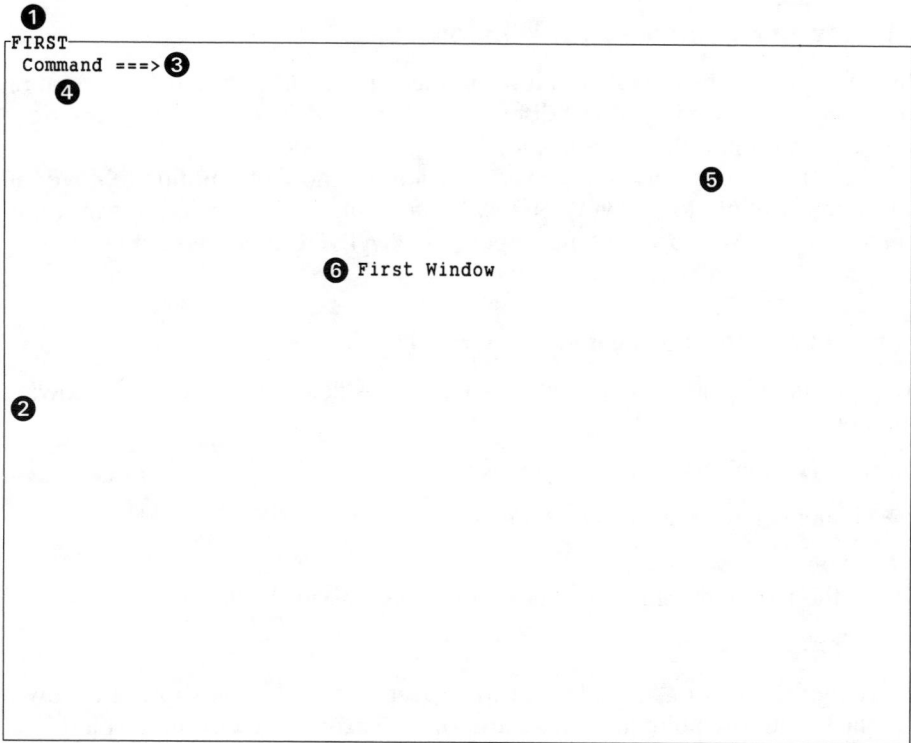

Display 5.1 A Simple Window

By default, the window has a black background with white text (or text in your monitor's color, on monochrome monitors). For readability, this book shows windows with a white background and black text. The window fills the entire display on your monitor. The circled numbers show the following parts of the window:

1. the window name
2. the border of the window
3. the command line
4. the message line (for messages from the SAS System)
5. the display
6. a field being displayed.

The %DISPLAY statement displays a window until one of the following happens:

- In a window with no fields that require input, you press ENTER.
- In a window with at least one field that requires input, you take some input action in all fields and press ENTER on the last field.

When one of these situations exists, the SAS System removes the display. Because this example displays only text, no fields require input and pressing ENTER removes the display.

While a window is being displayed, you can use some SAS Display Manager System commands with it, such as window call and sizing commands. You can also create customized commands. **CREATING AND DISPLAYING SYSTEMS OF WINDOWS** later in this chapter discusses using customized commands with windows.

Creating the Contents of a Window

This section uses the default window outline shown earlier to illustrate creating the contents of a window. It first discusses individual displays and then describes how to create more than one display for a given window.

Note: This section discusses basic principles without attempting to cover all syntax or all options for the %WINDOW statement. Detailed reference information for creating window contents appears in **%WINDOW Statement** in Chapter 3, "Macro Program Statements."

How the Contents of a Window Are Organized

An individual item in a window is called a *field*. A field consists of the following elements:

<location> item-to-display <options>

The elements have the following meanings:

location
>   is the row and column position in the display, in this form:

>   *<row> <column>*

>   Either the row or the column can appear first; this book shows the row first. The row pointer controls are #*macro-expression* (for an absolute row position) and / (to move to the next row). If you omit the row pointer control in the first field of a display, the item appears in the top row of the display. If you omit the pointer control in a later field, the macro processor continues to use the current row. The column pointer controls are @*macro-expression* (for an absolute column position) and +*macro-expression* (to move the number of columns specified). If you omit the column pointer control, the item appears in the first column after the left border. The macro processor evaluates *macro-expression* when it compiles the macro window; thus, the position of a field is fixed after the window is compiled.

item-to-display
>   can be either text enclosed in single or double quotes, a macro variable name (without an ampersand), or a macro expression that generates a macro variable name. You *must* enclose text in quotes; otherwise, the macro processor looks for a macro variable by that name. **Writing Constant Text** and **Writing Fields with Macro Variable Values** later in this chapter discuss writing these items in more detail.

options
> specify the attributes of the field such as highlighting, color, and whether a field containing a macro variable is protected from alteration.

All the fields in a window that are displayed at once form a *group*. This section discusses creating fields containing constant text.

Writing Constant Text

To write constant text in a field, take these steps:

1. Specify the row and column position of the field with pointer controls.
2. Enclose the constant text with quotes.
3. Add any options to describe the text.

You must enclose constant text in single or double quotes. If you do not, the macro processor treats the text as a macro variable name and attempts to retrieve a macro variable value. You can use macro expressions to generate the text; the macro expressions resolve when the %WINDOW statement executes, and the resulting text is stored as part of the window definition. Constant text in a display is always protected: you cannot enter new text over existing constant text when a window is displayed. If one field containing constant text overlaps another field containing constant text, only the field defined last appears. The SAS System writes a warning message in the SAS log.

The following example shows text created from character strings and macro variable references:

```
%window employee
        #5 a4 "Date of Access: &sysday, &sysdate.."
        #8 a10 "Employee Data Base"
        #17 a29 "Press ENTER to continue.";
```

This display contains three fields of text. The first field references macro variables SYSDAY and SYSDATE. Displaying this window with the following statement produces **Display 5.2**:

```
%display employee;
```

```
┌EMPLOYEE──────────────────────────────────────────────────────────────┐
│ Command ===>                                                          │
│                                                                       │
│                                                                       │
│                                                                       │
│     Date of Access: Monday, 23JUL90.                                  │
│                                                                       │
│                                                                       │
│            Employee Data Base                                         │
│                                                                       │
│                                                                       │
│                                                                       │
│                                                                       │
│                                                                       │
│                             Press ENTER to continue.                  │
│                                                                       │
│                                                                       │
│                                                                       │
│                                                                       │
│                                                                       │
│                                                                       │
│                                                                       │
│                                                                       │
│                                                                       │
└───────────────────────────────────────────────────────────────────────┘
```

Display 5.2   Window Containing Constant Text

For simplicity, this window uses the default attributes for display of text. Depending on your monitor, you can change the color of text and the highlighting attributes. For example, you can write the text

<u>ENTER</u>

by specifying ATTR=UNDERLINE, as shown:

```
%window employee
       #5 @4 "Date of Access: &sysday, &sysdate.."
       #8 @10 "Employee Data Base"
       #17 @29 "Press" @35 "ENTER" attr=underline
           @41 "to continue.";
```

Display 5.3 shows the underlined text.

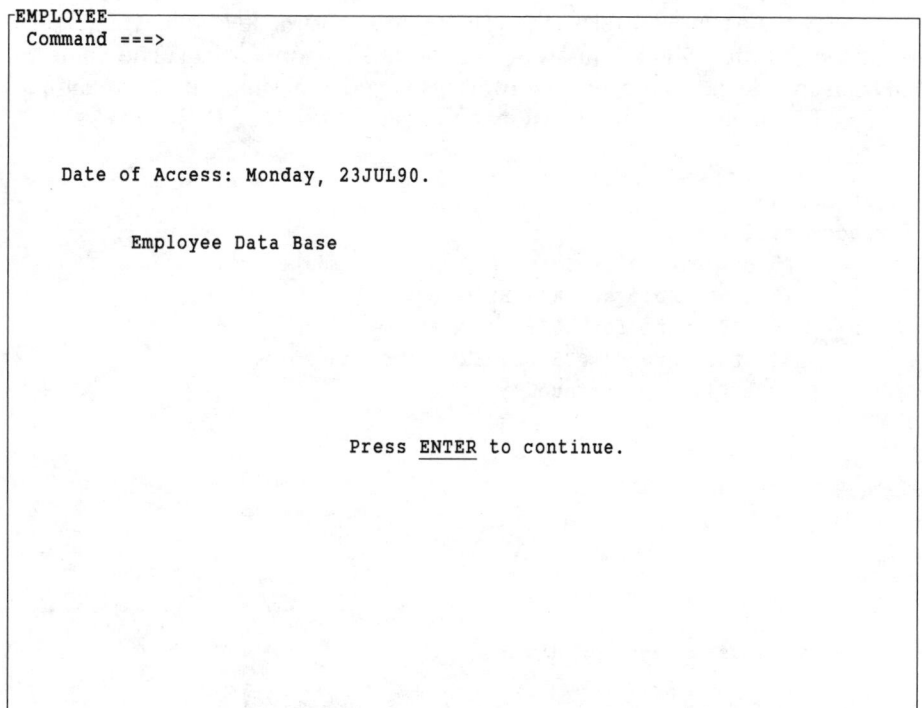

```
┌─EMPLOYEE─────────────────────────────────────────────────────────┐
│ Command ===>                                                      │
│                                                                   │
│                                                                   │
│     Date of Access: Monday, 23JUL90.                              │
│                                                                   │
│            Employee Data Base                                     │
│                                                                   │
│                                                                   │
│                                                                   │
│                                                                   │
│                        Press ENTER to continue.                   │
│                                                                   │
│                                                                   │
│                                                                   │
│                                                                   │
└───────────────────────────────────────────────────────────────────┘
```

Display 5.3   Underlining Text

Writing Fields with Macro Variable Values

At times you want information to change each time a window is displayed. For example, you may want to indicate which month of personnel records is being displayed, or you may want the user to select the month of records to be displayed. In that case, use macro variable values as part of the display.

Displaying a macro variable's value   The example in **Writing Constant Text** earlier in this chapter uses a macro variable reference to generate part of a text field. Once generated, the text field never changes. To display a value that can change each time the window is displayed—for example, the month for which you are accessing personnel data—give the name of the macro variable at the location you want. (Note that you use the macro variable name, not a macro variable reference.) The macro processor displays the current value of the variable.

Note the following points about displaying macro variable values:

- By default, you can change the value of a displayed macro variable; to prevent changes, use the PROTECT= option with the field.
- The macro processor displays as much as possible of the macro variable's value. If the length of the value changes, so does the display, except when the value would overlap another field.
- Serious problems can occur if one field overlaps another. Only the most recently defined field appears in the display; if both fields create macro variables, only the most recent macro variable is created. The SAS System writes a message in the SAS log indicating that fields overlap.

The simplest way to prevent fields from overlapping is to specify the length of the display field for the macro variable. The length of the display field does not affect the length of the variable; it simply controls the display.

The following example displays the value of macro variable MON, which identifies the month for which you are accessing the personnel data. The value of MON can change each time the window is displayed. (For simplicity, this example uses a %LET statement to create MON and assign it a value.) **Display 5.4** shows the display.

```
%let mon=jul;
%window employee
        #5 @4 "Date of Access: &sysday, &sysdate.."
        #8 @10 "Employee Data Base"
        #9 @10 "Data for" @19 mon 3
        #17 @29 "Press" @35 "ENTER" attr=underline
           @41 "to continue.";
```

```
┌EMPLOYEE─────────────────────────────────────────────────────┐
│ Command ===>                                                 │
│                                                              │
│                                                              │
│                                                              │
│    Date of Access: Monday, 23JUL90.                          │
│                                                              │
│        Employee Data Base                                    │
│        Data for jul                                          │
│                                                              │
│                                                              │
│                                                              │
│                    Press ENTER to continue.                  │
│                                                              │
│                                                              │
│                                                              │
│                                                              │
│                                                              │
│                                                              │
└──────────────────────────────────────────────────────────────┘
```

Display 5.4 Displaying a Fixed Number of Characters from a Macro Variable's Value

If the value of macro variable MON changes before the next time the macro processor displays window EMPLOYEE, the new value appears in the next display.

Entering values   When you create a field for input, it is important to give *the length of the input field* along with the macro variable name. (Using ATTR=UNDERLINE to underline the field shows users its length.) The length of the input field determines how many characters the user can enter for the value; it does not affect the length of the macro variable value the macro processor can store. If you omit the length, the macro processor uses either

- the length of the current value
- 8 bytes, if the macro variable has not been previously defined.

Assigning a length is important because some common macro program statements (such as %GLOBAL and %LOCAL) create macro variables with null values. If you define a macro variable in one of those statements and do not include a length for input, the macro processor does not allow the user to input any characters into the field.

For example, suppose you want the user to select the month to be examined in the employee database. The following %WINDOW statement both displays the current value of MON and instructs the user to select another month if the current month isn't the one he or she wants:

```
%let mon=jul;
%window employee
        #5 a4 "Date of Access: &sysday, &sysdate.."
        #8 a10 "Employee Data Base"
        #9 a10 "Data for" a19 mon 3
        #11 a4 "Or select another month (blank to quit):"
            a45 mon 3 attr=underline
        #17 a29 "Press" a35 "ENTER" attr=underline
            a41 "to continue.";
```

Suppose the current value of MON is **jul**. The value appears in each field that uses MON, as **Display 5.5** shows. To change the value, just type a new value in the input field.

```
┌EMPLOYEE─────────────────────────────────────────────────────────
│ Command ===>
│
│
│
│
│    Date of Access: Monday, 23JUL90.
│
│
│           Employee Data Base
│           Data for jul
│
│    Or select another month (blank to quit): jul
│
│
│
│
│                        Press ENTER to continue.
│
│
│
│
│
│
└─────────────────────────────────────────────────────────────────
```

Display 5.5 Displaying a Field for Entering a Value

Preventing entry of values   In the preceding example, you underline the field in which the user is to enter the new value, but nothing prevents the user from entering the new value in the wrong field—the field that reports the current data set instead of the field for selecting a new data set. The simplest way to prevent data entry is to protect the first MON field with the PROTECT= option; then the user can enter a value only in the selection field as you intended. The following code shows the PROTECT= option:

```
%window employee
        #5 @4 "Date of Access: &sysday, &sysdate.."
        #8 @10 "Employee Data Base"
        #9 @10 "Data for" @19 mon 3 protect=yes
        #11 @4 "Or select another month (blank to quit):"
             @45 mon 3 attr=underline
        #17 @29 "Press" @35 "ENTER" attr=underline
             @41 "to continue.";
```

To see how a protected field can be useful, consider this program:

```
%macro empl(mon);
    %display employee;
    %do %while(&mon ne);
        data temp;
            set in.&mon;
            more SAS statements
        run;
        %display employee;
    %end;
%mend empl;
```

Suppose you invoke macro EMPL as shown:

```
%empl(jul)
```

The macro processor first displays **Display 5.6**.

```
┌EMPLOYEE──────────────────────────────────────────────────────────┐
│  Command ===>                                                     │
│                                                                   │
│                                                                   │
│                                                                   │
│     Date of Access: Monday, 23JUL90.                              │
│                                                                   │
│                                                                   │
│           Employee Data Base                                      │
│           Data for jul                                            │
│                                                                   │
│     Or select another month (blank to quit): jul                  │
│                                                                   │
│                                                                   │
│                                                                   │
│                         Press ENTER to continue.                  │
│                                                                   │
│                                                                   │
│                                                                   │
│                                                                   │
│                                                                   │
└───────────────────────────────────────────────────────────────────┘
```

Display 5.6   Displaying the Initial Value

The SAS compiler receives these statements:

```
DATA TEMP;
   SET IN.JUL;
   more SAS statements
RUN;
```

Next, suppose you enter the value **aug**, as in **Display 5.7**.

```
┌EMPLOYEE─────────────────────────────────────────────────────┐
│ Command ===>                                                 │
│                                                              │
│                                                              │
│                                                              │
│     Date of Access: Monday, 23JUL90.                         │
│                                                              │
│                                                              │
│          Employee Data Base                                  │
│          Data for jul                                        │
│                                                              │
│     Or select another month (blank to quit): aug             │
│                                                              │
│                                                              │
│                                                              │
│                      Press ENTER to continue.                │
│                                                              │
│                                                              │
│                                                              │
│                                                              │
│                                                              │
└──────────────────────────────────────────────────────────────┘
```

Display 5.7   Changing the Value

The SAS compiler then sees these statements:

```
DATA TEMP;
   SET IN.AUG;
   more SAS statements
RUN;
```

When the user enters three blanks in the field, the loop ceases execution.

Creating Multiple Contents for a Window

At times you may want to define different sets of fields for the same window. All the fields in a window that appear at once are known as a group of fields; rather than using a single unnamed group as in the preceding sections, you can name groups of fields with the GROUP= option and display them individually.

Displaying different groups of text in a window is helpful both for keeping your windows organized (since you have fewer windows to keep track of) and for avoiding repeating window options that don't change (for example, if you have defined a particular size or position for a window).

For example, suppose the user may need to select either the month or the department to be analyzed in the employee database. A simple solution is to create window EMPLOYEE like this:

```
%window employee
      group=month
      #5 a4 "Date of Access: &sysday, &sysdate.."
      #8 a10 "Employee Data Base"
      #9 a10 "Data for" a19 mon 3 protect=yes
      #11 a4 "Or select another month (blank to quit):"
          a45 mon 3 attr=underline
      #17 a29 "Press" a35 "ENTER" attr=underline
          a41 "to continue.";

      group=dept
      #5 a4 "Date of Access: &sysday, &sysdate.."
      #8 a10 "Employee Data Base"
      #12 a10 "Report for all departments"
      #14 a4 "Or select a department" a27 dept 6 attr=underline
      #17 a29 "Press" a35 "ENTER" attr=underline
          a41 "to continue.";
```

This %WINDOW statement defines two groups of fields, and a %DISPLAY statement displays the one you name.* For example, to display the fields for selecting a month, specify this statement:

```
%display employee.month;
```

To display the fields for selecting a department, specify this statement:

```
%display employee.dept;
```

Display 5.8 shows the EMPLOYEE.DEPT group of fields.

---

* For more complex displays, see **CREATING AND DISPLAYING SYSTEMS OF WINDOWS** later in this chapter.

```
┌EMPLOYEE─────────────────────────────────────────────────────────────┐
│ Command ===>                                                         │
│                                                                      │
│                                                                      │
│                                                                      │
│    Date of Access: Monday, 23JUL90.                                  │
│                                                                      │
│                                                                      │
│          Employee Data Base                                          │
│                                                                      │
│                                                                      │
│          Report for all departments                                  │
│                                                                      │
│     Or select a department _____                                    │
│                                                                      │
│                                                                      │
│                         Press ENTER to continue.                     │
│                                                                      │
│                                                                      │
│                                                                      │
│                                                                      │
│                                                                      │
│                                                                      │
│                                                                      │
│                                                                      │
│                                                                      │
└──────────────────────────────────────────────────────────────────────┘
```

Display 5.8   Displaying a Group of Fields

Controlling the Appearance of a Window

The windows shown so far have occupied the entire display. However, you can also create windows in different sizes and different positions in the display.

To begin a window at a place other than the upper left corner of the display, use the IROW= and ICOLUMN= options in the %WINDOW statement. Specify the row, column, or both at which you want the window to start. Count the upper border of the default display as row 1 and the left border as column 1.

To control the number of rows and columns in the display (and therefore where the display ends), use the ROWS= and COLUMNS= options. The ROWS= option gives the number of rows the window is to contain *including the top and bottom borders, the command line or action bar, and the message line.* The COLUMNS= option gives the number of columns the window is to contain *including the left and right borders.** **Figure 5.1** illustrates these options.

---

* If you have worked with macro windows in Release 6.03, note that the row and column conventions are different in Release 6.06. In Release 6.03, the ROWS= and COLUMNS= values exclude the borders.

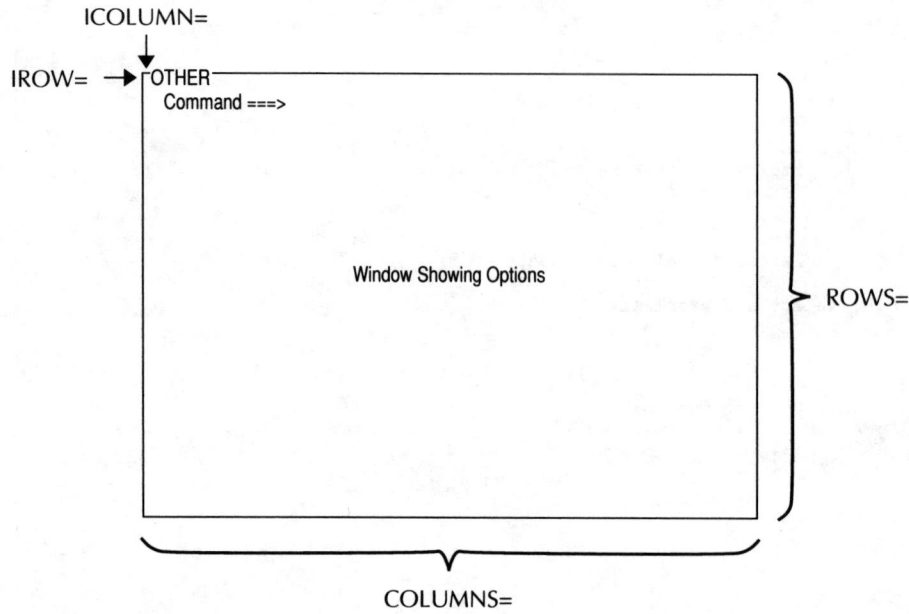

Figure 5.1   Options That Control the Size and Shape of Windows

For example, the following %WINDOW statement creates a window that partially overlays the PROGRAM EDITOR and LOG windows in display manager. **Display 5.9** illustrates the window created.

```
%window empsmall irow=4 rows=22 icolumn=10 columns=60
        #5 ə4 "Date of Access: &sysday, &sysdate.."
        #8 ə10 "Employee Data Base"
        #9 ə10 "Data for" ə19 mon protect=yes
        #11 ə4 "Or select another month (blank to quit):"
            ə45 mon 3 attr=underline
        #17 ə29 "Press" ə35 "ENTER" attr=underline
            ə41 "to continue.";
```

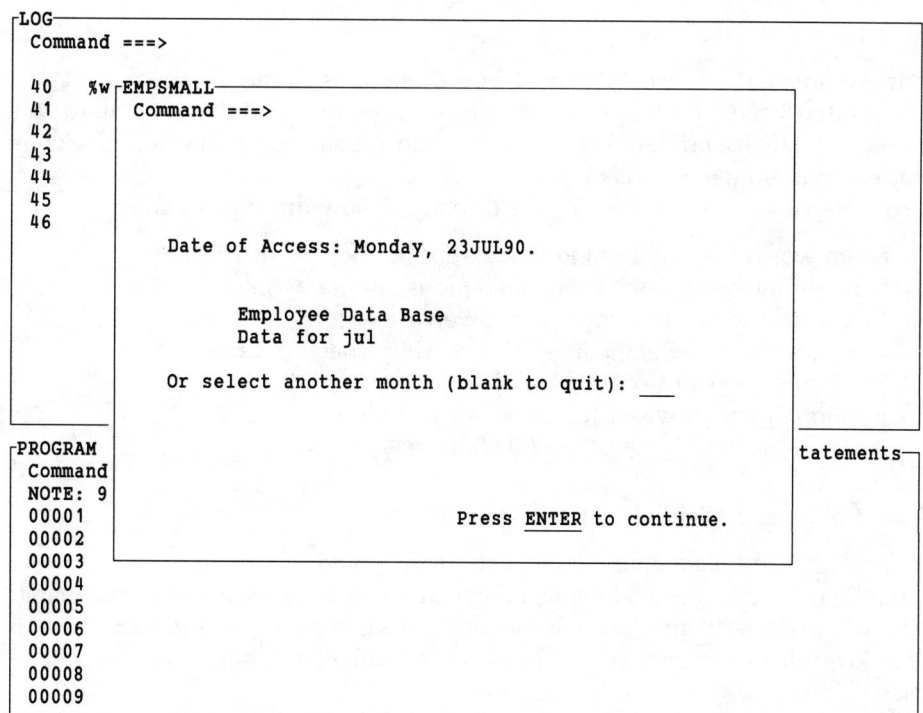

```
┌LOG──────────────────────────────────────────────────────────────────┐
│ Command ===>                                                         │
│                                                                      │
│  40    %w ┌EMPSMALL──────────────────────────────────────────┐      │
│  41       │  Command ===>                                     │      │
│  42       │                                                   │      │
│  43       │                                                   │      │
│  44       │                                                   │      │
│  45       │                                                   │      │
│  46       │                                                   │      │
│           │       Date of Access: Monday, 23JUL90.            │      │
│           │                                                   │      │
│           │                                                   │      │
│           │          Employee Data Base                       │      │
│           │          Data for jul                             │      │
│           │                                                   │      │
│           │       Or select another month (blank to quit): ___│      │
│           │                                                   │      │
├PROGRAM    │                                                   │tatements┤
│ Command   │                                                   │      │
│ NOTE: 9   │                                                   │      │
│ 00001     │               Press ENTER to continue.            │      │
│ 00002     │                                                   │      │
│ 00003     │                                                   │      │
│ 00004     └───────────────────────────────────────────────────┘      │
│ 00005                                                                │
│ 00006                                                                │
│ 00007                                                                │
│ 00008                                                                │
│ 00009                                                                │
└──────────────────────────────────────────────────────────────────────┘
```

Display 5.9   Displaying a Smaller Window

Depending on your operating system and monitor, you can use display manager commands to move a macro window, change its size, and change the color of various items in the displayed window. **%WINDOW Statement** in Chapter 3 lists the display manager commands available with macro windows.

Designing Effective Windows

When you design windows for users, remember that a user's perception of an application is greatly influenced by the appearance of the application's windows. Windows that are cluttered, difficult to read, difficult to understand, or visually unattractive can make users frustrated with the whole application.

In designing windows, one of the most important things to consider is the type of monitor that users of the application have. To make windows effective for all users, you should scale window text and fields to the smallest monitor on which an application runs. If some users have monochrome monitors and some have color, you should plan color and highlighting that produce attractive combinations of shading on monochrome displays.

When you plan the contents of a window, remember to give the user the following information:

- how to exit from a window without taking action
- how to respond to and release windows.

Books on designing application windows are available.*

---

* One example is Galitz, Wilbert O. (1985), *Handbook of Screen Format Design*, Wellesley, MA: QED Information Sciences, Inc.

Using Indention and Spacing

To make online displays easy to read, you should design them to be more open than printed pages. That is, there should be more blank background space on a window than on a printed page. Windows can appear cluttered when they contain less than 40 percent blank space.

To increase the readability of your displays, follow these guidelines:

- Make words, sentences, and paragraphs as short as possible.
- Make terminology concise, unambiguous, and consistent.
- Create text in mixed upper- and lowercase letters.
- Consider double-spacing lines of text when space permits.
- Separate blocks of text by blank lines.
- Position labels above or to the left of text blocks.
- Avoid using lines longer than 60 characters.

Using Colors and Highlighting

To use color and highlighting effectively, you should use them conservatively. Carefully planned color and highlighting can signal or prompt users and enable them to rapidly scan and locate information. Remember to find out whether all users have the same type of monitor and, in particular, whether all users have color monitors.

When you design windows with color, remember these guidelines:

- Avoid combining colors that are adjacent on the color wheel because they are harder to distinguish.
- Use contrasting colors for differentiation and bright colors for emphasis.
- Avoid combining complementary colors (opposites on the color wheel) for a window's background and text (for example, red text on green background) because these combinations can cause users to experience an unpleasant feeling of visual vibration.

CREATING AND DISPLAYING SYSTEMS OF WINDOWS

The windows shown so far in this chapter have been relatively simple, and the technique for displaying them—the %DISPLAY statement outside a macro definition—has also been simple. However, window definitions can contain more complex groups of fields. In addition, when you place %DISPLAY statements inside a macro definition instead of outside, you have more flexibility in what you display. Specifically, placing %DISPLAY statements inside a macro allows you to

- merge more than one group of fields into a single display
- use the SYSCMD automatic variable with %IF-%THEN statements to cause conditional display of various groups of fields.

This section describes how to use these two features. **HOW THE SAS SYSTEM PROCESSES WINDOWS** later in this chapter describes the technical aspects of displaying windows that make these features possible.

Displaying More Than One Group of Fields at the Same Time

An earlier example created two groups of fields for a window and allowed you to display either of them. For reference, the example below repeats that code:

```
%window employee
      group=month
      #5 @4 "Date of Access: &sysday, &sysdate.."
      #8 @10 "Employee Data Base"
      #9 @10 "Data for" @19 mon 3 protect=yes
      #11 @4 "Or select another month (blank to quit):"
         @45 mon 3 attr=underline
      #17 @29 "Press" @35 "ENTER" attr=underline
         @41 "to continue.";

      group=dept
      #5 @4 "Date of Access: &sysday, &sysdate.."
      #8 @10 "Employee Data Base"
      #12 @10 "Report for all departments"
      #14 @4 "Or select a department" @27 dept 6 attr=underline
      #17 @29 "Press" @35 "ENTER" attr=underline
         @41 "to continue.";
```

In this %WINDOW statement, three of the lines in each group of fields are identical. When you display a window outside a macro definition, you must repeat all the fields in each group because each %DISPLAY statement sets up an independent windowing environment; that is, no information is retained from one display to the next.

However, if you display the window (not define it) inside a macro definition, you can put the information that does not change into one group, the other information into other groups, and display the groups that you want. This %WINDOW statement divides the information into three groups:

```
%window employee
      group=base
      #5 @4 "Date of Access: &sysday, &sysdate.."
      #8 @10 "Employee Data Base"
      #17 @29 "Press" @35 "ENTER" attr=underline
         @41 "to continue.";

      group=month
      #9 @10 "Data for" @19 mon 3 protect=yes
      #11 @4 "Or select another month (blank to quit):"
         @45 mon 3 attr=underline

      group=dept
      #12 @10 "Report for all departments"
      #14 @4 "Or select a department" @27 dept 6 attr=underline;
```

Now place the %DISPLAY statements inside a macro definition, and display the groups of fields you want. In macro EMPDATA, shown here, you specify whether you want information by department or by month:

```
%macro empdata(show);
   %display employee.base noinput;
   %if &show=month %then %display employee.month;
   %else %if &show=dept %then %display employee.dept;
%mend empdata;
```

The NOINPUT option in the first %DISPLAY statement serves these two purposes:

- It tells the macro processor not to allow input in any fields of that group (although in this case, entering new values for the read-only variables SYSDAY and SYSDATE has no permanent effect).
- It tells the macro processor not to wait for you to press ENTER in that display before proceeding to the next action.

Therefore, invoking macro EMPDATA displays EMPLOYEE.BASE, followed immediately by either EMPLOYEE.MONTH or EMPLOYEE.DEPT, depending on the value of parameter SHOW. The following invocation produces **Display 5.10**:

```
%empdata(month)
```

```
┌EMPLOYEE────────────────────────────────────────────────────────────
 Command ===>




    Date of Access: Monday, 23JUL90.


         Employee Data Base
         Data for jul

    Or select another month (blank to quit): jul




                        Press ENTER to continue.
```

Display 5.10   Displaying Two Groups of Fields at Once

Changing a Display Conditionally

Suppose that, if the user initially displays the field for MONTH, you want him or her to be able to display the field for DEPT as well. You can assign a value from the window's command line to the automatic variable SYSCMD and then use the value of SYSCMD in a %IF-%THEN statement, as shown:

```
%macro empdata(show);
   %display employee.base noinput;
   %if &show=month %then
      %do;
          %display employee.month;
          %if %upcase(&syscmd)=DEPT %then %display employee.dept;
      %end;
   %else %if &show=dept %then %display employee.dept;
%mend empdata;
```

The value of SYSCMD works like a customized display manager command; you specify what the macro processor is to do when SYSCMD has a particular value. (If you have not specified any action, the macro processor accepts the value of SYSCMD but does not use it.) Now the following invocation produces the same display as before:

```
%empdata(month)
```

However, entering **dept** on the command line displays the DEPT fields.

   Display 5.11 shows the display of DEPT fields after you enter **dept** on the command line.

```
┌EMPLOYEE───────────────────────────────────────────────────────────────┐
│ Command ===>                                                           │
│                                                                        │
│                                                                        │
│                                                                        │
│                                                                        │
│    Date of Access: Monday, 23JUL90.                                    │
│                                                                        │
│                                                                        │
│           Employee Data Base                                           │
│           Data for jul                                                 │
│                                                                        │
│    Or select another month (blank to quit): jul                        │
│           Report for all departments                                   │
│                                                                        │
│    Or select a department _____                                       │
│                                                                        │
│                                                                        │
│                          Press ENTER to continue.                      │
│                                                                        │
│                                                                        │
│                                                                        │
│                                                                        │
│                                                                        │
│                                                                        │
└────────────────────────────────────────────────────────────────────────┘
```

Display 5.11   Entering a Customized Command and Seeing the Result

   You can also write customized messages on the window's message line by assigning a value to the automatic macro variable SYSMSG. For example, if the user enters a value other than **dept** on the command line, the macro processor can inform the user that **dept** is the only valid choice, as shown:

```
%macro empdata(show);
   %display employee.base noinput;
   %if &show=month %then
      %do;
         %display employee.month;
         %if %upcase(&syscmd)=DEPT %then %display employee.dept;
         %else %if &syscmd ne %then
            %do;
               %let sysmsg=
               %upcase(&syscmd) is not valid. You may choose: DEPT;
               %display employee.month;
            %end;
      %end;
   %else %if &show=dept %then %display employee.dept;
%mend empdata;
```

Suppose you invoke EMPDATA with a parameter value of **month** and enter **division** on the command line. **Display 5.12** shows the message.

```
┌EMPLOYEE────────────────────────────────────────────────────────────
 Command ===>
 DIVISION is not valid. You may choose: DEPT


    Date of Access: Monday, 23JUL90.


          Employee Data Base
          Data for jul

    Or select another month (blank to quit): jul




                         Press ENTER to continue.




 └──────────────────────────────────────────────────────────────────
```

Display 5.12 Response to an Invalid Choice

This example requires the user to reinvoke the macro to correct his or her selection. You can also write a loop that gives the user multiple opportunities to make the correction, as in the following macro:

```
%macro empdata(show);
    %local loop;
    %let loop=1;
    %display employee.base noinput;
    %if &show=month %then
        %do %until(&loop=0);
            %display employee.month;
            %if %upcase(&syscmd)=DEPT %then
                %do;
                    %display employee.dept;
                    %let loop=0;
                %end;
            %else %if &syscmd ne %then %let sysmsg=
                    %upcase(&syscmd) is not valid. You may choose: DEPT;
            %else %let loop=0;
        %end;
    %else %if &show=dept %then %display employee.dept;
%mend empdata;
```

The %DO %UNTIL loop executes at least once and continues executing until the value of macro variable LOOP is 0. When the user either requests the DEPT group or presses ENTER without requesting any group, the value of LOOP becomes 0 and the loop ceases to execute.

HOW THE SAS SYSTEM PROCESSES WINDOWS

This section describes some internal aspects of how the SAS System treats macro windows. Understanding the internal processing of macro windows helps you increase the efficiency of your programs containing windows.

Creating and Storing Windows

When the macro processor compiles a macro containing a %WINDOW statement, it stores the %WINDOW statement as text (discussed in Chapter 8, "How the SAS System Processes a Program"). During macro execution (or the execution of a %WINDOW statement in open code), the macro processor executes the %WINDOW statement to produce a utility file in the WORK library. The utility file remains in the WORK library until the end of the session. (You cannot view or manipulate window files.) Executing a %WINDOW statement is also called defining a window.

Macro variables created in a window are stored in the current referencing environment (see Chapter 2, "Macro Variables"). A macro window does not create a separate referencing environment.

The way the SAS System stores windows determines where you should create them. Because the macro processor creates windows at macro execution, defining a window inside a macro means that each time you invoke the macro, you re-create the window file. For efficiency, you should create macro windows in the outermost layer of nesting possible—either open code or, in a system of macros, in the controlling (driver) macro. That causes the macro window to be defined only once.

In the following example, the user must enter an expression to select observations from the employee database. The first version shows an inefficient construction, and the second shows an efficient one.

```
      /* inefficient for repeated executions */

%macro printit;
   %window getobs
           #5 @4 "Date of Access: &sysday, &sysdate.."
           #8 @10 "Employee Data Base"
           #9 @10 "Data for" @19 mon 3 protect=yes
           #11 @4 "Enter a SAS expression"
           #12 @4 "to choose the observations to be printed:"
           #14 @4 obs 50 attr=underline
           #17 @29 "Press" @35 "ENTER" attr=underline
               @41 "to continue.";

   %display getobs;
   proc print data=&syslast noobs;
      where &obs;
      title "Observations Where &obs";
   run;
%mend printit;
```

```
      /* efficient for repeated executions */

%window getobs
        #5 a4 "Date of Access: &sysday, &sysdate.."
        #8 a10 "Employee Data Base"
        #9 a10 "Data for" a19 mon 3 protect=yes
        #11 a4 "Enter a SAS expression"
        #12 a4 "to choose the observations to be printed:"
        #14 a4 obs 50 attr=underline
        #17 a29 "Press" a35 "ENTER" attr=underline
            a41 "to continue.";

%macro printit;
    %display getobs;
    proc print data=&syslast noobs;
        where &obs;
        title "Observations Where &obs";
    run;
%mend printit;
```

In the first example, each time you invoke macro PRINTIT you re-create the
GETOBS window. In the second example, you create GETOBS once and simply
display it each time you execute the macro. The SAS compiler sees the same code
in either case; the differences are the efficiency and that in the first example,
macro variable OBS is local to macro PRINTIT, whereas in the second example,
it is global.

In either case, invoking macro PRINTIT and responding as shown in **Display
5.13** causes the SAS compiler to see the statements shown after the window.

```
┌GETOBS──────────────────────────────────────────────────────────┐
│ Command ===>                                                    │
│                                                                 │
│                                                                 │
│                                                                 │
│                                                                 │
│    Date of Access: Monday, 23JUL90.                             │
│                                                                 │
│            Employee Data Base                                   │
│            Data for jul                                         │
│                                                                 │
│    Enter a SAS expression                                       │
│    to choose the observations to be printed:                    │
│                                                                 │
│    start>1980 and dept in ('MKT','SALES')_____    │
│                                                                 │
│                                                                 │
│                        Press ENTER to continue.                 │
│                                                                 │
│                                                                 │
│                                                                 │
│                                                                 │
│                                                                 │
│                                                                 │
│                                                                 │
│                                                                 │
└─────────────────────────────────────────────────────────────────┘
```

Display 5.13   Creating a Window to Specify a Condition

```
PROC PRINT DATA=IN.PERSDATA NOOBS;
   WHERE START>1980 AND DEPT IN('MKT','SALES');
   TITLE "Observations Where start>1980 and dept in('MKT','SALES')";
   RUN;
```

Displaying Windows

The SAS System displays macro windows through a windowing environment that is similar to the display manager windowing environment but is managed independently. The separate environment allows you to display a macro window from a line-oriented or noninteractive session as well as from a display manager session. (Note that windowing environments are not related to macro variable referencing environments.)

The way the macro processor uses the windowing environment depends on whether a %DISPLAY statement occurs outside or inside a macro definition. If it occurs outside, executing the statement creates the environment; when the window goes away, so does the environment. The next execution of a %DISPLAY statement creates a new windowing environment. As a result, you cannot maintain text from one display in order to merge it with another display; you must create all fields you intend to display at once in a single group.

If a %DISPLAY statement occurs inside a macro definition, the first %DISPLAY statement in the macro creates a windowing environment, and all subsequent %DISPLAY statements use that environment. Thus, executing multiple %DISPLAY statements from inside a macro is more efficient than executing the same number from outside a macro. In addition, inside a macro definition the NOINPUT option enables you to merge text from multiple groups without the user's having to press ENTER to bring up each subsequent group.

Earlier in this chapter, **Creating Multiple Contents for a Window** illustrates preparing text for display outside a macro and **Displaying More Than One Group of Fields at the Same Time** illustrates preparing text for display inside a macro.

Chapter 6
DATA Step Interfaces

The features shown earlier in this book affect SAS statements that are being compiled, or constructed. In particular, information provided by those statements and functions is constant during DATA step execution. Similarly, those features cannot transfer information produced by a DATA step to another step in the program. The features shown in this chapter operate on macro variables while the DATA step is executing; thus, an individual iteration of the DATA step can assign a value to or retrieve the value of a macro variable. The SYMPUT routine assigns values to macro variables during DATA step execution, and the SYMGET function retrieves values of macro variables during DATA step execution.

Contents

SYMGET Function

The SYMGET function returns the value of a macro variable to the DATA step during DATA step execution. The form of the SYMGET function is

SYMGET(*argument*)

where

> *argument*   identifies a macro variable. The forms of *argument* are given below.

The SYMGET function returns a character value. If you use the SYMGET function in an assignment statement without assigning a length to the target variable, the length is 200. If the length of the returned value is more than 200 characters, the returned value is truncated on the right. If the SYMGET function cannot locate the macro variable identified in *argument*, SYMGET returns a missing value, and the DATA step issues a message for an illegal argument to a function.

The argument of the SYMGET function can be any of the following:

- a character string representing the name of a macro variable (not a macro variable reference), as in this example:

```
%let g=good;
data test2;
   length x $ 4;
   set test1;
   x=symget('g');            /* Note absence of ampersand */
   y="&g";
run;
```

In each observation of data set TEST2, X has the value good. The assignment statement and the SYMGET function in it are executed in each iteration of the DATA step. The LENGTH statement assigns X the length 4; without the LENGTH statement, the SAS System assigns a length of 200.

For comparison, the second assignment statement receives the same value, good. The macro processor resolves the macro variable reference while the SAS compiler is compiling the DATA step. The SAS compiler sees the statement as

```
Y="good";
```

- the name of a DATA step character variable whose values are the names of macro variables, as in this example:

```
%let a1=begin;
%let a2=end;
%let a3=continue;
data one;
   length key $ 8;
   input code $ @@;
   key=symget(code);
   cards;
a1 a1 a2 a3 a1 a2
;

proc print;
   title "Data Set Produced Using SYMGET";
run;
```

In DATA step ONE, the character variable CODE has a value of **a1**, **a2**, or **a3**. Each time the assignment statement is executed, the SYMGET function selects the macro variable identified by CODE and returns the value of that macro variable. That value becomes the value of KEY for the current observation. The LENGTH statement assigns KEY the length 8; without that statement, the SAS System assigns a length of 200. **Output 6.1** shows the data set produced.

Output 6.1   DATA Step Values Returned by the SYMGET Function

```
         Data Set Produced Using SYMGET                       1

         OBS      KEY           CODE

           1      begin         a1
           2      begin         a1
           3      end           a2
           4      continue      a3
           5      begin         a1
           6      end           a2
```

If the value of CODE is not a valid SAS name, or if the macro processor cannot find a macro variable of that name, the SAS System prints a note that the function has an illegal argument and sets the resulting value to missing.

- a character expression, as in this example:

```
%let s1=a;
%let s2=b;
%let s3=c;
data test3;
   set test1;
   length score $ 8;
   score=symget('s'||left(_n_));
run;
```

Each time the DATA step executes, the SYMGET function first evaluates the character expression to construct a macro variable name; then it retrieves the value of that macro variable. In the first iteration of the DATA step, the SYMGET function combines the letter S and the left-aligned value of the automatic variable _N_ to form the name S1. Then it retrieves the value of macro variable S1, and the assignment statement assigns SCORE the value **a**. Similarly, the value of SCORE is **b** in the second observation and **c** in the third. If the data set TEST1 has more than three observations, subsequent iterations of the DATA step produce a note about an invalid argument to SYMGET and assign SCORE a missing value.

Examples

Example 1:   Retrieving a Different Macro Variable Value for Each BY Group

This example uses the SYMGET function to retrieve a different value for each BY group. Match the circled numbers to the paragraphs that follow.

```
data sales; ❶
   input revenue region $ @@;
   cards;
2000 north  2000 north  1600 south  3300 east
1500 east   2200 east   2400 west   2800 west
1400 west   1000 west   2800 south  3000 north
2100 south  1500 south  1800 south  1700 east
1000 north  1100 north  1600 east   1300 west
1600 east   3200 east   1700 south  1200 west
2400 west   3000 west   2000 north  1500 south
2800 south  3100 south  1200 east
;

proc sort;
   by region;
run;

proc univariate noprint; ❷
   output out=meddata median=medrev;
   var revenue;
   by region;
run;

data _null_; ❸
   set meddata;
   call symput('m'||left(_n_),medrev);
run;

data tophalf;
   retain medval 0; ❹
   set sales;
   by region;
   if first.region then
      do; ❺
         x+1;
         medval=symget('m'||left(x));
      end;
   if revenue>=medval; ❻
run;

proc print;
   id region;
   var revenue;
   title "Revenues At Or Above Median";
run;
```

1. The DATA SALES step creates a SAS data set containing several values of the variable REVENUE for each region (variable REGION). The PROC SORT step sorts the data by region.
2. The PROC UNIVARIATE step creates an output SAS data set containing the median value of REVENUE for each region.
3. The DATA _NULL_ step uses the SYMPUT routine (described later in this chapter) to create macro variables named M1, M2, and so on—one for each region. The value assigned to the macro variable is the value of the DATA step variable MEDREV for that observation—the median revenue for that region.
4. The DATA TOPHALF step first creates the variable MEDVAL that will contain the values retrieved by the SYMGET function.
5. When the IF condition is true, the sum statement increments the counter X; thus, X contains the number of the current BY group. The SYMGET function retrieves the value of the macro variable containing the median revenue for that region and assigns the value to MEDVAL. Because MEDVAL is retained, you need to execute the SYMGET function only once for each BY group.
6. The subsetting IF statement selects only observations with a value greater than the value of MEDVAL for that BY group, as shown in **Output 6.2**.

Output 6.2   Data Set Produced Using the SYMGET Function

```
                    Revenues At Or Above Median                    1

                    REGION    REVENUE

                    east       3300
                    east       2200
                    east       1700
                    east       3200
                    north      2000
                    north      2000
                    north      3000
                    north      2000
                    south      2800
                    south      2100
                    south      1800
                    south      2800
                    south      3100
                    west       2400
                    west       2800
                    west       2400
                    west       3000
```

Example 2:   Transferring Variable Information with the SYMGET Function and the SYMPUT Routine

This example transfers information from a data set created by the MEANS procedure into a data set containing salary information for employees of Dusty Department Store. The final report displays each employee's name, department, salary, and the employee's salary as a percentage of the department's total salary expenditure and of the store's total salary expenditure. Match the circled numbers to the explanations that follow.

```
data dusty; ❶
   input dept $ name $ salary @@;
   cards;
```

```
Bedding Reed 28000       Bedding Chee 26000
Bedding Parker 19000     Bedding George 18000
Bedding Joiner 18000     Carpets Hilliard 20000
Carpets Yao 22000        Carpets Jones 19000
Carpets McNair 20000     Carpets Thomas 22000
Gifts Diaz 18000         Gifts Pardo 29000
Gifts Rankin 17000       Gifts Hassan 20000
Kitchen White 18000      Kitchen Banks 24000
Kitchen Marks 19000      Kitchen Cannon 25000
Video Jones 19000        Video Smith 18000
Video Kushnir 25000      Video Morse 26000
;

proc means noprint;
   class dept;
   var salary;
   output out=stats sum=s_sal;
run;

proc print data=stats;
   var dept s_sal;
   title "Summary of Salary Information";
   title2 "for Dusty Department Store";
run;

data _null_; ❷
   set stats;
   if _n_=1 then call symput('s_tot',s_sal); ❸
   else call symput('s'||dept,s_sal); ❹
run;

data new; ❺
   set dusty;
   pctdept=(salary/symget('s'||dept))*100; ❻
   pcttot=(salary/&s_tot)*100; ❼
run;

proc print data=new split="*";
   label dept="Department"
         name="Employee"
         pctdept="Percent of*Department*Salary"
         pcttot="Percent of*Store *Salary";
   format pctdept pcttot 4.1;
   title "Salary Profiles for Employees";
   title2 "of Dusty Department Store";
run;
```

1. The DATA DUSTY step creates a SAS data set containing each employee's department, name, and salary, and the PROC MEANS step produces an output data set named STATS that contains the sum of salaries (variable S_SAL) for each department and for the store as a whole. The PROC PRINT step prints data set STATS.
2. The DATA _NULL_ step creates macro variables and assigns them values from STATS.
3. The first observation in STATS contains information about salaries for all employees (variable S_SAL in combination with a missing value for DEPT). Therefore, in the first iteration of the DATA _NULL_ step, the SYMPUT routine places the sum of salaries for all employees into the value of macro variable S_TOT.

4. In the second iteration, the SYMPUT routine creates a macro variable by concatenating the letter S and the value of the DEPT variable, in this case `Bedding`. Macro variable SBEDDING contains the sum of the salaries of employees in the Bedding department. Subsequent executions of the DATA step produce analogous macro variables for other departments. In all, the DATA _NULL_ step produces six macro variables: one for each of the five departments, plus one for the store as a whole.

5. The DATA NEW step creates the final data set to be used in the report. It calculates each employee's salary as a percentage of the departmental salary expenditure (PCTDEPT) and as a percentage of the store's total salary expenditure (PCTTOT). The PROC PRINT step after the DATA step prints the report.

6. In the expression that calculates PCTDEPT, the SYMGET function forms the macro variable name by concatenating the letter S and the value of DEPT.

7. PCTTOT is created by dividing the employee's salary by the total of salaries in the store. Because the total does not change during the execution of the DATA step, a macro variable reference is a more efficient way than the SYMGET function to retrieve the value of S_TOT.

Output 6.3 shows data set STATS and the report produced from data set NEW.

Output 6.3   Intermediate Data Set and Final Report

```
                  Summary of Salary Information                    1
                    for Dusty Department Store

              OBS       DEPT        S_SAL

               1                   470000
               2      Bedding      109000
               3      Carpets      103000
               4      Gifts         84000
               5      Kitchen       86000
               6      Video         88000
```

```
                  Salary Profiles for Employees                    2
                     of Dusty Department Store

                                             Percent of   Percent of
                                             Department      Store
      OBS    Department   Employee   SALARY    Salary       Salary

       1      Bedding      Reed       28000    25.7          6.0
       2      Bedding      Chee       26000    23.9          5.5
       3      Bedding      Parker     19000    17.4          4.0
       4      Bedding      George     18000    16.5          3.8
       5      Bedding      Joiner     18000    16.5          3.8
       6      Carpets      Hilliard   20000    19.4          4.3
       7      Carpets      Yao        22000    21.4          4.7
       8      Carpets      Jones      19000    18.4          4.0
       9      Carpets      McNair     20000    19.4          4.3
      10      Carpets      Thomas     22000    21.4          4.7
      11      Gifts        Diaz       18000    21.4          3.8
      12      Gifts        Pardo      29000    34.5          6.2
      13      Gifts        Rankin     17000    20.2          3.6
      14      Gifts        Hassan     20000    23.8          4.3
      15      Kitchen      White      18000    20.9          3.8
      16      Kitchen      Banks      24000    27.9          5.1
      17      Kitchen      Marks      19000    22.1          4.0
      18      Kitchen      Cannon     25000    29.1          5.3
      19      Video        Jones      19000    21.6          4.0
      20      Video        Smith      18000    20.5          3.8
      21      Video        Kushnir    25000    28.4          5.3
      22      Video        Morse      26000    29.5          5.5
```

SYMPUT Routine

The SYMPUT routine assigns a value produced in the DATA step to a macro variable. If the macro variable does not exist, the SYMPUT routine creates it. The form of the SYMPUT routine is

SYMPUT(*name*,*value*)

where

    name   contains the name of the macro variable. The forms *name* can take are described below.

    value   contains the value to be assigned. The forms *value* can take are described below.

You must use the SYMPUT routine as part of the CALL statement.

Each execution of the SYMPUT routine assigns a value to one macro variable. In most cases, a macro variable created by the SYMPUT routine is global; for details, see **Creating a Variable with the SYMPUT Routine** in Chapter 2, "Macro Variables."

Note: The most important fact to remember in using the SYMPUT routine is that it assigns the value of the macro variable during DATA step execution, but macro variable references resolve during the compilation of a step or global statement used outside a step. As a result, the following are true:

- You cannot use a macro variable reference to retrieve a macro variable's value in the same DATA step in which the SYMPUT routine assigns that value.
- To reference a value in a global statement following the DATA step (for example, a TITLE statement), you must first explicitly force the DATA step to execute with a RUN statement.

For further explanation, see **Referencing Values Assigned by the SYMPUT Routine** later in this section.

In the argument of the SYMPUT routine, *name* can be any of the following:

- a character string enclosed in quotes that is a valid SAS name, as in this example:

```
call symput('new',value);
```

The SYMPUT routine assigns *value* to a macro variable named NEW.
- the name of a DATA step character variable whose values are valid SAS names. The value of the variable in the current observation gives the name of the macro variable. This example shows the correct form:

```
data a;
   input person $;
   call symput(person,value);
   cards;
Ann
Tom
Bill
;
```

The SYMPUT routine assigns *value* to three macro variables named ANN, TOM, and BILL.

- a character expression. For example, this statement builds a macro variable name of the form MV*n* by combining the character string MV and the left-aligned value of _N_:

```
call symput('mv'||left(_n_),value);
```

This form is useful for creating a series of macro variables.

In the argument of the SYMPUT routine, *value* can be any of the following:

- a string enclosed in quotes. For example, this statement assigns the string **test value** to the macro variable identified in *name*:

```
call symput(name,'test value');
```

- the name of a DATA step variable. The value of the variable in the current observation is assigned as the value of the macro variable. The variable can be numeric or character; if the variable is numeric, the SAS System performs an automatic numeric-to-character conversion and writes a message in the log. **How the SYMPUT Routine Formats the Values It Assigns** later in this section describes the rules the SYMPUT routine follows in assigning values of DATA step variables to macro variables.

  Consider the following example:

```
data b;
   input city $;
   call symput(name,city);
   cards;
Raleigh
Cary
Apex
;
```

Each time the CALL SYMPUT statement executes, the value of CITY for the current observation is assigned to the macro variable named in *name*. This form is most useful when *name* is also the name of a SAS variable or a character expression that contains a SAS variable because a unique macro variable name and value can be created from each observation. (If *name* is a character string, the SYMPUT routine creates only one macro variable, and its value changes in each iteration of the DATA step. Only the value assigned in the last iteration remains after DATA step execution is finished.)

- a DATA step expression. The value returned by the expression in the current observation is assigned as the value of the macro variable in *name*. If the expression is numeric, the SAS System performs an automatic numeric-to-character conversion and writes a message in the log. **How the SYMPUT Routine Formats the Values It Assigns** later in this section describes the rules the SYMPUT routine follows in assigning values of DATA step expressions to macro variables.

  The following example uses a DATA step function to generate *value*:

```
data c;
   input holiday mmddyy.;
   call symput(name,put(holiday,worddate.));
   cards;
070490
;
```

The macro variable identified in *name* receives the value **July 4, 1990**.

Referencing Values Assigned by the SYMPUT Routine

One of the most common problems in using the SYMPUT routine is being unable to reference a macro variable value assigned by SYMPUT. The failure generally occurs when the statement referencing that macro variable is compiled before the CALL SYMPUT statement assigning its value executes. Chapter 8, "How the SAS System Processes a Program," gives details on compilation and execution, but the following examples illustrate two common situations.

Referencing a Value in a DATA Step

Suppose you must decide whether to insert some statements into a DATA step, depending on whether the SAS data set is the one you want. You read a value from the first observation of the SAS data set, use the SYMPUT routine to create a macro variable containing the value, and then decide whether to execute the rest of the macro based the DATA step value. This example shows a common mistake and how to correct it:

```
    /* first attempt--incorrect */
%macro quick(company);
    data newco;
        set oldco;
        if _n_=1 then call symput('firmname',firm);
    %if &firmname=&company %then
        %do;
            year=year+10;
            capital=capital+50000;
        %end;
    run;
%mend quick;


%quick(Ramos Foods)
```

Invoking macro QUICK causes the SAS compiler to see the following statements:

```
DATA NEWCO;
    SET OLDCO;
    IF _N_=1 THEN CALL SYMPUT('FIRMNAME',FIRM);
```

The SAS System does not execute the DATA step at this point because the SAS compiler is still compiling statements—it has not reached a step boundary, such as another DATA or PROC statement or a RUN statement. Therefore, the CALL SYMPUT statement does not execute. The next statement the macro processor encounters is the %IF statement, containing this condition:

```
&firmname=&company
```

The macro processor cannot resolve the reference &FIRMNAME because the SYMPUT routine has not yet created the macro variable FIRMNAME. The macro processor issues a warning that the reference &FIRMNAME is not recognized and then interprets the ampersand in &FIRMNAME as the AND operator. The macro ceases execution because the AND operator cannot begin a logical expression.*

---

* Using the %NRQUOTE function around &FIRMNAME changes the problem but does not solve it. In this case, the macro processor compares the nine-character string `&firmname` to the value of COMPANY, as shown:

```
&firmname=Ramos Foods
```

The comparison is never true.

To correct the problem, place the CALL SYMPUT statement in a separate step that executes before the %IF statement, as shown here:

```
    /* second version--correct */
%macro quick2(company);
    data _null_;
        set oldco;
        call symput('firmname',firm);
        stop;
    run;
    %if &firmname=&company %then
        %do;
            data newco;
                set oldco;
                year=year+10;
                capital=capital+50000;
            run;
        %end;
%mend quick2;


    %quick2(Ramos Foods)
```

In this example the macro processor first generates the DATA _NULL_ step. When the SAS compiler encounters the RUN statement, the SAS System executes the step and the SYMPUT routine assigns a value to the macro variable FIRMNAME (for example, `Ramos Foods`). Then the macro processor executes the %IF-%THEN statement with this condition:

```
    Ramos Foods=Ramos Foods
```

The %IF condition is true, and the macro processor generates the next DATA step, containing the two assignment statements.

Referencing a Value in a Global Statement

A second common problem occurs when you assign a value to a macro variable in a DATA step and use it in a following global statement (such as a TITLE statement) without explicitly ending the DATA step. In this case, the SAS System compiles the global statement with the DATA step—before the SYMPUT routine assigns the value to the macro variable. Therefore, the global statement does not contain the value of the macro variable.

The following example illustrates the problem:

```
    /* first attempt--incorrect */
data new;
    set old end=last;
    if profit>0 then p+1;
    if last then call symput('prof',left(p));

    /* program to print the data */
title "Data Set Showing &prof Observations with Profit";
footnote "For Patel Products Ltd.";
proc print data=new;
run;
```

The second IF-THEN statement is the last executable statement you write in the DATA step, but neither the comment, TITLE, nor FOOTNOTE statement signals a step boundary. Therefore, compilation of the DATA step continues until the

SAS System reaches the PROC PRINT statement. The TITLE statement containing the macro variable reference is compiled as part of the DATA step, and the SYMPUT routine has not executed to create macro variable PROF when the TITLE statement references PROF. The macro variable reference passes into the SAS compiler without resolution, and the SAS System issues a warning message. The SAS compiler sees this title:

```
TITLE "Data Set Showing &prof Observations with Profit";
```

To make the value of PROF available to the TITLE statement, you must create a step boundary between the DATA step and the TITLE statement so that the DATA step executes before the SAS System compiles the TITLE statement. The following example creates a step boundary with a RUN statement:

```
    /* correct method */
data new;
    set old end=last;
    if profit>0 then p+1;
    if last then call symput('prof',left(p));
run;


    /* program to print the data */
title "Data Set Showing &prof Observations with Profit";
footnote "For Patel Products Ltd.";
proc print data=new;
run;
```

Now the SAS compiler recognizes the end of the DATA step at the first RUN statement. The SAS System ceases compiling statements at that point and executes the DATA step. During the last iteration of the DATA step, the SYMPUT routine executes and assigns a value to macro variable PROF. For example, if 15 observations in the data set have a positive value of PROFIT, the SYMPUT routine assigns PROF the value 15. The SAS compiler sees this title:

```
TITLE "Data Set Showing 15 Observations with Profit";
```

The following section, **How the SYMPUT Routine Formats the Values It Assigns**, describes the use of the LEFT function in the argument of the SYMPUT routine.

How the SYMPUT Routine Formats the Values It Assigns

The SYMPUT routine uses certain formatting rules when it assigns a value to a macro variable. The first two sections, **Character Values** and **Numeric Values**, discuss those rules. The third section, **Preventing Numeric-to-Character Conversion Messages**, gives examples of how to avoid the message that appears by default when you assign a numeric DATA step value to a macro variable with SYMPUT.

Character Values

If the *value* argument of the SYMPUT routine is a character variable, the SYMPUT routine writes it using the $w. format, where w is the length of the variable. Therefore, a value shorter than the length of the DATA step variable is written with trailing blanks. For example, consider this program:

```
data char1;
    input c $;
    call symput('char',c);
    cards;
x
;
```

Because the length of the DATA step variable C is 8 by default, the SYMPUT routine uses the $8. format, and the value of CHAR contains the letter **x** followed by seven trailing blanks. If you use the value of CHAR in a SAS operation that does not trim trailing blanks, the blanks can produce unexpected results. For example, the following statements produce **Output 6.4**:

```
data char2;
   length newchar $ 3;
   newchar="&char"||"yz";
run;

proc print data=char2;
   title "Using &char in Concatenation";
   title2 "Unwanted Blanks and Truncation";
run;
```

Output 6.4   Using a Left-aligned Value Produced from a DATA Step
Character Variable

```
                      Using x          in Concatenation                    1
                      Unwanted Blanks and Truncation

                              OBS     NEWCHAR

                               1        x
```

Because the length of variable NEWCHAR is 3, the value of NEWCHAR is **x** followed by two blanks; the characters **yz** are truncated. In addition, the title contains unwanted blanks. To eliminate the blanks, use the TRIM function in the *value* argument of the SYMPUT routine, as shown here:

```
data char3;
   input c $;
   call symput('char',trim(c));
   cards;
x
;

data char4;
   length newchar $ 3;
   newchar="&char"||"yz";
run;

proc print;
   title "Using &char in Concatenation";
   title2 "Intended Result";
run;
```

The program now produces **Output 6.5**.

Output 6.5   Trimming Blanks before Assigning the Value

```
         Using x in Concatenation                      2
            Intended Result

             OBS     NEWCHAR

              1       xyz
```

Numeric Values

If the *value* argument is a numeric variable, the SYMPUT routine writes it using the default format for DATA step numeric variables, the BEST12. format. The resulting value is a 12-byte string with the value right-aligned within it. For example, the following program assigns the value of a numeric DATA step variable to macro variable NUM:

```
data num1;
   x=1;
   call symput('num',x);
run;
```

If you use the value of NUM in a SAS operation that does not trim leading blanks, the right alignment can produce unexpected results. For example, the following statements produce **Output 6.6**:

```
data num2;
   length result $ 10;
   result='abc'||"&num";
run;

proc print data=num2;
   title "Study of &num";
   title2 "Unwanted Blanks and Truncation";
run;
```

Output 6.6   Using a Right-aligned Value Produced from a DATA Step
            Numeric Variable

```
            Study of        1                    1
       Unwanted Blanks and Truncation

             OBS     RESULT

              1       abc
```

Both the title and the value of RESULT contain undesired blanks. Because the length of variable RESULT is 10, RESULT is composed of the characters **abc** and the first seven characters of the value of NUM—all blanks. The value of NUM is truncated before the 1. In addition, the title contains unwanted blanks. To eliminate the blanks, use the LEFT function to left-align the value before the SYMPUT routine assigns the value to NUM. The following example eliminates the unwanted blanks:

```
data num3;
   x=1;
   call symput('num',left(x));
run;

data num4;
   length result $ 10;
   result='abc'||"&num";
run;

proc print data=num4;
   title "Study of &num";
   title2 "Intended Result";
run;
```

The result of the PROC PRINT step appears in **Output 6.7**.

Output 6.7   Removing Leading Blanks before Assigning the Value

```
                        Study of 1                              2
                       Intended Result

                   OBS      RESULT

                    1        abc1
```

Preventing Numeric-to-Character Conversion Messages

When the DATA step issues a note that numeric-to-character conversion has been performed in an argument of the SYMPUT routine, you can eliminate the note by using the PUT function to perform the conversion explicitly, as in these examples:

```
call symput('mv'||left(put(_n_,4.)),value);
call symput('num',left(put(x,12.)));
```

Use a format wide enough to contain all possible digits in the value of the numeric variable.

Examples

Example 1:   Executing a Macro Based on a DATA Step Value

Suppose you want to extract observations dated October 1 through October 15, 1991 (variable SALEDATE) from SAS data set SALES and add them to data set SAVE.MAINFILE. Because you do not know whether any sales occurred during the period, you do not know whether you need to execute a PROC APPEND step. If you place the PROC APPEND step inside a macro, you can execute it conditionally as part of a %IF-%THEN statement. Use the SYMPUT routine to create a macro variable to be used in the %IF condition. Match the numbers in this example to the numbered paragraphs that follow the code:

```
data temp;
   set sales end=final;
   if '01oct91'd<=saledate<='15oct91'd then
      do; ❶
         output;
         n+1;
      end;
   if final and n then call symput('check','yes'); ❷
   else if final then call symput('check','no');
   drop n;
run;

%macro app;
   %if &check=yes %then
      %do; ❸
         proc append base=save.mainfile data=temp;
         run;
      %end;
%mend app;

%app ❹
```

1. If a value of SALEDATE falls in the period, the DATA step outputs the observation to TEMP and increments the value of N.
2. If the value of N is greater than 0 during the last execution of the DATA step, the SYMPUT routine assigns macro variable CHECK the value **yes**. Otherwise, during the last execution of the DATA step, CHECK receives the value **no**.
3. In macro APP, the value of CHECK determines whether the macro generates the PROC APPEND step.
4. When execution reaches the macro call %APP, if the value is **yes**, the next step in the SAS program is the following:

```
PROC APPEND BASE=SAVE.MAINFILE DATA=TEMP;
RUN;
```

Otherwise the PROC APPEND step is not generated.

Example 2:   Generating PROC Steps Using DATA Step Values

This example uses CALL SYMPUT statements to create macro variables containing the current BY value, the mean salary in each BY group, and the number of BY groups in the SAS data set. Macro PLOTIT uses those values in the PROC PLOT steps it generates. Match the circled numbers to the explanations that follow.

```
data employ; ❶
   input sex $ age salary @@;
   cards;
m 21 17000   f 26 19000   m 32 27000   m 30 27000
m 21 16500   f 27 26000   f 23 21000   m 24 21500
f 22 15900   m 23 22000   f 24 21000   f 25 23000
f 33 31000   f 31 30000
;
```

```
proc sort;
   by sex;
run;

proc means noprint; ❷
   by sex;
   var salary;
   output out=outmean mean=msal;
run;

data _null_; ❸
   set outmean end=eof;
   call symput('group'||left(_n_),trim(sex));
   call symput('ref'||left(_n_),msal);
   if eof then call symput('total',_n_);
run;

%macro plotit;  ❹
   %local i;
   proc plot data=employ;
      title "Age * Salary";
   %do i=1 %to &total;
      where sex="&&group&i";
      plot age*salary / href=&&ref&i;
      title2 "Group=&&group&i";
   run;
   %end;
   quit;
%mend plotit;

%plotit
```

1. The DATA EMPLOY step creates the SAS data set to be analyzed, and the SORT procedure sorts EMPLOY by variable SEX.
2. The MEANS procedure calculates the mean salary for each BY group (stored in variable MSAL of data set OUTMEAN).
3. A DATA _NULL_ step reads data set OUTMEAN and uses the SYMPUT routine to create macro variables containing the mean salary for each group, an identifier for each group, and the number of groups in the data set. In all, the DATA _NULL_ step creates five macro variables: GROUP1, REF1, GROUP2, REF2, and TOTAL.
4. Macro PLOTIT generates PROC PLOT steps. Macro PLOTIT first creates a local macro variable named I to be used as the index variable in the iterative %DO loop. The loop is executed the number of times given by TOTAL (that is, once for each BY group). Macro PLOTIT generates a RUN group with a WHERE statement that selects observations in the current BY group. The HREF= option draws a reference line on the plot at the location indicated by the current REFn macro variable. The TITLE2 statement receives the name of the BY group (the value of the current GROUPn macro variable). The RUN statement causes execution of the current group of statements (because PROC PLOT is an interactive procedure). The QUIT statement ends the execution of the PLOT procedure.

Macro PLOTIT generates the following statements:

```
PROC PLOT DATA=EMPLOY;
   TITLE "Age * Salary";
   WHERE SEX="f";
   PLOT AGE*SALARY / HREF=23362.5;
   TITLE2 "Group=f";
RUN;
   WHERE SEX="m";
   TITLE2 "Group=m";
   PLOT AGE*SALARY / HREF=21833.333333;
RUN;
QUIT;
```

Chapter 7

The Autocall Facility

The autocall facility enables you to store macro source code in external files and invoke macros as you need them without having to define or include them in the current program or session. The autocall facility lets you accumulate useful macro source code in libraries for easy execution.

This chapter describes how to create and use autocall macros, and describes some autocall macros in libraries supplied by SAS Institute.

Contents

USING THE AUTOCALL FACILITY

As an introduction to autocall processing, the following example shows how to use an autocall macro in a SAS session. Without worrying about formal definitions or naming rules just yet, suppose you create a file named PRTDATA in an autocall library. File PRTDATA contains the following statements:

```
%macro prtdata;
   proc print;
   run;
%mend prtdata;
```

Then you submit the following SAS program:

```
data drug403;
   merge in.clinic in.trial;
   by drug403;
run;

   %prtdata
```

When the macro processor attempts to execute macro PRTDATA, it does not find a macro definition for PRTDATA in your program. Without the autocall facility, the macro processor issues a warning message and passes the macro call %PRTDATA into the SAS program. The SAS System then issues an error message because %PRTDATA is not an acceptable SAS statement.

If you enable the autocall facility with the MAUTOSOURCE system option and associate an autocall library with your SAS job or session using the SASAUTOS= system option, the macro processor takes the additional step of searching the autocall library for a file named PRTDATA (or PRTDATA.SAS, depending on your operating system). The autocall facility locates file PRTDATA, brings the statements it contains into the program, and processes all of the statements in the file. This includes compiling the macro named PRTDATA and executing it to produce the SAS statements for a PROC PRINT step.

Things you need to know in order to use the autocall facility efficiently and effectively include

- creating and using autocall libraries
- setting SAS system options to use the autocall facility
- understanding autocall library operations
- debugging autocall macros
- improving autocall efficiency.

Creating and Using Autocall Libraries

An autocall library is an aggregate storage location containing individual library members, each of which contains a macro definition.

Note: Different operating systems call an aggregate storage location by different names, such as a directory, a maclib, a text library, or a partitioned data set. For complete details on the nature of aggregate storage locations at your site, see the SAS documentation for your operating system.

To use an aggregate storage location as a SAS autocall library, do the following:

- Name members within the library the same as the names of macros they contain. For example, the statements defining a macro you would invoke by typing %SPLIT must be in a library member named SPLIT.

    Note: On operating systems that allow filenames with extensions, you must name autocall macro library members with a SAS-type extension, usually .SAS. Look at the autocall macros on your system provided by SAS Institute to determine whether names of library members containing macros must have a SAS-type extension at your site. See **Setting SAS System Options to Use the Autocall Facility** later in this chapter for instructions on finding and viewing your autocall libraries supplied by SAS Institute.

- In your program or SAS session, identify the library as an autocall library with the SASAUTOS= system option. There are several ways to do this, and you can specify more than one library at a time, as described in **Setting SAS System Options to Use the Autocall Facility** later in this chapter.

When storing members in an autocall library, remember the following:

- Although the SAS System does not restrict the type of material you place in an autocall library, you should store only autocall library members in it to avoid confusion.
- Although the SAS System lets you include more than one macro definition in an autocall library member as well as open code, you should generally keep only one macro in any autocall library member to avoid confusion. If you need to keep several macros in the same autocall library member, keep related macros together.

Setting SAS System Options to Use the Autocall Facility

SAS system options are instructions that control the way the SAS System performs operations. These four SAS system options control the autocall facility and other related macro features:

IMPLMAC
    causes the macro processor to recognize statement-style macro invocations (described in **Macro Invocations** in Chapter 3, "Macro Program Statements"). NOIMPLMAC disables statement-style macro invocations. This is important for the autocall facility since it determines whether you can invoke statement-style macros in your autocall libraries using a statement-style invocation. See **Improving Autocall Efficiency** later in this chapter for a discussion of how the use of statement-style macros in autocall affects performance.

MAUTOSOURCE
    enables the autocall facility. NOMAUTOSOURCE disables the autocall facility.

MRECALL
    causes the macro processor to search autocall libraries for a library member that was not found in a previous search. NOMRECALL, the default, causes the macro processor to search autocall libraries only at the first invocation of any autocall macro.

SASAUTOS=*library-specification* |
        (*library-specification-1*, . . . ,*library-specification-n*)
    specifies the autocall library or libraries. *Library-specification* can be
        - a SAS fileref.
        - the name of an aggregate storage location on your operating system enclosed in quotes.
        - a concatenated list of filerefs or aggregate storage location names enclosed in quotes (or both) that are enclosed in parentheses and separated by either blanks or commas. Concatenated lists can contain any mixture of filerefs and aggregate storage location

names in any order. See **Understanding Autocall Library Operations** in this chapter for a discussion of how the autocall facility uses these lists.

Note: See the SAS documentation for your operating system for complete details on specifying the physical names of external files, including details about using operating-system-specific filerefs.

To see the settings of all of these system options, look at the output of the OPTIONS procedure, or check the OPTIONS window in the SAS Display Manager System. In most cases, the default fileref or filerefs associated with the SASAUTOS= option are for the autocall library or libraries supplied by SAS Institute to your site.

See Appendix 1, "SAS System Options Used with the Macro Facility," for a discussion of how to specify system options and for more complete descriptions of all system options used with macro processing.

Understanding Autocall Library Operations

The following sections contain details about the mechanics of the autocall system.

How the SAS System Locates and Processes Libraries

The SAS System looks for autocall library members in libraries you specify with the SASAUTOS= system option. When you specify autocall libraries and then invoke an uncompiled macro, the SAS System does the following:

1. opens all of the libraries it can open
2. searches each one for a member with the same name as the macro you invoked.

When the SAS System finds a library member with that name, or that name with a SAS-type extension on systems with filename extensions, the macro processor does the following:

1. compiles all of the source statements in that member, including any and all macro definitions
2. executes any open code (macro statements or SAS source statements not within any macro definition) in that member
3. executes the macro within it with the name you invoked.

Note: If an autocall library member contains more than one macro, the macro processor compiles all of the macros but executes only the macro with the name you invoked.

Any open code statements in the same autocall library member as a macro execute only the first time you invoke the macro. When you invoke the macro later in the same session, the SAS System only executes the macro.

If you change the SASAUTOS= specification, the SAS System stores the new specification until you invoke an uncompiled autocall macro. Then, the SAS System closes all opened libraries and opens all the newly specified libraries that it can open.

How the SAS System Responds to Missing Libraries

The SAS System responds to missing autocall libraries during autocall processing in different ways depending on how many libraries you specify and how you specify them.

Single autocall library If you specify an undefined fileref or a nonexistent aggregate storage location as an autocall library, the SAS System sets the NOMAUTOSOURCE system option when you first invoke an uncompiled macro and issues a warning message that the autocall facility has been suspended. To continue autocall processing, specify the MAUTOSOURCE and the MRECALL system options, respecify the SASAUTOS= system option with corrected library information, and invoke the macro again. Remember to specify the NOMRECALL system option the next time in your session you have an opportunity to do so.

Concatenated list of libraries The SAS System sets the NOMAUTOSOURCE system option when you first invoke an uncompiled macro if you specified a concatenated list of libraries containing either of the following:

- an undefined fileref
- a nonexistent aggregate storage location name enclosed in quotes, if no other library successfully opened.

If you specify a concatenated list of libraries containing a nonexistent aggregate storage location name enclosed in quotes, but at least one of the other libraries you specified successfully opened, the SAS System provides no warning and does not set the NOMAUTOSOURCE option when you first invoke an uncompiled macro. Every invocation of an uncompiled macro from this point on causes the SAS System to attempt to open any unopened autocall libraries.

Example of misspelled fileref Suppose you submit the following statements:

```
filename autmac 'aggregate-storage-location ';
options sasautos=autmic;
%split
```

The FILENAME statement associates the fileref AUTMAC with the aggregate storage location you use as an autocall library. Your library contains a member with a macro called SPLIT, and no other macro called SPLIT has yet been compiled during the current SAS session. The OPTIONS statement contains the misspelled fileref AUTMIC. The SAS System responds with these messages:

```
1    filename autmac 'aggregate-storage-location ';
2    options sasautos=autmic;
3    %split
     -
     180
WARNING: No logical assign for filename AUTMIC.
WARNING: Source level autocall is not found or cannot be opened.
         Autocall has been suspended and OPTION NOMAUTOSOURCE has been
         set.  To use the autocall facility again, set OPTION
         MAUTOSOURCE.
WARNING: Apparent invocation of macro SPLIT not resolved.
ERROR 180-322: Statement is not valid or it is used out of proper order.
```

To resume macro processing, submit the following statements:

```
;
options mrecall mautosource sasautos=autmac;
%split
```

The first semicolon signals the end of the invalid SAS statement that the invocation of macro SPLIT became, enabling the SAS System to correctly recognize the subsequent statements. You need to include this first semicolon only in interactive line mode or display manager mode. In batch or noninteractive modes, simply fix the error and resubmit your program.

Changing Autocall Libraries in an Interactive Session

When you specify a concatenated list of all your autocall libraries in the SASAUTOS= option, all of your autocall macros are available at once. However, if you specify only some autocall libraries in the concatenation (for example, if you are testing members in a particular library), you may accidentally invoke an autocall macro that is not in any of the current autocall libraries. In this case, the autocall facility does not locate the right library member, and the macro facility cannot resolve the macro invocation. If the MERROR system option is in effect, the macro processor issues a warning message.

To search another library for that member, change the value of the SASAUTOS= option to include the new library, or add the library to the current concatenated list of libraries with the display manager OPTIONS window or an OPTIONS statement. Then, specify the MRECALL system option and invoke the macro again. The MRECALL option causes the autocall facility to search your autocall libraries for an uncompiled macro each time you invoke that macro. (By default, the NOMRECALL option causes the autocall facility to search your autocall libraries for an uncompiled macro only once, when you first invoke it.)

For example, suppose one of your autocall libraries contains this macro named SHOW:

```
%macro show;
    this is macro show
%mend show;
```

In the SAS session shown in **Output 7.1**, you first request macro SHOW from a library with the fileref ABC. When you discover member SHOW is not in that library, you change the SASAUTOS= specification to add the autocall library with fileref XYZ and invoke the macro again.

Output 7.1   Searching Different Libraries for an Autocall Member

```
5            filename abc 'agg.stor.locn1';
WARNING: Apparent invocation of macro SHOW not resolved.
6            options sasautos=abc;
7            run;
8            %put %show;
%show
9            filename xyz 'agg.stor.locn2';
10           options sasautos=(abc xyz) mrecall;
11           run;
12           %put %show;
this is macro show
13           options nomrecall;
14           run;
```

To make your program more efficient, you should specify the MRECALL option only when you need it, such as when developing or testing autocall macros. In the preceding example, as soon as you locate macro SHOW, you should specify the NOMRECALL option so that the autocall facility searches your autocall libraries for an uncompiled macro only once. Leaving the MRECALL option in effect slows down macro processing with unnecessary searches of your autocall libraries.

Debugging Autocall Macros

When the autocall facility locates an autocall library member and brings it into your session, the macro processor compiles any macros in that library member. For the rest of your SAS session, the SAS System stores the compiled macros in a catalog in the WORK library. Under no circumstances does the autocall facility use an autocall library member when a compiled macro with the same name already exists. Thus, if you invoke an autocall macro and discover you made an error when you defined it, you must correct the autocall library member for future use and compile the corrected version directly in your program or session.

Correcting Errors in Display Manager

To debug an autocall macro in a display manager session, do the following:

1. Use the INCLUDE command to bring the autocall library member into the SAS PROGRAM EDITOR window.
2. Correct the error.
3. Store a copy of the corrected macro in the autocall library.
4. Submit the macro definition from the PROGRAM EDITOR window.

The macro processor then compiles the corrected version, replacing the incorrect compiled macro. The corrected, compiled macro is now ready to execute at the next invocation.

Correcting Errors in Interactive Line Mode

To debug an autocall macro in an interactive line mode session, do the following:

1. Enter your text editor.
2. Correct the autocall library member.
3. Use a %INCLUDE statement to bring the corrected library member into your SAS session.

The macro processor then compiles the corrected version, replacing the incorrect compiled macro. The corrected, compiled macro is now ready to execute at the next invocation.

Improving Autocall Efficiency

Efficient use of the autocall facility depends on how and why you use the autocall facility. Techniques that save CPU time or disk storage can be less convenient for you as a programmer or an end user. The nature of your work also has an impact on what kind of efficiencies are important to you.

Efficient Autocall Applications

In general, the autocall facility is relatively more useful and efficient for production because there is usually no need to debug autocall macros. This is especially true if many users share a common autocall library and many application programs use tested, production-level autocall macros.

The autocall facility is the best way to store extensions to the SAS language in the form of utility routines and complete macro subsystems. You don't have to remember to retrieve key subroutines at DATA or PROC step boundaries with the %INCLUDE statement when you use the autocall facility, and you limit the number of macros compiled to those you use.

Inefficient Autocall Applications

The autocall facility is relatively less useful during program development, which is when error checking and debugging occur. Since you need to retrieve and replace code anyway, the autocall facility provides less convenience for the same overhead.

Since program development often focuses on discrete sections of an application, there is less need to have all utility macros available at one time. Using concatenated lists of autocall libraries is not as great a convenience if you only need a handful of macros from any given library.

During program development, use the %INCLUDE statement or the INCLUDE display manager command to retrieve macros during your SAS session.

Efficiency Tips

Here are some general tips for processing efficiently with the autocall facility:

- Avoid specifying the MAUTOSOURCE and IMPLMAC system options together if you have no statement-style macros in your code. This keeps the macro processor from checking every autocall library each time it encounters the name of a potential statement-style macro at the beginning of any SAS source statement.
- Always specify the NOMRECALL option immediately after you successfully locate and compile a macro using the MRECALL option. This keeps the macro processor from needlessly checking autocall libraries for undefined previously invoked macros.
- Be aware of the efficiency trade-off between using many autocall libraries with fewer macros per library versus using fewer autocall libraries with more macros per library. Having fewer libraries means fewer file operations but less flexibility in storing logical groupings of macros. Many small libraries are sometimes better when developing macros, and a few large libraries are better when using production-level macros.

See Appendix 3, "Macro Efficiency and Debugging," for a more complete discussion of using the entire macro facility efficiently.

AUTOCALL LIBRARY SUPPLIED BY SAS INSTITUTE

SAS Institute supplies libraries of autocall macros to each SAS site. Which libraries you receive depend on the SAS products you use. If your site has installed these autocall libraries and uses the standard configuration of the SAS System supplied by the Institute, the only thing you need to do to begin using those macros is to specify the MAUTOSOURCE system option. Then invoke the macros as needed. If your site has not installed any autocall libraries or has modified the configuration of the SAS System, see your SAS Software Consultant for information on how to access the macros.

Macros in the Base SAS Software Autocall Library

Members of the base SAS software autocall library contain macros written at the Institute as working examples of ways in which you can use the autocall facility and as examples of extensions to the SAS System. Additional macros may be added to the library in the future. The following list gives invocations and descriptions for some autocall macros used with base SAS software. You can obtain more information by browsing the comments at the beginning of each member.*

Even though the macros available in the autocall libraries supplied by SAS Institute to your site are working utility programs, you can also use them as models for your own routines. In addition, you can call them in macros you write yourself.

---

* If your site has licensed additional SAS software products, the library may contain additional macros to be used with those products. Macros used with other products in the SAS System are described in the documentation for those products.

Note: Refer to the SAS documentation for your operating system for information about the default autocall library supplied by SAS Institute or contact your SAS Software Representative.

%CMPRES(*argument*)

compresses multiple blanks within *argument* into a single blank and removes leading and trailing blanks from it. *Argument* can be text or any macro expression. The result is not quoted, even if *argument* is quoted. To return a quoted value, use macro QCMPRES, described later in this section. For example, the statements

```
%let a=first     value;
%let b=%cmpres(&a);
%put &b;
```

produce the following line:

```
first value
```

%DATATYP(*argument*)

returns a value of NUMERIC when *argument* consists of digits and, optionally, a leading plus or minus sign, a decimal, or a scientific or floating-point exponent (E or D in upper- or lowercase). Otherwise, it returns the value CHAR. For example, the statements

```
%let a=500;
%let b=-325;
%let c=2.3E1;
%let d=DEC90;
%put a is %datatyp(&a) and b is %datatyp(&b);
%put c is %datatyp(&c) and d is %datatyp(&d);
```

produce the following text:

```
a is NUMERIC and b is NUMERIC
c is NUMERIC and d is CHAR
```

%LEFT(*argument*)

left-aligns *argument* by removing leading blanks. The result is unquoted, even if *argument* is quoted. To return a quoted value, use macro QLEFT, described later in this section. The LEFT and QLEFT macros are analogous to the DATA step LEFT function. For example, the statements

```
%let a=%str(   m e m o);
%let b=%left(&a);
%put *&a* *&b*;
```

produce the following text:

```
*   m e m o* *m e m o*
```

%QCMPRES(*argument*)

compresses multiple blanks within *argument* into a single blank and removes leading and trailing blanks. The result is automatically quoted with the same kind of quoting produced by the %NRBQUOTE function. For example, the statements

```
%let x=5;
%let y=10;
%let a=%nrstr(%eval(&x   +    &y));
%put *%qcmpres(&a)*  **%cmpres(&a)**;
```

produce the following line:

```
*%eval(&x + &y)* **15**
```

%QLEFT(*argument*)

left-aligns the value of *argument* by removing leading blanks. The result is quoted with the same kind of quoting produced by the %NRBQUOTE function. The QLEFT and LEFT macros are analogous to the DATA step LEFT function. The statements

```
%let d=%nrstr(   &sysday   );
%put *&d* *%qleft(&d)* *%left(&d)*;
```

produce the following text:

```
*   &sysday   * *&sysday   * *Tuesday   *
```

%QTRIM(*argument*)

trims trailing blanks from *argument* and quotes the result with the same kind of quoting produced by the %NRBQUOTE function. The QTRIM and TRIM macros are analogous to the DATA step TRIM function. For example, executing the following statements on January 28, 1990:

```
%let date=%nrstr(   &sysdate   );
%put *&date* *%qtrim(&date)* *%trim(&date)*;
```

produces the following text:

```
*   &sysdate   * *   &sysdate* *   28JAN90*
```

%TRIM(*argument*)

trims trailing blanks from *argument*. The result is unquoted, even if the argument is quoted. To return a quoted value, use macro QTRIM, described earlier in this section. The TRIM and QTRIM macros are analogous to the DATA step TRIM function. For example, the statements

```
%let x=%str(Cary   );
%let y=%trim(&x);
%put ***&x*** ***&y***;
```

write the following line:

```
***Cary   *** ***Cary***
```

%VERIFY(*source,excerpt*)

returns the position of the first character in *source* that is not also present in *excerpt*. If all characters in *source* are present in *excerpt*, VERIFY returns a 0. The VERIFY macro is analogous to the DATA step VERIFY function. For example, the statements

```
%let x=temperature;
%let y=time;
%put ***%verify(&x,&y)***;
```

write the following line:

```
***4***
```

SPECIAL TOPICS

How the SAS® System Processes a Program

Macro Compilation and Execution

Macro Quoting

Chapter 8

How the SAS® System Processes a Program

This chapter and Chapter 9, "Macro Compilation and Execution," describe a typical pattern that the SAS System in general and the macro facility in particular follow to process a program. These chapters are helpful in understanding advanced aspects of macro quoting, how macro execution interacts with the rest of a SAS program, and how to control the timing of macro execution in your programs.

Note: These chapters present advanced topics in an extremely simplified form. They are not intended as a detailed representation of how SAS software works. You can write many macro programs without knowing the material in these chapters; however, as you write larger, more complex macro systems, this material becomes helpful.

Contents

Figures

HOW THE SAS SYSTEM INTERPRETS SAS STATEMENTS

On a fundamental level, all macro processor activity and all interactions between the macro processor and the rest of the SAS System are based on how the SAS System interprets the statements you submit. This section illustrates the processing of a simple SAS program. You can use the model shown here to trace the execution of any SAS program, with or without macro processor activity.

Figure 8.1 shows a simple SAS program that displays sales data.

```
data sales(drop=lastyr);
   infile in1;
   input m1-m12 lastyr; total=m12+lastyr;
run;
%let list=m1 m7 m12 total;
proc print;
   var &list;
run;
```

Figure 8.1 SAS Program for Displaying Sales Data

In this example, the DATA step represents a portion of a SAS program without macro activity. The %LET statement and the PROC PRINT step represent a portion of a program with macro activity. (This example uses a %LET statement and macro variable reference for simplicity, but a macro definition and invocation work the same way in this respect. Chapter 9 illustrates processing a macro definition and an invocation.)

SAS Programs without Macro Activity

Input Stack to Word Queue

The SAS System treats lines in a program as elements in an *input stack*. The first line in the program that is available for use is called the top of the input stack. The SAS System reads words from the top of the input stack. At the beginning of the sales program, the DATA statement is the top of the input stack.

A part of the SAS System called the *word scanner* reads the input stack word by word and transfers one word at a time into the *word queue*. **Figure 8.2** shows the parts of a typical word queue.

Position	Word
1	
2	
3	
4	Macro Boundary
5	
6	

Figure 8.2   Typical SAS Word Queue

This word queue contains six positions labeled 1 to 6; word 1 is the top of the queue, and word 6 is the bottom. The macro boundary is shown here to complete the diagram; it is discussed in Chapter 10, "Macro Quoting."

When the word scanner begins reading the sales program, it places the first word in the top line of the input stack into the bottom of the word queue, as in **Figure 8.3**.

Position	Word
1	
2	
3	
4	
5	
6	DATA

from input stack ⟶

Figure 8.3   First Word Entering Word Queue

As the word scanner continues to place words in the word queue, the first word moves toward the top of the queue. **Figure 8.4** shows how the word queue fills up as the word scanner reads the first statement.*

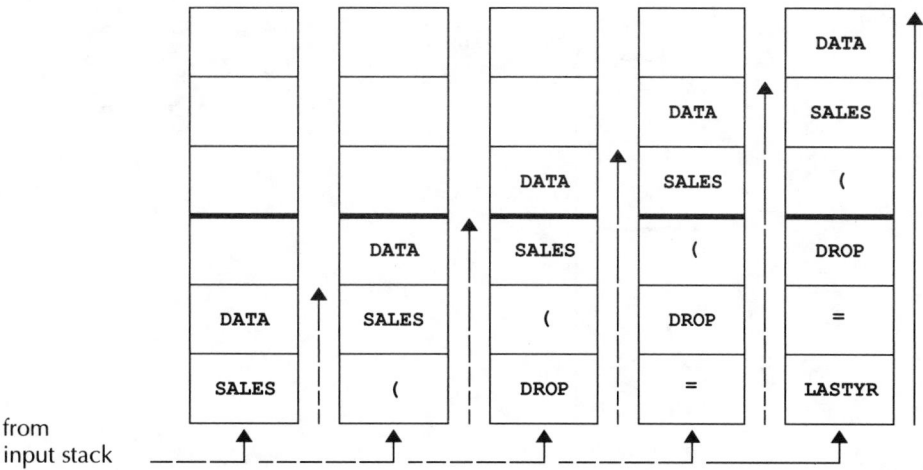

Figure 8.4   Additional Words Entering Word Queue

At this point, the word queue contains some items that look more or less like English words (DATA, SALES, DROP, and LASTYR) and some items that do not (the left parenthesis and the equal sign). In SAS processing, many items that do not look like English words are still considered words and occupy separate positions in the word queue. Another name for a word in the SAS System is a *token*. Tokens are discussed in **TOKENIZATION** later in this chapter. **Figure 8.5** shows that the words now in the word queue have been removed from the input stack.

```
                        );
    infile in1;
    input m1-m12 lastyr; total=m12+lastyr;
run;
%let list=m1 m7 m12 total;
proc print;
    var &list;
run;
```

Figure 8.5   Input Stack after Words Have Been Removed

Word Queue to Compiler

Parts of the SAS System that use words (such as the SAS compiler or the display manager processor) obtain words from the top of the word queue. **Figure 8.6**

---

* **Figure 8.4** and some other figures show several stages of the word queue side by side to save space. Remember that the diagrams represent one word queue that changes over time.

shows the SAS compiler requesting words from the word queue after a word reaches the top of the queue.*

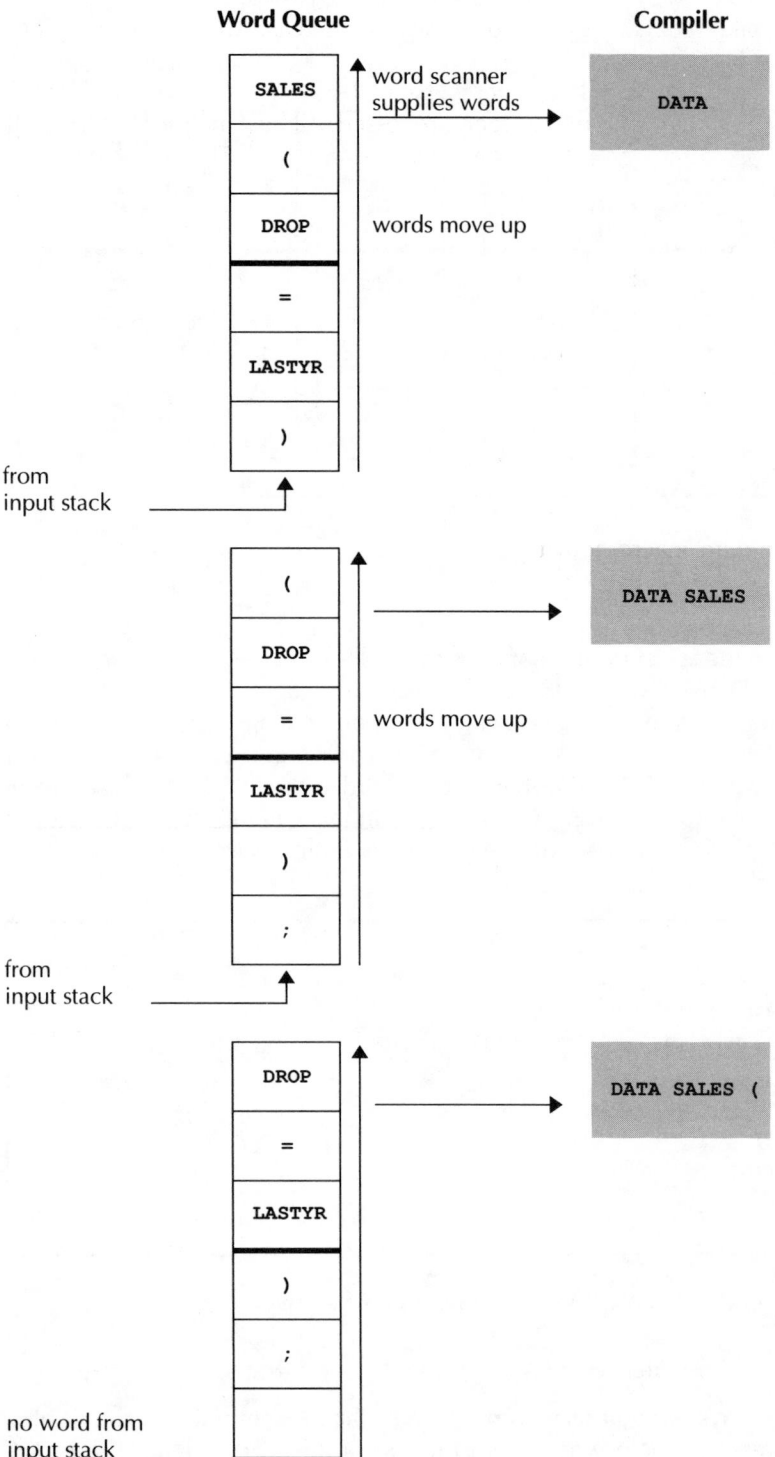

Figure 8.6   How the Compiler Receives a Statement

---

* Note that these illustrations show a simple view of the word queue, and many activities not shown here occur in the queue.

The compiler continues to request words until a statement is complete, and the word scanner continues to supply them. (However, as a very general rule, the word scanner allows only one SAS statement in the word queue at a time.) The same process occurs as the SAS System encounters each new statement. When the compiler recognizes the end of a step (in this case, the RUN statement), the step is executed.

In a SAS program with no macro processor activity, this process repeats without change until the entire program has been processed. All information that the SAS compiler receives comes from the program you submitted. (The only exception is the %INCLUDE statement, which puts new entries on the input stack and therefore new words in the word queue.)

SAS Programs with Macro Activity

Macro processor activity can generate new SAS statements and parts of SAS statements that become new entries on the input stack.

Input Stack to Word Queue and Word Queue to SAS Compiler or Macro Processor

The second part of the sales program, shown in **Figure 8.7**, illustrates processing a SAS program with macro activity.

```
%let list=m1 m7 m12 total;
proc print;
   var &list;
run;
```

Figure 8.7   Part of a SAS Program That Requires Macro Activity

The SAS System begins to process this part of the program as it did the first part. The compiler requests a word, and the word scanner begins to read words and place them into the word queue. If the word scanner recognizes a percent sign or an ampersand followed by a nonblank character in the word queue, the word scanner triggers the macro processor to examine those tokens. If the macro processor recognizes the tokens (for example, as a macro language keyword), the macro processor requests additional words if necessary and performs the activity indicated, as shown in **Figure 8.8**.

1. Compiler requests word. Word scanner begins to place words into word queue.

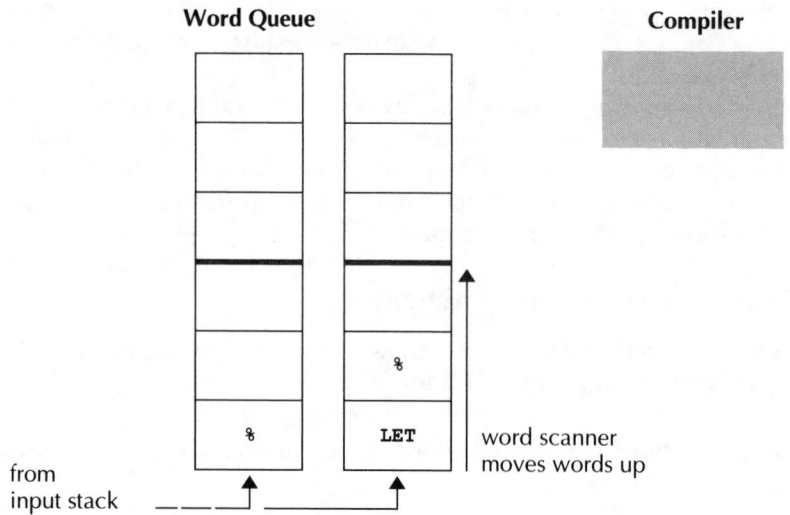

2. Word scanner recognizes a percent sign not followed by a blank in word queue and triggers the macro processor to examine tokens. Macro processor recognizes a %LET statement; requests words until it encounters a semicolon (using its own word queue, not shown); and stores the macro variable and value in a symbol table.

Macro Processor Symbol Table

Name	Value
LIST	m1 m7 m12 total

Figure 8.8 Activating the Macro Processor: %LET Statement

From the time the word scanner triggers the macro processor until that macro processor action is complete, all actions occur in the macro processor's word queue. The rules are the same as for the main word queue; the macro processor uses a separate queue so that its actions do not affect the main word queue. During internal macro processor activity, no activity occurs in the main word queue or the SAS compiler.

The word scanner then reads the PROC PRINT statement and sends it to the SAS compiler.

Macro Processor to Input Stack

After the compiler has received the complete PROC statement, the compiler requests words again. **Figure 8.9** shows what happens when the word scanner encounters an ampersand followed by a nonblank character.

1. Compiler requests word. Word scanner begins to place words into word queue.

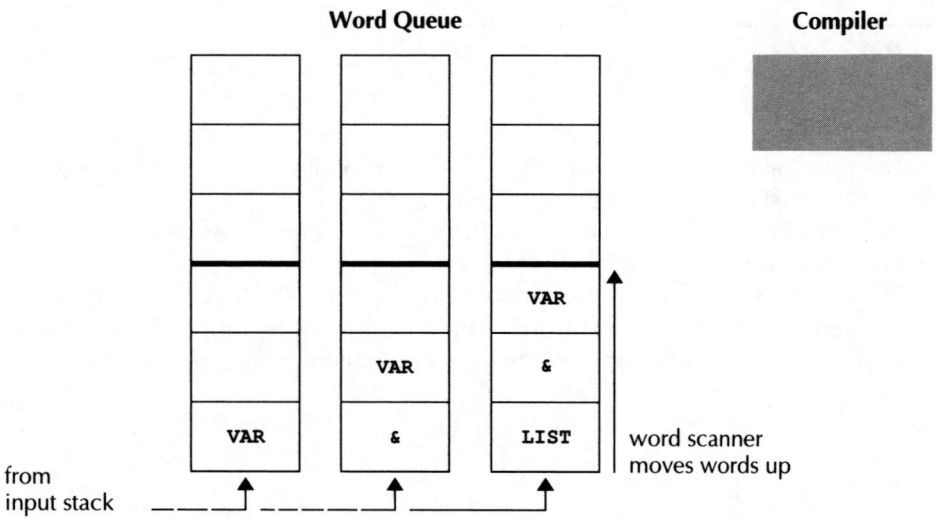

2. Word scanner recognizes an ampersand not followed by a blank in word queue and triggers macro processor to examine tokens. Macro processor recognizes a macro variable reference and retrieves value.

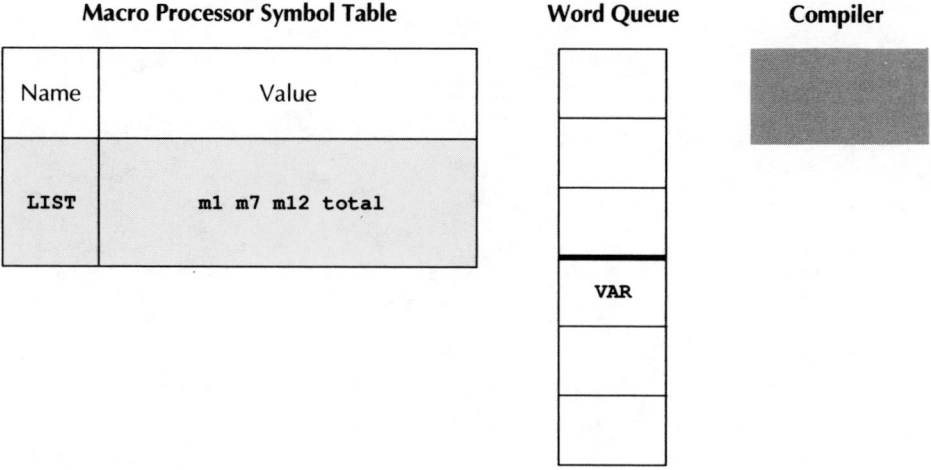

Figure 8.9 Processing a Macro Variable Reference

The macro processor places text generated by resolving a macro variable reference on the input stack. **Figure 8.10** shows the input stack now.

```
m1 m7 m12 total
              ;
run;
```

Figure 8.10   Input Stack after Macro Processor Generates Text

The text that results from resolving the macro variable reference is the new top of the input stack. The semicolon shown on the second line is the semicolon remaining in the VAR statement, which the word scanner was reading when it encountered the macro variable reference.

Processing of the statement continues in **Figure 8.11**. The SAS compiler continues to request words, and the word scanner continues to supply them (turning control over to the macro facility as necessary), until the entire program has been read.

1. Compiler requests words. Word scanner places words into word queue; when a word
   reaches word 1, word scanner supplies that word to compiler.

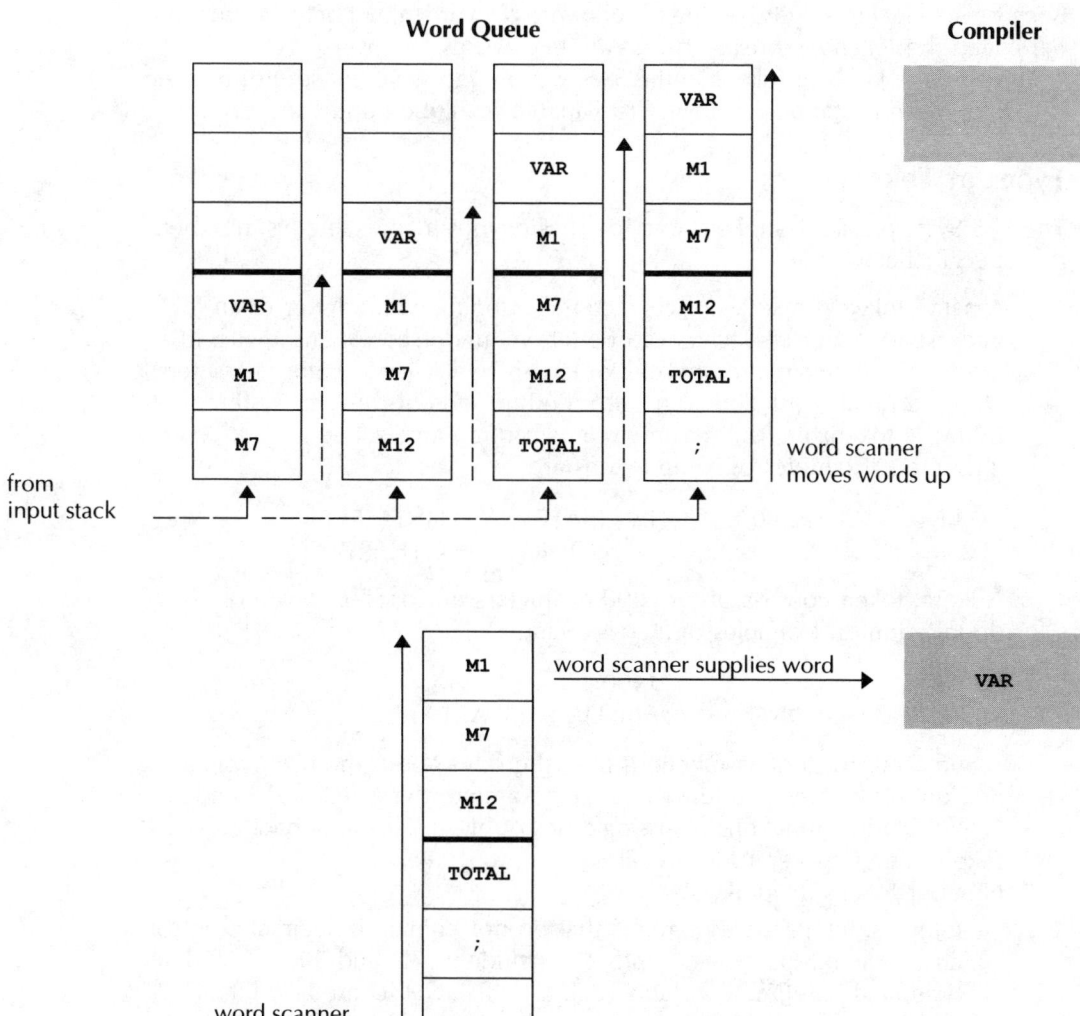

Figure 8.11   Processing Text Generated by Macro Processor

Summary

The SAS compiler (or certain other parts of the SAS System) requests one word
at a time from the word queue. The word scanner supplies the words. If the word
scanner detects a percent sign or ampersand followed by a nonblank character
in the next to the last word in the word queue, the word scanner triggers the
macro processor. The macro processor performs the activity indicated and returns
any text generated to the top of the input stack, ahead of the text remaining in
the program. The word scanner resumes supplying words from the top of the
input stack to the word queue. When a DATA or PROC step is completed during
this process, it is executed.

TOKENIZATION

A program first appears to the SAS System as a continuous series of characters. Because activity in the word queue occurs word by word, a part of the word scanner called the *tokenizer* breaks the stream into words, or *tokens*.

Knowing the kinds of tokens in the SAS System and what constitutes a token is helpful in understanding both macro variable resolution and macro quoting.

Types of Tokens

The SAS System classifies tokens into four basic types: names, literals, numbers, and special characters.

1. A name token is a series of characters beginning with a letter or an underscore. Later characters can be letters, underscores, and digits. In most SAS processing, the maximum length of a name is eight characters. However, that restriction comes from other parts of the SAS System, not from the tokenizer. The maximum length of a name token is 200 characters. Examples of name tokens are

DATA	YEAR_90	UNIVARIATE	LINESLEFT	_N_
F25	_TEST	DESCENDING	OTHERWISE	_1

2. A literal token consists of 1 to 200 characters enclosed in single or double quotes. Examples of literals include

'CARY'	"1990"
'DR. KEMPLE-LONG'	"AMELIA EARHART"

   Some macro quoting functions alter the rules about the use of single and double quotes in a few cases. For example, the %BQUOTE and %NRBQUOTE functions treat single or double quotes as separate tokens. See Chapter 10 for details.

3. Number tokens include
   - integers. Integers are numbers that do not contain a decimal point or an exponent. Examples of integers include 1, 72, and 5000. SAS date, time, and datetime constants such as '24AUG90'D are also integers.
   - real (floating-point) numbers. Floating-point numbers contain a decimal point or an exponent. Examples include numbers such as 2.35, 5., 2.3E1, and 5.4E-1.

   Although the macro processor uses number tokens, it treats them as strings. (However, an explicit or implicit %EVAL function assigns numeric properties to integers.) Note that the macro processor does not interpret SAS date, time, and datetime constants as number tokens; thus, you cannot use the %EVAL function to convert them to their corresponding integers. **MACRO EXPRESSIONS** in Chapter 9 discusses how the macro processor uses integer tokens.

4. All characters except letters, numbers, and the underscore are special characters. Examples of special characters include

   = + − % & ; ( )

   Most special characters are single tokens. However, the blank is not a token, although it can end a name or number token. A single or double quote either marks the boundary of a literal token or is a character within a literal token, but it is not itself a token. (Chapter 10 discusses situations in which single and double quotes become separate tokens.) A period can sometimes be part of another token (for example, as a decimal in a number such as 2.5 or as a delimiter in a macro variable reference such as &A.B). In addition, some two-character operators, such as ** and <=, form a single token.

A token ends when the tokenizer encounters one of the following:

- the beginning of a new token
- a blank after a name or number token
- in a literal token, a quote of the same type that began the token that is not followed by another quote of that type.

The maximum length of any token is 200 characters.

How the SAS System Tokenizes Statements

The first SAS statement in the sales program earlier in this chapter contains eight tokens (four names and four special characters):

Input Stack	Tokens
`data sales(drop=lastyr);`	`data■sales■(■drop■=■lastyr■)■;`

The following examples show how the SAS System tokenizes other statements:

1. This statement contains one name, one number, and two special characters:

   `x5=123.4;`   `x5■=■123.4■;`

2. This statement contains three names, one number, and six special characters. The blanks do not count as tokens.

   `x6 = x5 + ( x4 * 12.5 );`   `x6■=■x5■+■(■x4■*■12.5■)■;`

3. This statement contains one name, one literal, and two special characters:

   `site="Spivey's Corner";`   `site■=■"Spivey's Corner"■;`

4. This statement contains three names and four special characters. The period following ONE is a delimiter for the macro variable reference and is part of the macro variable name token.

   `%put &one.&two;`   `%■put■&■one.■&■two■;`

5. This statement contains three names and seven special characters. Because a blank is not a token, the condition is "the value of X equals null."

   `%do %while(&x= );`   `%■do■%■while■(■&■x■=■)■;`

Exercises

Understanding tokenization is helpful in understanding many features of SAS software. For practice, try tokenizing the examples that follow. The correct tokenization is shown following the examples.

1. `if score>40 then do;`

2. `title "Quality Control";`

3. `today=date();`

4. `input@3name$@10sex 1.;`

5. `%let a=&x&y;`

6. `%macro schedul(date,time=);`

7. `%let n&i=%eval(&x1+10);`

8. `%do %until(%substr(&a,1,4)=data);`

Answers to Tokenization Exercises

Statement	Tokenization
1. `if score>40 then do;`	`if■score■>■40■then■do■;`
2. `title "Quality Control";`	`title■"Quality Control"■;`
3. `today=date();`	`today■=■date■(■)■;`
4. `input@3name$@10sex 1.;`	`input■@■3■name■$■@■10■sex■1.■;`
5. `%let a=&x&y;`	`%■let■a■=■&■x■&■y■;`
6. `%macro schedul(date,time=);`	`%■macro■schedul■(■date■,■time■=■)■;`
7. `%let n&i=%eval(&x1+10);`	`%■let■n■&■i■=■%■eval■(■&■x1■+■10■)■;`
8. `%do %until(%substr(&a,1,4)=data);`	`%■do■%■until■(■%■substr■(■&■a■,■1■,■4■)■=■data■)■;`

Chapter 9

Macro Compilation and Execution

Macro compilation and execution are separate processes from DATA or PROC step compilation and execution. Understanding the difference between macro compilation and execution and the activities that occur in each process will help you understand both macro expression evaluation (discussed in this chapter) and macro quoting (discussed in Chapter 10, "Macro Quoting"). This chapter first describes macro compilation and execution and then points out some special features of macro execution. The last section of the chapter discusses macro expressions and the way the macro processor evaluates arithmetic and logical expressions.

Contents

MACRO COMPILATION AND EXECUTION

This section first shows how the macro processor compiles a macro and then how macro execution occurs. The last part of this section shows how macro compilation and execution interact with other SAS compilation and execution.

Macro Compilation

Chapter 8, "How the SAS System Processes a Program," shows how the SAS System processes a program containing a %LET statement and a macro variable reference. The SAS System uses the same process when the program contains a macro definition and macro invocation.

Compiling a Simple Macro

Suppose the sales program shown in Chapter 8 continues with a macro definition, an invocation, and a PROC MEANS step:

```
%macro app;
   %if &sysday=Friday %then
      %do;
         proc append base=save.sales data=current;
         run;
      %end;
%mend app;
%app
proc means;
   var total;
run;
```

As Chapter 8 shows, when the SAS compiler requests a word, the word scanner places words in the word queue. When the SAS System reaches this part of the sales program, the word queue looks like **Figure 9.1.***

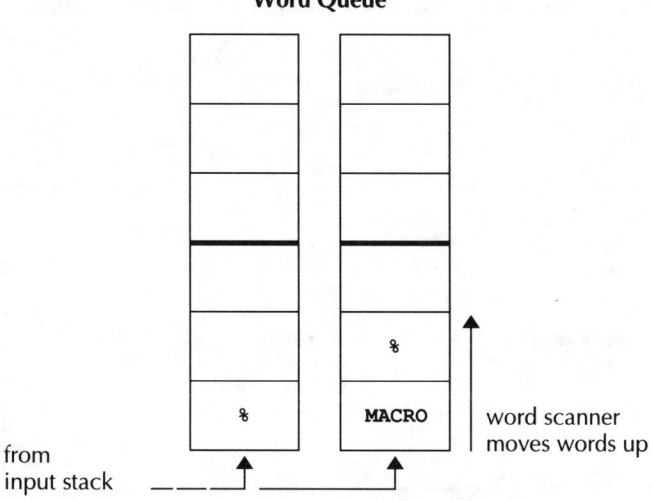

Word Queue

from
input stack

word scanner
moves words up

Figure 9.1   Macro Definition Entering Word Queue

---

* Note that this figure shows two stages of activity in the word queue, not two word queues.

When the word scanner detects a percent sign followed by a nonblank character (the %MACRO keyword in the sales program), the word scanner triggers the macro processor. The macro processor examines the tokens, recognizes the beginning of a macro definition, and begins to compile the macro.

During macro compilation, the macro processor

- records the name of the macro and the names and default values of any parameters
- compiles and stores all macro program statements for that macro
- stores all noncompiled items in the macro as text.

If the macro processor detects a syntax error while compiling the macro, the macro processor continues to compile it, checks the syntax in the rest of the macro, and issues messages for any additional errors it finds. However, the macro processor does not store the macro for execution. A macro that the macro processor compiles but does not store is called a *dummy macro*.

Result of Macro Compilation

Compiling a macro produces a member in a SAS catalog in the WORK library consisting of compiled macro program statements and text. However, the SAS System does not currently support copying or renaming macros as it does other members of catalogs.

The distinction between compiled macro program statements and stored text is important for macro execution (discussed in the next section). Examples of items stored as text include the following:

- macro variable references
- nested macro invocations
- nested macro definitions
- macro functions, except %STR and %NRSTR
- arithmetic and logical macro expressions
- names and values of local macro variables
- text to be written by %PUT statements
- field definitions in %WINDOW statements
- model text for SAS statements and SAS Display Manager System commands.

Figure 9.2 shows the compiled items in macro APP in red and items stored as text in black.

```
%macro app;
   %if &sysday=Friday %then
      %do;
          proc append base=save.sales data=current;
          run;
      %end;
%mend app;
```

Figure 9.2   Compiled Items and Stored Text in a Compiled Macro

Note the following points about macro compilation:

- The macro processor receives the result of the %STR and %NRSTR functions, not the functions and their arguments. The %STR and %NRSTR functions are described in Chapter 10.
- When the macro processor recognizes the beginning of a nested macro definition, the macro processor stores all subsequent tokens as the text of the nested macro until it encounters a %MEND statement for that macro. It does not compile the nested macro as it is compiling the outer macro. (See **Executing Nested Macro Definitions** later in this chapter for an example of how the macro processor compiles and executes a nested macro definition.)

Macro Execution

Macro execution consists of a series of simple actions that occur over and over. This section first illustrates how a simple macro executes within a SAS program and then discusses other points about macro execution.

Executing a Simple Macro

Figure 9.3 shows the lines remaining in the sales program after the macro processor compiles macro APP.

```
%app
proc means;
   var total;
run;
```

Figure 9.3   Sales Program Showing Macro Invocation

The word scanner begins to place words into the word queue again, as shown in **Figure 9.4**.

Word Queue

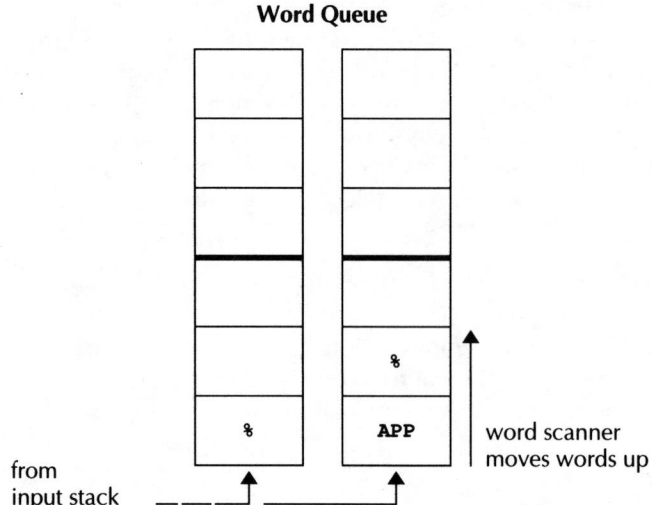

Figure 9.4   Macro Invocation Entering Word Queue

The macro processor recognizes a macro invocation and begins to execute macro APP. During macro execution, the macro processor

- executes compiled macro program statements
- places noncompiled items on the input stack as text
- reads text that the word scanner has placed in the word queue.

Execution of macro APP proceeds as follows:

1. The macro processor first encounters the compiled %IF statement. The macro processor executes the statement and recognizes that the next item will be stored text containing the %IF condition.
2. The macro processor places the following text on the input stack ahead of the remaining text in the program (the PROC MEANS step):

    &sysday=Friday

    Figure 9.5 shows the input stack now.

```
&sysday=Friday
proc means;
   var total;
run;
```

Figure 9.5   Text for %IF Condition on Input Stack

3. The word scanner reads the tokens & and SYSDAY into the word queue and triggers the macro processor.

4. The macro processor resolves the reference &SYSDAY (for example, into **Friday**) and places the result on top of the input stack, ahead of the remaining text in the program. **Figure 9.6** shows the input stack at this point.

```
Friday
        =Friday
proc means;
   var total;
run;
```

Figure 9.6 Input Stack after Macro Variable Reference Is Resolved

5. The word scanner then reads **Friday=Friday** word by word from the input stack and places the tokens into the word queue. Because the macro processor needs a condition for the %IF statement, the word scanner passes the text to the macro processor.
6. The macro processor evaluates the expression **Friday=Friday** (using the implicit %EVAL function) and, because the expression is true, proceeds to the %THEN statement.
7. The macro processor executes the compiled %THEN statement and proceeds to the compiled %DO statement.
8. The macro processor executes the compiled %DO statement and recognizes that the next item is stored text.
9. The macro processor places the stored text on top of the input stack, ahead of the text that remains in the program. **Figure 9.7** shows the text remaining in the program at this point.

```
proc append base=save.sales data=current;
run;
proc means;
   var total;
run;
```

Figure 9.7 Generated Text on Top of Input Stack

10. The word scanner reads the generated text from the input stack, places the tokens into the word queue, and (because there are no macro language triggers in the text) passes the tokens to the parts of the SAS System that request them.
11. The PROC APPEND step executes.
12. The macro processor recognizes the end of the %DO group at the %END statement and proceeds to the %MEND statement.
13. The macro processor executes the %MEND statement, and macro APP ceases execution.

The execution of macro APP shows the pattern of simple actions performed again and again. On a fundamental level, macro execution is the continuous cycle shown in **Figure 9.8**.

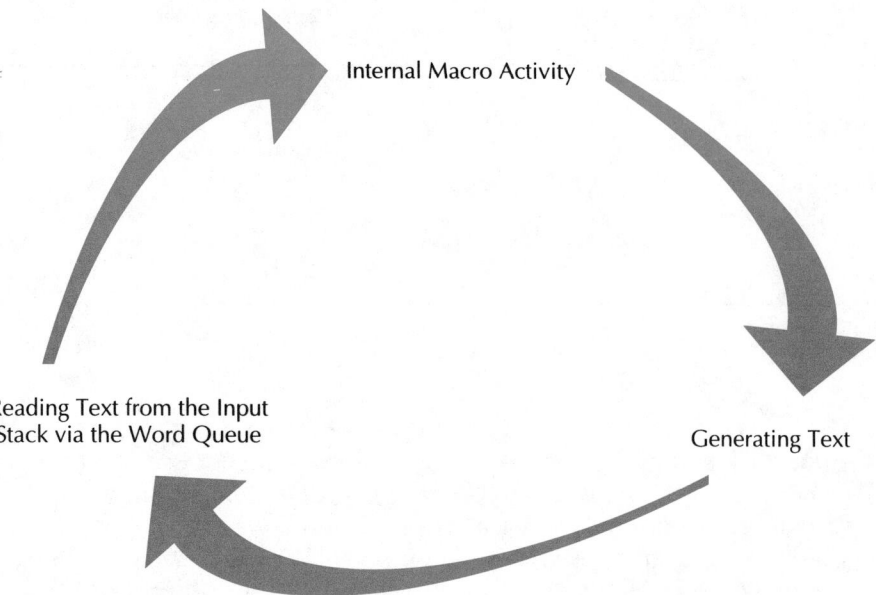

Internal Macro Activity

Reading Text from the Input
Stack via the Word Queue

Generating Text

Figure 9.8   Macro Execution

This cycle gives the macro processor much of its flexibility. The following sections show how this cycle affects the way the macro processor executes the macros you write.

Executing Nested Macro Definitions

Each time macro execution reaches a nested macro definition, the macro processor generates the nested macro definition as text and places it on the input stack. The word scanner then scans the definition and the macro processor compiles it. If you nest the definition of a macro that does not change, you cause the macro processor to compile the same macro each time that section of the outer macro is executed. You need to nest a macro definition only if you need to change the definition of that macro based on values known during the execution of the outer macro. To nest a macro's referencing environment, simply nest the macro invocation.

These examples illustrate the difference between nesting a macro definition and nesting a macro call:

```
%macro big1(year,product);
    %*nested definition--inefficient for repeated executions;
    %macro fn;
        footnote "Statistics for &product in &year";
    %mend fn;
    data stats;
        set in.archive;
        if product="&product" and year="&year";
    run;
    proc means;
        %fn
    run;
%mend big1;
```

```
%big1(90,coffee)

%macro big2(year,product);
   %*nested call only--efficient for repeated executions;
   data stats;
      set in.archive;
      if product="&product" and year="&year";
   run;
   proc means;
      %fn
   run;
%mend big2;

%macro fn;
   footnote "Statistics for &product in &year";
%mend fn;


%big2(90,coffee)
```

In the first example, each time you invoke macro BIG1, the macro processor generates the definition of macro FN as text, recognizes a macro definition, and compiles macro FN. In the second example, you move the definition of FN outside the definition of BIG2 so that FN is compiled only once. In both examples, the values of PRODUCT and YEAR are available to FN because the invocation of FN is within the definition of BIG1 or BIG2.

Executing Nested Macro Invocations

When macro execution reaches a nested macro invocation, the macro processor generates the invocation as text and puts the text on the input stack. The word scanner places those tokens into the word queue, recognizes a macro call, and triggers the macro processor. The macro processor temporarily suspends execution of the outer macro and executes the nested macro before performing any other activity. When the nested macro ceases execution, the macro processor performs the next action in the execution of the outer macro.

Recursive execution   *Recursive* execution occurs when a macro, while executing, invokes itself. You can also create recursive execution by calling a second macro from within the currently executing macro, a third macro from within the second macro, and so on, until you invoke a macro that invokes the original macro. Macro FACT, shown here, uses recursive execution to produce the factorial of parameter NUM:

```
%macro fact(num);
   %if &num=0 or &num=1 %then 1;
   %else %eval(&num*%fact(%eval(&num-1)));
%mend fact;
```

Macro FACT executes recursively because the %EVAL function contains a call to macro FACT; the macro processor simply reinvokes macro FACT while executing the %EVAL function. Invoking FACT as

```
%put ***%fact(4)***;
```

writes this line:

```
***24***
```

Recursive execution is a specialized technique and macro programs rarely require it.

Executing Macro Functions

The macro processor generates macro functions, except the %STR and %NRSTR functions, as text and places the text on the input stack. The word scanner places those tokens into the word queue, recognizes the trigger *%name*, and invokes the macro processor. (Remember that the macro processor receives the result of the %STR or %NRSTR function, not the function itself.) If you misspell the name of a macro function, the macro processor does not recognize the name of the function, but it does recognize the pattern *%name(values)*—that is, a macro invocation with parameter values. Therefore, the macro processor attempts to invoke a macro of that name. If the macro processor cannot find that macro, it leaves those tokens in the word queue. In addition, it produces the following warning message:

```
WARNING: Apparent invocation of macro macroname not resolved.
```

When those tokens reach the SAS compiler, they usually cause an error message because few SAS statements accept the percent sign.

Interaction of Compilation and Execution

This chapter and the preceding one illustrate the relationship between macro compilation and execution and other SAS System compilation and execution. The relationship can be summarized as follows:

- The SAS compiler and other parts of the SAS System request words from the word queue. The compiler compiles each statement.
- When the compiler has received a complete DATA or PROC step, the step executes.
- During macro compilation, neither macro execution, SAS compilation, nor SAS execution occurs in that environment. (However, if you submit part of a macro definition from the display manager PROGRAM EDITOR window or a full-screen procedure program screen, you can invoke macros from the command line before you submit the rest of the macro definition.)
- When macro execution begins, the SAS compiler and other parts of the SAS System continue to request words from the word scanner. During macro execution, the macro processor places a piece of text on the input stack and pauses while the word scanner processes that text. When the word scanner needs more words, it triggers macro execution to produce the next piece of text. Thus, SAS compilation can alternate closely with macro execution. When the SAS compiler has received a complete step, the SAS System executes that step. Because the word scanner does not supply words during SAS execution, the word scanner does not need to trigger macro execution at that time. After the current SAS step has executed, portions of the SAS System begin to request words again; thus, the word scanner triggers macro execution to produce another piece of text if necessary.

MACRO EXPRESSIONS

A *macro expression* is a sequence of macro operators and operands. Any item stored as text can be an operand. The most common operands are macro variable references, macro invocations, macro functions, model text for SAS statements and display manager commands, and (in the argument of the %EVAL function) integers. Operators include arithmetic and logical operators (described in **Arithmetic and Logical Expressions** later in this section) and grouping parentheses. All of the following are macro expressions:

```
&new
&a=&b
100
%start
%scan(&a,1)
%eval(&x+100)
&a ne and &b=yes
```

An important group of macro expressions consists of expressions evaluated with the %EVAL function: arithmetic and logical expressions. This section concentrates on those expressions.

Arithmetic and Logical Expressions

Because the macro language is a string-handling facility, the macro processor treats all tokens (including those that look like integers) as strings. The macro processor uses the %EVAL function (whether you specify it or the macro facility makes an automatic call to it) each time the macro facility requires a token to have numeric properties. (**Table 9.2**, later in this chapter, shows features of the macro language that use an implicit %EVAL function.)

Arithmetic Expressions

In the following example, both %PUT statements include an arithmetic expression:

```
%let a=2;
%let b=3;
%put %eval(&a*&b);
%put %substr(&sysday,1,&a*&b);
```

In the first %PUT statement, an explicit %EVAL function multiplies the value of A by the value of B. In the second %PUT statement, the macro processor positions itself in the value of SYSDAY with numbers obtained from the second and third arguments of the %SUBSTR function. The macro processor makes an implicit call to the %EVAL function to treat those arguments as numbers. Although the first example uses the %EVAL function explicitly and the second example uses it implicitly, the rules for evaluating the expression are the same in both cases.

Logical Expressions

Logical expressions include comparisons such as those in the following %IF conditions:

```
%macro bkup;
   %if &sysday=Friday %then %put do a full backup today;
   %put %eval(&sysday=Friday);
%mend bkup;


%bkup
```

```
%macro compare(test=0);
   %if &test %then %put test is true;
   %put %eval(&test);
%mend compare;


%compare(test=5)
```

The %IF statement in each example automatically invokes the %EVAL function to make the comparison. If an explicit comparison such as the one in the first example is true, the %EVAL function returns the value 1; if it is false, the function returns a 0. In implied comparisons such as macro COMPARE, the condition is true if variable TEST has a numeric value other than 0 and false if the value of TEST is 0. A character value or a null value produces an error.

Rules for Arithmetic and Logical Evaluation

The use of %EVAL resembles the use of expressions in the DATA step in most ways; however, the following characteristics of %EVAL are different from the way the DATA step handles expressions:

- The %EVAL function performs only integer arithmetic. It does not use or recognize fractions. See **Using Integer Arithmetic in the Macro Facility** later in this chapter for more information.
- Because the macro facility uses only integers, the range of acceptable numbers is less than in the DATA step. (The DATA step stores all numbers in floating-point form, which can represent much larger numbers than integer form.) The range of representable integers in the macro facility is $\pm 2,147,483,647$.
- The %EVAL function does not recognize operators for concatenation, minimum, or maximum.
- Expressions in which comparison operators surround a macro expression, as in $10 < \&X < 20$, may or may not be the equivalent of a DATA step compound expression (depending on what the macro expression resolves into). To be safe, write the connecting operator explicitly, as in the expression $10 < \&X$ AND $\&X < 20$.

Table 9.1 lists the operators available to the %EVAL function, their symbols, and their mnemonic forms. The order in which operations are performed in the macro language is the same as in the DATA step. As in the DATA step, operations within parentheses are performed first.

Table 9.1 Macro Language Operators

Operator	Mnemonic	Name	Precedence
**		exponentiation	1
+		positive prefix	2
−		negative prefix	2
¬ ^ ~	NOT	logical not★	3
*		multiplication	4
/		division	4
+		addition	5
−		subtraction	5
<	LT	less than	6
<=	LE	less than or equal	6
=	EQ	equal	6
¬= ^= ~=	NE	not equal★	6
>	GT	greater than	6
>=	GE	greater than or equal	6
&	AND	logical and	7
|	OR	logical or	8

★ The symbol to use depends on your keyboard.

Using Integer Arithmetic in the Macro Facility

Integer arithmetic is arithmetic that uses only integers. Values containing characters other than digits (for example, decimal points) are illegal.

Performing Arithmetic Calculations

In the macro facility, the following statements all perform calculations on integers and yield integer results:

```
%let a=%eval(1+2);
%let b=%eval(10*3);
%let c=%eval(4/2);
```

The values assigned to A, B, and C are 3, 30, and 2, respectively. However, in the statements

```
*wrong;
%let d=%eval(1.5+2.5);
```

the %EVAL function causes the error message

```
ERROR: A character operand was found in the %EVAL function or
%IF condition where a numeric operand is required. The condition
was:  1.5+2.5
```

because the macro facility treats a value containing a decimal as a string. In the following example, the %EVAL function assigns E the integer value 30 but issues an error message for the second expression:

```
*right;
%let e=%eval(10+20);


*wrong;
%let f=%eval(10.0+20.0);
```

The values 10.0 and 20.0 are not integers; the decimals indicate fractional parts in which the fraction is 0. Thus, the macro facility treats them as strings. As a simple rule, remember that you cannot perform an arithmetic calculation on a value containing a decimal.

If you perform division on integers that would ordinarily result in a fraction, integer arithmetic discards the fractional part. For example, the following statements assign I the value 1:

```
%let g=5;
%let h=3;
%let i=%eval(&g/&h);
```

As another example, the following statement tests whether J is even because only an even number can be divided by 2 and the result multiplied by 2 to obtain the original number:

```
%if (&j/2)*2=&j %then
    %do;
```

Performing Comparisons

Although you cannot perform arithmetic calculations on noninteger values, you can use them in comparisons.

In making character comparisons, the macro processor compares strings character by character until it reaches either a pair of characters that do not match or the end of the strings. If one string contains fewer characters than the other, the shorter string is padded with trailing blanks. The macro processor treats a comparison between a character string and an integer as a comparison between two character strings.

The macro processor uses the same collating sequence as the SORT procedure (described in the *SAS Procedures Guide, Version 6, Third Edition*).

For example, macro TEST compares noninteger character strings to see which is larger:

```
%macro test(first,second);
    %if &first>&second %then %put &first>&second;
    %else %if &first=&second %then %put &first=&second;
    %else %put &first<&second;
%mend test;
```

Suppose you use the following invocation:

```
%test(2.50,2.50)
```

The macro processor compares the 2s, the periods, the 5s, and then the 0s. Because all of them are equal, the macro processor writes this message:

```
2.50=2.50
```

Suppose you invoke TEST with the following:

```
%test(2.6,2.50)
```

In this case, the macro processor compares the 2s, the periods, and then the characters 6 and 5. Because 6 is larger, the macro processor writes the following line:

```
2.6>2.50
```

Finally, consider this invocation:

```
%test(2.5,2.50)
```

The macro processor compares the 2s, the periods, and the 5s; then it compares a padded blank in the first value to the 0 in the second value. Because a blank is smaller than a 0, the macro processor writes the following line:

```
2.5<2.50
```

Using Automatic Evaluation

When a macro language feature automatically uses the %EVAL function, using an explicit %EVAL function causes two evaluations to be performed. Consider these two examples:

```
*inefficient;
title "Data for %substr(&sysdate,%eval(%length(&sysdate)-4),5)";

*efficient;
title "Data for %substr(&sysdate,%length(&sysdate)-4,5)";
```

In the first example, the explicit evaluation returns a value of 2 or 3 (depending on whether the value of SYSDATE contains six or seven characters), and the implicit %EVAL function performs the evaluation

```
%eval(2)
```

or

```
%eval(3)
```

Because the result of evaluating an integer is that integer, the second example, which uses only the implicit evaluation, is more efficient.

Any macro language feature that requires a numeric value automatically invokes the %EVAL function. **Table 9.2** shows in boldface the macro language features that automatically invoke the %EVAL function.

Table 9.2 Automatic Evaluation in Macro Language Features

%DO *macro-variable*=**expression** %TO **expression** <%BY **expression**>;

%DO %UNTIL(**expression**);

%DO %WHILE(**expression**);

%IF **expression** %THEN *statement*;

%QSCAN(*argument*,**expression**<,*delimiters*>)

%QSUBSTR(*argument*,**expression**<,**expression**>)

%SCAN(*argument*,**expression**<,*delimiters*>)

%SUBSTR(*argument*,**expression**<,**expression**>)

Timing of Arithmetic and Logical Evaluation

At macro compilation, the macro processor stores arithmetic and logical expressions as text. At macro execution, the macro processor generates the text, reads it, and performs the evaluation. This fact has some important consequences:

- You can determine all elements of an expression, including operators, at macro execution.
- In some cases, the macro processor detects a null argument for an implicit %EVAL function at macro compilation. The macro processor detects all other syntax errors in arithmetic and logical expressions at macro execution.

In this example, you control the form of the evaluation through macro parameter values because you specify the operator for the evaluation at macro execution:

```
%macro ev1(left,operator,right);
    %if &left &operator &right %then %put &left &operator &right;
    %else %put condition was &left &operator &right--not true;
%mend ev1;
```

```
%ev1(10,>,5)
```

When you invoke macro EV1, the condition of the %IF statement becomes

```
10 > 5
```

and the %PUT statement writes the following:

```
10 > 5
```

In the following example, the macro processor detects a syntax error only at macro execution:

```
%macro ev2;
    %*call macro endweek or daily;
    %*note missing operator;
    %if &sysday Saturday %then %endweek;
    %else %daily;
%mend ev2;
```

```
%ev2
```

During compilation, the macro processor recognizes that the %IF statement contains a condition and stores the following text:

```
&sysday Saturday
```

During execution, the macro processor places the text on the input stack, reads and resolves the reference &SYSDAY (for example, into **Saturday**), and then reads the rest of the condition. When the macro processor receives the complete expression without encountering an operator, it issues an error message.

Chapter 10
Macro Quoting

This chapter discusses ways to make the macro processor treat an item as text rather than as a symbol in the macro language. The process is known as *macro quoting*. The first section of this chapter, **OVERVIEW OF MACRO QUOTING**, defines macro quoting and answers some common questions about it. The section **USING MACRO QUOTING FUNCTIONS** describes the tasks that macro quoting involves and illustrates the function used for each task. **UNQUOTING QUOTED TEXT** describes how to use the %UNQUOTE function and gives some technical background on when you need to use it. The last section, **REFERENCE TABLES**, gives some tables you can use as references on macro quoting.

Contents

OVERVIEW OF MACRO QUOTING

To make the macro processor treat an item as text rather than as a symbol in the macro language, you use a process known as macro quoting. This section introduces macro quoting through questions and answers.

What Is Macro Quoting?

The macro processor is extremely flexible and can generate all kinds of text. Because the macro processor allows you to generate all sorts of characters as text, and because the macro language is composed of some of the same characters, eventually a question arises: is the macro processor supposed to treat a particular character—for example, a semicolon—as text, or as a symbol in the macro language?

If you do not indicate otherwise, the macro processor interprets any item that can be part of the macro language as part of the macro language, not as text. The steps you take to cause the macro processor to treat a certain item as text rather than as part of the macro language are called *macro quoting*. (*Treating an item as text* and *removing the significance of an item* are other phrases that refer to the concept of macro quoting.)

As a simple example, suppose you want to assign the following text to a macro variable named P:

```
proc print; run;
```

If you plan the %LET statement as follows, you create an ambiguous situation:

```
%let p=proc print; run;;
```

Are the semicolons that follow PRINT and RUN part of the value of P, or does one of them end the %LET statement? If you do not tell the macro processor what to do, it treats the semicolon after PRINT as the end of the %LET statement; the value of P is

```
proc print
```

and the characters

```
run;;
```

are simply the next part of the program. To assign the PROC PRINT step as the value of P, you must quote the semicolons. You quote them by using a macro quoting function, introduced in the next section.

Why Are There Macro Quoting Functions?

In DATA and PROC steps, a single or double quote indicates that the SAS System is to treat an item as text. (The term *quoting* comes from the use of these characters.) For example, in this DATA step the SAS System treats the first occurrence of ONE as a variable name and the second occurrence as a group of characters to be assigned as the value of Y:

```
data new;
   set old;
   x=one;
   y='one';
run;
```

Enclosing the characters in quotes causes the SAS System to treat the two statements differently.

In the macro facility, constant text often includes single and double quotes. Therefore, it is not convenient to use those characters to mark items to be treated as text. Instead, the macro language encloses text to be quoted in the argument of a function. Functions that quote text are known as *quoting functions*.

To assign the text

```
proc print; run;
```

as the value of macro variable P, enclose the value in the quoting function %STR, as shown here:

```
%let p=%str(proc print; run;);
```

The beginning of the function, %STR followed by an opening parenthesis, indicates the beginning of a string, and the closing parenthesis indicates the end of the string. The macro processor treats the semicolons within the function as text and the semicolon outside the function as the end of the %LET statement.

What Are the Different Kinds of Quoting Functions?

In Version 6, the macro language has three types of quoting functions:

compilation functions
> cause the macro processor to treat items as text while compiling (constructing) a macro or while compiling a macro program statement in open code. The %STR and %NRSTR functions are compilation functions.

execution functions
> cause the macro processor to treat as text items that result from resolving a macro expression (such as a macro variable reference, a macro invocation, or the argument of an implicit %EVAL function). They are called execution functions because resolution occurs during macro execution or during execution of a macro program statement in open code. The macro processor resolves the expression as far as possible, issues any warning messages for macro variable references or macro invocations it cannot resolve, and quotes the result. The %QUOTE and %NRQUOTE functions quote most resolved items; if the value contains an unmatched, unmarked quote or parenthesis,* use the %BQUOTE-%NRBQUOTE pair instead.

function that prevents resolution
> causes the macro processor to treat the value of a macro variable as a "picture" during macro execution. It treats the value as text, without beginning the process of resolution. The %SUPERQ function prevents resolution of a macro variable's value. Note: The %SUPERQ function takes as its argument a macro variable *name* (or a macro expression that yields a macro variable name). The argument must not be a reference to the macro variable whose value you are quoting.

Within the compilation and execution categories, functions occur in pairs: one plain function and a similar function whose name begins with the letters NR. In each case, the plain function quotes the items in its category except for the ampersand and percent sign. The function beginning with NR quotes the ampersand and percent sign also.

---

* Table 10.1 describes marking unmatched quotes and parentheses.

How Much Text Should You Enclose in a Quoting Function?

In each of the following statements, the macro processor treats the quoted semi-colons as text:

```
%let p=%str(proc print; run;);
%let p=proc %str(print;) %str(run;);
%let p=proc print%str(;) run%str(;);
```

The value of P is the same in each case:

```
proc print; run;
```

Why are the different combinations possible?

When you enclose text in a quoting function, the macro processor quotes only the items that the function recognizes. Other text enclosed in the function remains unchanged.* In the preceding examples, the semicolon is one of the characters that the %STR function recognizes; thus, %STR quotes it and leaves the other characters in the argument unchanged. You can include any amount of text in the argument of a quoting function along with the item to be quoted. In general, enclose a group of text in a quoting function that makes the code easy to read.

When Do You Quote Items?

The macro facility allows you as much flexibility as possible in designing your macros. You need to quote an item only when the macro processor would otherwise interpret the item as part of the macro language rather than as text. For example, in this statement you must quote the first two semicolons to make them part of the text:

```
%let p=%str(proc print; run;);
```

However, in macro PR, shown here, you do not need to quote the semicolons after PRINT and RUN:

```
%macro pr(start);
   %if &start=yes %then
      %do;
         %put proc print requested;
         proc print;
         run;
      %end;
   %mend pr;
```

Because nothing in macro PR causes the macro processor to expect a semicolon within the %DO group, the macro processor treats the semicolons after PRINT and RUN as text.

Although it is not possible to give a series of rules that cover every situation, **USING MACRO QUOTING FUNCTIONS** later in this chapter describes broad categories of tasks and the quoting function to use for each. In addition, **REFERENCE TABLES** at the end of this chapter gives tables that compare various items that require quoting and the functions that quote them.

---

* In general, macro quoting functions take advantage of the fact that more hexadecimal combinations are possible in each byte than are needed to represent the symbols on a keyboard. When a macro quoting function recognizes an item to be quoted, the macro processor replaces the item with an unused hexadecimal combination. Unquoting a value (discussed later in this chapter) restores the original item.

What Is Unquoting?

Items that have been affected by a quoting function, such as the first two semicolons in the value of macro variable P in the preceding section, remain quoted as long as the item is being used by the macro processor.* When you use the value of P later in a macro program statement, as in

```
%if &ready=yes %then &p;
```

you do not need to quote the reference; the semicolons were already quoted by the %STR function and remain quoted. However, when the macro processor generates the value of P, the SAS System restores the meaning of the semicolons later so that the SAS compiler can compile a PROC PRINT step. Restoring the significance of an item affected by a quoting function is known as *unquoting* the item.

If you need to restore the meaning of an item that is used by the macro processor rather than generated as text, you must unquote it with the %UNQUOTE function (discussed in **UNQUOTING QUOTED TEXT** later in this chapter).

When the macro processor generates text from a quoted item, as in the value of P above, you can usually allow the SAS System to unquote the quoted items automatically. However, in a few cases, quoting text changes the way the word scanner tokenizes it. (The word scanner and tokenization are discussed in Chapter 8, "How the SAS System Processes a Program.") In those cases, allowing the SAS System to unquote the text automatically results in SAS statements that look correct but which the SAS compiler does not recognize. To cause the word scanner to tokenize those items as you intended, enclose them in the %UNQUOTE function. The section **UNQUOTING QUOTED TEXT** later in this chapter contains an example of using the %UNQUOTE function to restore normal tokenization.

USING MACRO QUOTING FUNCTIONS

This section describes the tasks for which you need to use quoting functions and the function to use for each task.

Quoting at Macro Compilation

If an item affects the way the macro processor constructs macro program statements, you must quote the item during macro compilation (or the compilation of a macro program statement in open code). The two macro compilation functions are %STR and %NRSTR. They differ only in their effect on ampersands and percent signs.

Quoting Most Items: The %STR Function

The %STR function works on text that is present when the macro processor is compiling a macro (or a macro program statement used in open code). It allows the macro processor to compile a macro or a macro program statement as you intended, without misinterpreting items as part of the macro language rather than as text. Because the %STR function works during macro compilation, the macro processor does not receive the function itself; it simply receives the quoted text.

---

* However, using a quoted argument in the %SCAN, %SUBSTR, and %UPCASE functions returns an unquoted result.

The %LET statement in **OVERVIEW OF MACRO QUOTING** earlier in this chapter illustrates using %STR to create the proper value for a macro variable, as shown:

```
%let p=%str(proc print; run;);
```

The value of P is

```
proc print; run;
```

If the value contains an unmatched (unpaired) quote or parenthesis, you must place a percent sign before that character in order for the %STR function to accept it. The following %LET statement shows an unmatched quote:

```
%let p=%str(proc print; title "O%'Brien Project"; run;);
```

The value of P is now

```
proc print; title "O'Brien Project"; run;
```

Table 10.1 at the end of this chapter illustrates how to mark unmatched quotes and parentheses.

Macro KEEPIT1, below, shows how the %STR function works in a macro definition:

```
%macro keepit1(size);
    %if &size=big %then %str(keep city _numeric_;);
    %else %str(keep city;);
%mend keepit1;
```

The invocation

```
%keepit1(big)
```

produces this statement:

```
KEEP CITY _NUMERIC_;
```

When you use the %STR function in the %IF-%THEN statement, the macro processor interprets the first semicolon after the word %THEN as text. The second semicolon ends the %THEN statement, and the %ELSE statement immediately follows the %THEN statement. Thus, the macro processor compiles the statements as you intended. However, if you omit the %STR function, the macro processor interprets the first semicolon after the word %THEN as the end of the %THEN clause and the next semicolon as constant text. Because constant text cannot appear between a %THEN and a %ELSE clause, the macro processor does not compile the macro. Instead, it issues an error message.

In the %ELSE statement, the %STR function causes the macro processor to treat the first semicolon in the statement as text and the second one as the end of the %ELSE clause. Therefore, the semicolon that ends the KEEP statement is part of the conditional execution. If you omit the %STR function, the first semicolon ends the %ELSE clause and the second semicolon is outside the conditional execution. It is generated as text each time the macro executes. (In this example, the placement of the semicolon does not affect the SAS code.) Again, using %STR causes macro KEEPIT1 to compile as you intended.

Quoting the & and % in Addition: The %NRSTR Function

The %NRSTR function quotes the same items as the %STR function and also quotes the ampersand and percent sign. Thus, the macro processor does not recognize any macro language triggers in text quoted with the %NRSTR function.

For example, the following macro definition contains patterns that the macro processor would ordinarily recognize as macro variable references:

```
%macro credits(d=%nrstr(Mary&Stacy&Joan Ltd.));
   footnote "Designed by &d";
%mend credits;
```

Using %NRSTR causes the macro processor to treat &STACY and &JOAN simply as part of the text in the value of D; the macro processor does not issue warning messages for unresolvable macro variable references. Therefore, invoking macro CREDITS with the default value of D, as in

```
%credits()
```

generates this FOOTNOTE statement:

```
FOOTNOTE "Designed by Mary&Stacy&Joan Ltd.";
```

If you omit the %NRSTR function, the macro processor attempts to resolve the references &STACY and &JOAN as part of the resolution of &D in the FOOTNOTE statement. The macro processor issues these warning messages:

```
WARNING: Apparent symbolic reference STACY not resolved.
WARNING: Apparent symbolic reference JOAN not resolved.
```

Example: Comparing the %STR and %NRSTR Functions   Macro KEEPIT2, shown here, illustrates a case in which you use both %STR and %NRSTR:

```
%macro keepit2(size,var);
   data new;
      set old;
      date="&sysdate"d;
      format date mmddyy.;
   %if &size=big %then %str(keep city date &var;);
   %else %str(keep city date;);
   run;
   proc print;
      title "&var City and Date (Created with %nrstr(&SYSDATE))";
   run;
%mend keepit2;
```

Invoking macro KEEPIT2 on January 12, 1990, with

```
%keepit2(big,Cost Profit)
```

generates these statements:

```
DATA NEW;
   SET OLD;
   DATE="12JAN90"D;
   FORMAT DATE MMDDYY.;
   KEEP CITY DATE COST PROFIT;
RUN;
PROC PRINT;
   TITLE "Cost Profit City and Date (Created with &SYSDATE)";
RUN;
```

In macro KEEPIT2, you must quote the KEEP statements so that the macro compiles as you intend. Because you want the reference &VAR in the %THEN clause to resolve to the value you specify in the invocation, you use %STR, which allows the resolution of macro variable references in its argument. However, when you create the TITLE statement in the macro definition, you know that you want to use the string &SYSDATE as part of the title. By enclosing it in the %NRSTR function, you cause the macro processor to treat it as text rather than as a macro variable reference.

Quoting Resolved Values during Macro Execution

To quote the result produced by resolving items during macro execution, you usually use the %QUOTE or %NRQUOTE function. As with the %STR and %NRSTR functions, a percent sign must precede an unmatched quote or parenthesis. If it is not practical to mark the unmatched characters (for example, in user-supplied values), use the %BQUOTE and %NRBQUOTE pair instead.* In each pair, the function beginning with NR affects the same items as the plain function and also affects the ampersand and percent sign. **Table 10.3** in **REFERENCE TABLES** later in this chapter shows the items that each function affects.

Quoting Most Items: The %QUOTE Function

The %QUOTE function works on values that result from resolving a macro expression (usually a macro variable reference or a macro invocation). Because the macro processor resolves expressions during macro execution, this function also works during macro execution. It prevents the macro processor from treating items that should be considered text as part of the macro language during macro execution.

For example, suppose macro ORDER produces part of a DATA step for use in a supermarket's inventory control. Macro ORDER generates an IF statement with a code for the fruit you specify (`gr` for grapefruit, `or` for orange, and so on). You define macro ORDER as

```
%macro order(fruit);
   %if %quote(&fruit) ne %then
      %do;
         if frutcode="&fruit";
         %put request accepted;
      %end;
   %else %put fruit code missing;
%mend order;
```

Then you invoke ORDER in the following program:

```
data temp;
   set in.stock;
   %order(or)
run;
```

The SAS compiler sees the program

```
DATA TEMP;
   SET IN.STOCK;
   IF FRUTCODE="or";
RUN;
```

In the %IF condition, the reference &FRUIT resolves to the quoted value `or`, and the macro processor compares the text `or` to a null string. If you omit the

---

* This discussion presents the %QUOTE and %NRQUOTE functions as the way to quote resolved items and reserves the %BQUOTE and %NRBQUOTE functions for special cases. It is also possible to use the %BQUOTE and %NRBQUOTE functions to quote all resolved items and eliminate the %QUOTE-%NRQUOTE pair. Use the method you prefer. Also note that this discussion applies only to Version 6 of SAS software. If you plan to transfer programs to a host executing Version 5, you should read **Comparing the %BQUOTE function in Version 5 and Version 6** later in this section.

%QUOTE function, the macro processor treats **or** as the mnemonic operator OR and produces an error message for the invalid expression

```
or ne
```

The important point is that the reference &FRUIT does not cause a problem during macro compilation; the values to which it resolves during macro execution may cause problems. Therefore, you need a function that quotes resolved values: %QUOTE.

Passing in a value that requires quoting   Using an execution-time quoting function in the macro definition, as shown in macro ORDER, is the simplest and best way to have the macro processor accept resolved values that cause problems. However, if you discover that you need to pass in parameter values such as **or** when a macro has not been defined with an execution-time quoting function, you can do so by quoting the value in the invocation. The logic of the process is as follows:

1. When you quote an item in the macro facility, it remains quoted as long as it is within the macro facility (unless you use the %UNQUOTE function).
2. The macro processor constructs the complete macro invocation before beginning to execute the macro.
3. Therefore, you can quote the value in the invocation with the %STR function. Although the quoting is not needed when the macro processor is constructing the invocation, the value is quoted when macro execution begins and therefore does not cause problems during macro execution.

For example, suppose a similar macro named ORDERX does not contain the %QUOTE function. You can pass in the value **or** with the following invocation:

```
%orderx(%str(or))
```

However, placing the quoting function in the macro definition makes the macro much easier to use.

Example: Comparing the %QUOTE and %STR Functions   This example illustrates the difference between the %QUOTE and %STR functions. Match the circled numbers to the paragraphs below.

```
%macro notes(client,sponsor=%str(Designs-For-You, Inc.)); ❶
    %if %quote(&client) ne and %quote(&sponsor) ne %then ❸
        %str(title "Survey for &client"; ❷
            title2 "Sponsored by &sponsor";);
    %else %put Either client or sponsor was missing.;
%mend notes;

%notes(A+B Video) ❹
%notes(Fundays (Ltd.),sponsor=Trimway Health/Fitness Spa) ❺
```

1. You must quote SPONSOR's default value, `Designs-For-You, Inc.`, during macro compilation so that the comma does not indicate a new parameter name. The default value also contains hyphens; the %STR function recognizes them and quotes them, although they do not cause problems in the macro definition.
2. In the %THEN clause, the quoted semicolons end the TITLE and TITLE2 statements, and the semicolon outside the %STR function ends the %THEN clause at macro compilation.

3. Nothing in the macro variable references &CLIENT and &SPONSOR requires quoting when the macro is being compiled; therefore, you do not need the %STR function. However, you know that the values to which those references resolve may contain characters that require quoting, and you also know that the resolved values do not contain any unmatched quotes or parentheses. Therefore, you use the %QUOTE function. (If the resolved value may contain unmatched quotes or parentheses, use the %BQUOTE function.)

4. In the first execution of macro NOTES, the value of CLIENT contains a plus sign. The %QUOTE function in the %IF condition quotes the result of resolving &CLIENT; thus, the implicit %EVAL function in the %IF condition does not treat the plus sign as an operator. The second %QUOTE function has no effect in this execution of NOTES because the default value of SPONSOR was quoted by the %STR function, and the hyphens remain quoted during macro execution. The first execution of macro NOTES generates these statements:

```
TITLE "Survey for A+B Video";
TITLE2 "Sponsored by Designs-For-You, Inc.";
```

5. In the second execution of NOTES, the value of CLIENT contains a set of parentheses. The %QUOTE function quotes the parentheses and prevents the implicit %EVAL function from treating them as an operator. In addition, the new value of SPONSOR contains a slash. The %QUOTE function surrounding &SPONSOR quotes the slash so that the implicit %EVAL function does not interpret the slash as a division operator. The macro processor generates these statements:

```
TITLE "Survey for Fundays (Ltd.)";
TITLE2 "Sponsored by Trimway Health/Fitness Spa";
```

Quoting Unmatched, Unmarked Quotes and Parentheses: The %BQUOTE Function

The %BQUOTE function treats all parentheses and quotes produced by resolving macro variable references or macro calls as special characters to be quoted. (It does not quote parentheses or quotes that are not produced by resolution.) Therefore, it does not matter whether quotes and parentheses in the resolved value are matched; each one is quoted individually.

Another result of the %BQUOTE function is that a single or double quote produced by resolution within the %BQUOTE function becomes a separate token; the word scanner does not use it as the boundary of a literal token in the word queue. If generated text that was once quoted by the %BQUOTE function looks correct but the SAS System does not accept it, you may need to use the %UNQUOTE function (described later in this chapter) to restore normal tokenization.

In the following example, a DATA step creates a character value containing a single quote and assigns that value to a macro variable. Macro READIT then uses the %BQUOTE function to allow a %IF condition to accept the unmatched single quote:

```
data test;
   store="Susan's Office Supplies";
   call symput('s',store);
run;
```

```
%macro readit;
    %if %bquote(&s) ne %then %put valid;
    %else %put null value;
%mend readit;

    %readit
```

When you assign the value `Susan's Office Supplies` to STORE in the DATA step, enclosing the character string in double quotes allows you to use an unmatched single quote in the string. The SAS System stores the value of STORE as

```
Susan's Office Supplies
```

and the SYMPUT routine assigns that value (containing an unmatched single quote) as the value of macro variable S. If you do not use the %BQUOTE function when you reference S in macro READIT, the macro processor issues an error message for an invalid operand in the %IF condition.

Comparing the %BQUOTE function in Version 6 and Version 5   In Version 6, the %BQUOTE function quotes mnemonic operators such as AND and EQ. In Version 5, it does not. Consider the following example:

```
data _null_;
    input place $ 1-40;
    call symput('name',place);
    cards;
Bruce's, Lynn's, and Len's office
;

%macro test;
    %if %bquote(&name) ne %then %put %bquote(&name);
    %else %put name was null;
%mend test;

    %test
```

The value of the DATA step variable PLACE contains both unmatched quotes and the mnemonic operator **and**. In Version 6, the %BQUOTE function quotes those characters. Therefore, the %IF condition executes correctly and the %PUT statement produces the following:

```
Bruce's, Lynn's, and Len's office
```

For comparison, in Version 5 the %BQUOTE function quotes only the single quotes. In the %IF condition, the macro processor interprets the string **and** as a mnemonic operator and issues an error message.

The same principle applies to other quoting functions that quote unmatched quotes and parentheses: %NRBQUOTE, %QSCAN, %QSUBSTR, %QUPCASE, and %SUPERQ. In Version 6, all of these functions quote mnemonic operators; in Version 5, they do not. If you write programs that may be executed under Version 5 as well as under Version 6, you must observe the distinction between the Version 6 and Version 5 functions (described in more detail in the *SAS Guide to Macro Processing, Version 5 Edition*).

Quoting the & and % in Addition: The %NRQUOTE and %NRBQUOTE Functions

The %NRQUOTE and %NRBQUOTE functions are extremely specialized, and you seldom need them in macro programs. However, they are useful when you want a value to be resolved *when first encountered,* if possible, but you do not want any ampersands in the result to be interpreted as operators by an explicit or implicit %EVAL function. As with the %BQUOTE and %QUOTE functions, use the %NRBQUOTE function rather than the %NRQUOTE function if the value may contain unmatched, unmarked quotes or parentheses. **Table 10.3** in **REFERENCE TABLES** later in this chapter details the items that the %NRBQUOTE function quotes.

If the argument of the %NRQUOTE or %NRBQUOTE function contains an unresolvable macro variable reference or macro invocation, the macro processor issues a warning message before it quotes the ampersand or percent sign (assuming the SERROR or MERROR system option is in effect). To suppress the message, use the %SUPERQ function (discussed later in this chapter) instead.

Using the %NRQUOTE function   In the following program, you plan to enter company names as the value of the automatic variable SYSBUFFR. Some company names contain items that could cause problems. For example, the following name contains an ampersand that does not indicate a macro variable reference:

    A&A Autos

Names like this one present two problems: the macro processor attempts to locate a nonexistent macro variable, and if you use the value in a comparison, the implicit %EVAL function treats the ampersand as an operator.

Macro FIRMS shows the use of %NRQUOTE to build a macro that accepts the name **A&A Autos**:

```
%macro firms;
    %global code;
    %put Enter the name of the company;
    %input;
    %let name=%nrquote(&sysbuffr);
    %if &name ne %then %let code=valid;
    %else %let code=invalid;
    %put &name is &code;
%mend firms;
```

Invoking FIRMS and responding with

    A&A Autos

results in the SAS log shown in **Output 10.1**.

Output 10.1   Using the %NRQUOTE Function

```
1     %macro firms;
2        %global code;
3        %put Enter the name of the company;
4        %input;
5        %let name=%nrquote(&sysbuffr);
6        %if &name ne %then %let code=valid;
7        %else %let code=invalid;
8        %put &name is &code;
9     %mend firms;
10    %firms
Enter the name of the company
WARNING: Apparent symbolic reference A not resolved.
A&A Autos is valid
```

The macro processor uses the name **A&A Autos** three times after you enter it: when assigning the value of NAME, in the %IF condition, and in the %PUT statement. You receive only one warning message, in the %LET statement, because the macro processor attempts to resolve &A when it resolves &SYSBUFFR. However, the %NRQUOTE function quotes the string **&A** in the value of NAME, and the macro processor does not attempt to resolve it again. Therefore, the macro processor does not issue a warning message when it resolves &NAME in the %IF condition or in the %PUT statement. In addition, the ampersand does not cause an error in the %IF condition.

Using the %NRBQUOTE function   Names of some firms may contain an unmatched, unmarked quote as well as an ampersand that does not indicate a macro variable reference, as in the following:

```
Santos&D'Amato, Inc.
```

In a resolved value, the %NRBQUOTE function quotes the same items as the %NRQUOTE function and also unmatched, unmarked quotes and parentheses.

The following example modifies macro FIRMS to accept names that contain both *&name* patterns and unmatched quotes:

```
%macro firms2;
   %global code;
   %put Enter the name of the company;
   %input;
   %let name=%nrbquote(&sysbuffr);
   %if &name ne %then %let code=valid;
   %else %let code=invalid;
   %put &name is &code;
%mend firms2;
```

If you invoke FIRMS2 and respond with

```
Santos&D'Amato, Inc.
```

you get the result shown in **Output 10.2**.

Output 10.2   Using the %NRBQUOTE Function

```
11    %macro firms2;
12       %global code;
13       %put Enter the name of the company;
14       %input;
15       %let name=%nrbquote(&sysbuffr);
16       %if &name ne %then %let code=valid;
17       %else %let code=invalid;
18       %put &name is &code;
19    %mend firms2;
20    %firms2
Enter the name of the company
WARNING: Apparent symbolic reference D not resolved.
Santos&D'Amato, Inc. is valid
```

The macro processor accepts both the ampersand and the unmatched quote, and the ampersand does not interfere with the %EVAL function. As it did with **A&A Autos**, the macro processor issues a warning message because it could not locate macro variable D from **&D'Amato** when it resolved the reference &SYSBUFFR.

Preventing Resolution of a Macro Variable's Value

The %SUPERQ function locates the macro variable named in its argument and quotes the value of that macro variable without permitting any resolution to occur. It quotes all items that may require quoting at macro execution. Because %SUPERQ does not attempt any resolution of its argument, the macro processor does not issue any warning messages that a macro variable reference or a macro invocation has not been resolved. Therefore, even when using the %NRQUOTE or %NRBQUOTE function allows the program to work correctly, you can use the %SUPERQ function to eliminate unwanted warning messages from the SAS log. Note that the argument of %SUPERQ must be a single macro variable name.

This example shows how the %SUPERQ function affects two macro invocations, one for a macro that has been defined and one for an undefined macro:

```
%macro a;
   %put this is a;
%mend a;

%macro test;
   %put Enter two values;
   %input;
   %put %superq(sysbuffr);        /* Note absence of ampersand */
%mend test;
```

Suppose you invoke macro TEST and respond to the prompt as shown:

```
%test
Enter two values:
%a %x
```

The %PUT statement simply writes the following line:

```
%a %x
```

It does not invoke macro A, and it does not issue a warning message that %X was not resolved.

The following two examples compare the %SUPERQ function with other macro quoting functions.

Example: Using the %SUPERQ function to prevent warning messages   The discussions of the %NRQUOTE and %NRBQUOTE functions showed that those functions cause the macro processor to attempt to resolve the patterns &*name* and %*name* the first time it encounters them; if the macro processor cannot resolve them, it quotes the ampersand or percent sign so that later uses of the value do not cause the macro processor to recognize them. However, if the MERROR or SERROR option is in effect, the macro processor issues a warning message that the reference or invocation was not resolved.

Macro FIRMS3, shown here, adapts examples from the %NRQUOTE and %NRBQUOTE discussions to show how the %SUPERQ function can prevent unwanted warning messages:

```
%macro firms3;
    %global code;
    %put Enter the name of the company;
    %input;
    %let name=%superq(sysbuffr);
    %if &name ne %then %let code=valid;
    %else %let code=invalid;
    %put &name is &code;
%mend firms3;
```

If you invoke macro FIRMS3 twice and respond with the companies

```
A&A Autos
Santos&D'Amato
```

you get the SAS log shown in **Output 10.3**.

Output 10.3   Using %SUPERQ to Prevent Warning Messages

```
21    %macro firms3;
22        %global code;
23        %put Enter the name of the company;
24        %input;
25        %let name=%superq(sysbuffr);
26        %if &name ne %then %let code=valid;
27        %else %let code=invalid;
28        %put &name is &code;
29    %mend firms3;
30    %firms3
Enter the name of the company
A&A Autos is valid
31    %firms3
Enter the name of the company
Santos&D'Amato is valid
```

Example: Using the %SUPERQ function to enter macro keywords   Suppose you create an online training system in which users can enter problems and questions that another macro prints for you later. The user's response to a %INPUT statement is assigned to a local macro variable and then to a global macro variable. Because the user is asking questions about macros, he or she may enter all sorts of macro variable references and macro calls as examples of problems, as well as unmatched, unmarked quotes and parentheses. If you quote the response with %QUOTE, you have to use several %PUT statements to warn the user about responses that cause problems. If you use %BQUOTE, you need fewer instructions to the user, and if you use the %SUPERQ function, you need fewer still. Macros ASK1, ASK2, and ASK3 show how the macro code becomes simpler as you change quoting functions.

Macro ASK1 shows the warnings you must include in a macro when you quote the user's response with %QUOTE. Match the circled numbers to the paragraphs that follow.

```
%macro ask1;
    %global a;
    %local x; ❶
    %put Describe the problem.;
    %put Do not use macro language keywords, macro calls,;
    %put or macro variable references.;
    %put You must mark any unmatched quotes or parentheses;
    %put with a percent sign.;
    %put Enter /// when you are finished.;
    %do %until(%quote(&sysbuffr) eq %str(///)); ❷  ❸
        %input; ❹
        %let x=&x %quote(&sysbuffr); ❺
    %end;
    %let a=&x; ❻
    %mend ask1;
```

1. The local variable X contains the user's response, and the global variable A makes the value available to other macros in the training system.
2. In the %DO %UNTIL statement, the %QUOTE function prevents any evaluation of items in the value of SYSBUFFR by the implicit %EVAL function. Because the %QUOTE function does not quote all items that a user may enter, you must issue a long list of warning messages to try to prevent the user from entering values that the %QUOTE function does not handle.
3. The three slashes are enclosed in the %STR function to prevent the implicit %EVAL function from treating the slashes as division operators. Note: The slashes do not cause a problem at compilation because the %EVAL function works at execution. However, because the slashes are visible when you create the macro, you can use %STR.
4. Each execution of the %INPUT statement assigns one line of text as the value of SYSBUFFR.
5. The %QUOTE function in the value of X quotes any unmatched quotes or parentheses *that the user has marked with a percent sign* before assigning the value to X.
6. Because a quoted value remains quoted, you do not have to quote the value of A.

The user can invoke macro ASK1 and enter a problem as shown:

```
%ask1
Describe the problem.
Do not use macro language keywords, macro calls,
or macro variable references.
You must mark any unmatched quotes or parentheses
with a percent sign.
Enter /// when you are finished.
I created a macro variable inside a macro, but I couldn%'t use
it later in my program. Why?
///
```

Macro ASK1 is lengthy, and it requires the user to mark the unmatched quote in the response. Macro ASK2, below, shows how the macro looks when you use the %BQUOTE function:

```
%macro ask2;
   %global a;
   %local x;
   %put Describe the problem.;
   %put Do not use macro language keywords, macro calls,;
   %put or macro variable references.;
   %put Enter /// when you are finished.;
   %do %until(%bquote(&sysbuffr) eq %str(///));
      %input;
      %let x=&x %bquote(&sysbuffr);
   %end;
   %let a=&x;
%mend ask2;
```

Macro ASK2 does not include a warning about unmatched quotes and parentheses. The user can invoke macro ASK2 and enter a problem as shown:

```
%ask2
Describe the problem.
Do not use macro language keywords, macro calls,
or macro variable references.
Enter /// when you are finished.
Why didn't my macro run when I called it? (It had three
parameters, but I wasn't using any of them.) It ran
after I submitted the next statement.
///
```

Notice that both the first and second lines of the response contain an unmatched, unmarked quote and parenthesis. Macro ASK3, shown here, modifies macro ASK2 so that the %INPUT statement accepts macro language keywords and does not attempt to resolve macro calls and macro variable references:

```
%macro ask3;
   %global a;
   %local x;
   %put Describe the problem.;
   %put Enter /// when you are finished.;
   %do %until(%superq(sysbuffr) eq %str(///));      /* No ampersand */
      %input;
      %let x=&x %superq(sysbuffr);                  /* No ampersand */
   %end;
   %let a=&x;
%mend ask3;
```

The user can invoke macro ASK3 and enter a response as shown:

```
%ask3
Describe the problem.
Enter /// when you are finished.
My macro ADDRESS starts with %MACRO ADDRESS(COMPANY,
CITY);. I called it with %ADDRESS(SMITH-JONES, INC., BOSTON),
but it said I had too many parameters. What happened?
///
```

The response contains a macro language keyword, a macro invocation, and unmatched parentheses.

Character Functions That Perform Quoting

The %QSCAN, %QSUBSTR, and %QUPCASE functions work exactly like the %SCAN, %SUBSTR, and %UPCASE functions except that they quote the returned value. (The %SCAN, %SUBSTR, and %UPCASE functions return an unquoted result, even if the argument was quoted.) The items quoted are the same as those quoted by the %NRBQUOTE function.

Quoting a Scanned Excerpt: The %QSCAN Function

The following macro uses the %QSCAN function to assign items in the value of SYSBUFFR as the values of separate macro variables. Match the circled numbers to the paragraphs below.

```
%macro splitit;
   %put What character separates the values?; ❶
   %input;
   %let s=%bquote(&sysbuffr); ❷
   %put Enter three values.;
   %input;
   %local i;
   %do i=1 %to 3; ❸
      %global x&i;
      %let x&i=%qscan(%superq(sysbuffr),&i,&s); ❹
   %end;
%mend splitit;


%splitit
What character separates the values?
#

Enter three values.
Fischer Books#Smith&Sons#Sarah's Sweet Shoppe ❺
```

1. This question allows you to choose a delimiter for the %QSCAN function that does not appear in the values you are going to enter.
2. Quoting the value of SYSBUFFR with the %BQUOTE function allows the user to choose a quote or parenthesis as a delimiter if necessary.
3. The iterative %DO loop creates a global macro variable for each segment of SYSBUFFR and assigns it the value of that segment.
4. The %SUPERQ function quotes the value of SYSBUFFR in the first argument of the %QSCAN function. It prevents any resolution of SYSBUFFR.
5. The %QSCAN function returns quoted segments of the value of SYSBUFFR; thus, the unmatched quote in **Sarah's Sweet Shoppe** and the &name pattern in **Smith&Sons** do not cause problems.

Quoting a Substring: The %QSUBSTR Function

Macro QLEFT (discussed in Chapter 7, "The Autocall Facility") is an autocall macro supplied by SAS Institute that illustrates the %QSUBSTR function. Match the circled numbers to the paragraphs that follow.

```
%macro qleft(text); ❶
   %local i;
   %if %length(&text)=0 %then %let text=%str( ); ❸
   %let i=%verify(&text,%str( )); ❷
   %if &i %then %qsubstr(&text,&i); ❹
%mend qleft;
```

1. Macro QLEFT returns a quoted value without leading blanks.
2. The VERIFY macro in the SAS autocall library determines the position of the first nonblank character in parameter TEXT.
3. If the value of TEXT is null, QLEFT assigns a value of blank so that macro VERIFY returns a 0.
4. If the position is not 0 (that is, a nonblank character is present), the %QSUBSTR function generates a quoted value beginning at that position in the value of TEXT.

Quoting Text Converted to Uppercase: The %QUPCASE Function

Suppose, in the user training macro shown earlier, you want to use the word **STOP** instead of three slashes to indicate the end of input. Now you must convert the response to uppercase before using it in the %DO %UNTIL expression. Macro ASK4 modifies macro ASK3 to illustrate the %QUPCASE function. Match the circled numbers with the explanations that follow.

```
%macro ask4;
   %global a;
   %local x;
   %put Describe the problem.;
   %put Enter STOP when you are finished.; ❶
   %do %until(%qupcase(%superq(sysbuffr)) eq STOP); ❷
      %input;
      %let x=&x %superq(sysbuffr);
   %end;
   %let a=&x; ❸
%mend ask4;


%ask4
Describe the problem.
Enter STOP when you are finished.
Why can't I use &A or %B as a macro name in a %MACRO statement?
stop
```

1. Because a user may enter the string **stop** in either lower- or uppercase, you must convert the value of SYSBUFFR to uppercase before comparing it to **STOP**.
2. The %SUPERQ function prevents resolution of the value of SYSBUFFR. The %QUPCASE function converts that value to uppercase while maintaining the quoting.
3. The %LET statement does not convert the user's response to uppercase; the value is assigned to variable X as the user entered it.

The response contains an unmatched quote, the mnemonic operator OR, and a macro keyword.

UNQUOTING QUOTED TEXT

In general, quoted items do not cause problems—you quoted them in order to make the macro processor treat them as text. This section discusses situations in which you need to unquote quoted text with the %UNQUOTE function and gives some background on why you need to use it.

If you do not use the %UNQUOTE function, the SAS System unquotes quoted tokens when they cross the macro boundary in the word queue, shown in **Figure 10.1.**

Word Queue

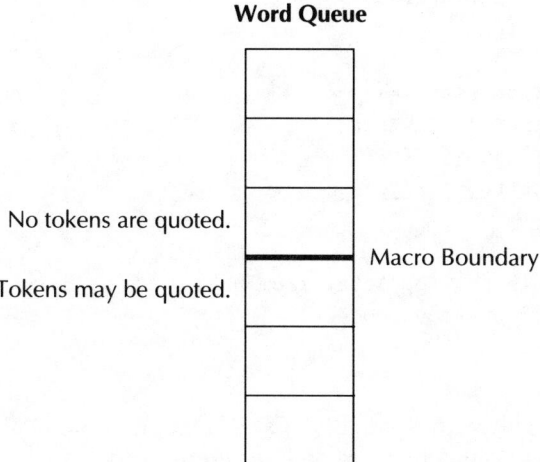

Figure 10.1 describes the following elements:

No tokens are quoted.

Macro Boundary

Tokens may be quoted.

Figure 10.1 Macro Boundary in Word Queue

Unquoting tokens automatically at the macro boundary allows the following statement to store a value containing quoted semicolons, whereas the SAS compiler later receives a PROC PRINT step in which the semicolons work normally:

```
%let p=%str(proc print; run;);
```

At times, you need to unquote the tokens before they reach the macro boundary; in that case, you must use the %UNQUOTE function. Situations in which you may need to unquote a token are

- when you need to use a quoted token with its original meaning later in the macro
- when a quoting function has altered the tokenization of input.

Both of these cases are described below.

Restoring the Meaning of a Token Later in a Macro

The following example illustrates using a value twice: once in quoted form and once in unquoted form.

Suppose macro ANALYZE is part of a system that allows you to compare the output of two statistical models interactively. First, you enter an operator to specify the relationship you want to test (one result greater than another, equal to another, and so forth). Macro ANALYZE tests the quoted value of the operator to verify that you have entered it correctly, uses the unquoted value to compare the values indicated, and writes a message. Match the circled numbers to the paragraphs below.

```
%macro analyze(stat);
   data _null_;
      set out1;
      call symput('v1',&stat);
   run;
   data _null_;
      set out2;
      call symput('v2',&stat);
   run;
```

```
      %put Preliminary test. Enter the operator.;
      %input;
      %let op=%bquote(&sysbuffr); ❶
      %if &op=%str(=<) %then %let op=%str(<=); ❷    ❸
      %else %if &op=%str(=>) %then %let op=%str(>=);
      %if &v1 %unquote(&op) &v2 %then ❹
         %put You may proceed with the analysis.;
      %else
         %do;
            %put &stat from out1 is not &op &stat from out2.;
            %put Please check your previous models.;
         %end;
   %mend analyze;
```

1. You quote the value of SYSBUFFR with the %BQUOTE function, which quotes resolved items including unmatched, unmarked quotes and parentheses (but excluding the ampersand and percent sign).

2. The %IF condition compares the value of OP to a string to see whether the value of OP contains the correct symbols for the operator. If the value contains symbols in the wrong order, the %THEN statement corrects the symbols. Because a quoted value remains quoted, you do not need to quote the reference &OP in the left side of the %IF condition.

3. Because you can see the characters in the right side of the %IF condition and in the %LET statement when you define the macro, you can use the %STR function to quote them. Quoting them once at compilation is more efficient than quoting them at each execution of ANALYZE.

4. To use the value of OP as the operator in the %IF condition, you must restore the meaning of the operator with the %UNQUOTE function.

Restoring Normal Tokenization

When a quoting function has altered the normal tokenization of text, mysterious-looking problems may occur. The most common symptom is that the SAS statements generated by a macro look correct, but the SAS System is not processing them as you expect. You can use the example below as a reference when your programs show similar problems.

In the following example, you enter a value enclosed in single quotes in response to a %INPUT statement. Macro ASSIGN1 quotes the response with the %BQUOTE function, in case you entered an unmatched quote, and then generates an assignment statement. However, ASSIGN1 does not produce the result you intended. Match the circled numbers to the paragraphs below.

```
   options mprint; ❶
   %macro assign1;
      %*first try--wrong;
      %put Input a value enclosed in single quotes.; ❷
      %input;
      %let x=%bquote(&sysbuffr); ❸
      %let qfirst=%qsubstr(&x,1,1); ❹
      %let qlast=%qsubstr(&x,%length(&x),1);
```

```
%if &qfirst=%str(%') and &qlast=%str(%') %then
    %do; ❺
        status=&x;
        run;
    %end;
%else
    %do;
        %put The value you gave was &x..;
        %put The value must be surrounded by single quotes.;
        %put Please call this macro again and enter a valid value.;
    %end;
%mend assign1;
```

1. The MPRINT option, described in Appendix 1, "SAS System Options Used with the Macro Facility," displays SAS statements produced by macro execution.
2. The %PUT statement prompts you for a character literal to be used in an assignment statement.
3. Because a user may enter an unmatched quote by mistake, you enclose the value of SYSBUFFR in the %BQUOTE function before you assign it to X.
4. These two statements identify the first and last characters entered.
5. The %IF statement tests whether the first and last characters of the value input are single quotes. If so, ASSIGN1 generates the assignment statement. If not, ASSIGN1 writes messages to the user.

Suppose you invoke ASSIGN1 in the following program:

```
data new;
    set old;
    %assign1
```

When the macro processor prompts you with

```
Input a value enclosed in single quotes.
```

you respond with the following:

```
'ok'
```

Output 10.4 shows the SAS log that results from macro ASSIGN1.

Output 10.4   DATA Step Generated by ASSIGN1

```
38    options mprint;
39    %macro assign1;
40        %*first try--wrong;
41        %put Input a value enclosed in single quotes.;
42        %input;
43        %let x=%bquote(&sysbuffr);
44        %let qfirst=%qsubstr(&x,1,1);
45        %let qlast=%qsubstr(&x,%length(&x),1);
46        %if &qfirst=%str(%') and &qlast=%str(%') %then
47            %do;
48                status=&x;
49                run;
50            %end;
51        %else
52            %do;
53                %put The value you gave was &x..;
54                %put The value must be surrounded by single quotes.;
55                %put Please call this macro again and enter a valid value.;
56            %end;
57    %mend assign1;
```

(continued on next page)

```
(continued from previous page)

58    data new;
59       set old;
60       %assign1
Input a value enclosed in single quotes.
NOTE: Line generated by the macro variable "X".
60    'ok'
      -
      386
MPRINT(ASSIGN1):    STATUS='OK';
MPRINT(ASSIGN1):    RUN;

ERROR 386-185: Expecting an arithmetic expression.

NOTE: The SAS System stopped processing this step because of errors.
WARNING: The data set WORK.NEW may be incomplete.  When this step was
         stopped there were 0 observations and 3 variables.
NOTE: The DATA statement used 0.06 CPU seconds and 1851K.
```

In the statements displayed by the MPRINT option, the statement

```
STATUS='OK';
```

looks like an ordinary assignment statement, but the SAS System issues error messages. Why?

The word scanner usually reads a statement of this type as four tokens: STATUS, =, 'ok', and ;. However, because you quoted the value of SYSBUFFR with the %BQUOTE function, the single quotes surrounding OK are now separate special-character tokens. The word scanner places them in the word queue separately instead of using them as the boundaries of the literal token 'ok'. Therefore, the SAS compiler receives an assignment statement whose value contains the name token OK and two special-character tokens. Because this form of the assignment statement is not acceptable, the SAS compiler issues error messages.

To cause the word scanner to use the single quotes as boundaries of the literal token 'ok', you must unquote them before the word scanner reads them. Macro ASSIGN2 shows the corrected macro, and **Output 10.5** shows the SAS log that results.

```
%macro assign2;
   %*second try--right;
   %put Input a value enclosed in single quotes.;
   %input;
   %let x=%bquote(&sysbuffr);
   %let qfirst=%qsubstr(&x,1,1);
   %let qlast=%qsubstr(&x,%length(&x),1);
   %if &qfirst=%str(%') and &qlast=%str(%') %then
      %do;
         status=%unquote(&x);
         run;
      %end;
   %else
      %do;
         %put The value you gave was &x..;
         %put The value must be surrounded by single quotes.;
         %put Please call this macro again and enter a valid value.;
      %end;
%mend assign2;
```

Output 10.5   DATA Step Produced Correctly

```
71  %macro assign2;
72      %*second try--right;
73      %put Input a value enclosed in single quotes.;
74      %input;
75      %let x=%bquote(&sysbuffr);
76      %let qfirst=%qsubstr(&x,1,1);
77      %let qlast=%qsubstr(&x,%length(&x),1);
78      %if &qfirst=%str(%') and &qlast=%str(%') %then
79          %do;
80              status=%unquote(&x);
81              run;
82          %end;
83      %else
84          %do;
85              %put The value you gave was &x..;
86              %put The value must be surrounded by single quotes.;
87              %put Please call this macro again and enter a valid value.;
88          %end;
89  %mend assign2;
90  data new;
91      set old;
92      %assign2
Input a value enclosed in single quotes.
MPRINT(ASSIGN2):    STATUS='ok';
MPRINT(ASSIGN2):    RUN;

NOTE: The data set WORK.NEW has 100 observations and 3 variables.
NOTE: The DATA statement used 0.06 CPU seconds and 1851K.
```

Enclosing the macro variable reference in the %UNQUOTE function causes the word scanner to interpret the characters 'ok' as a literal token, and the SAS compiler receives an acceptable SAS statement.

REFERENCE TABLES

This section gives several tables you can use as a reference for macro quoting.

Marking Unmatched Quotes and Parentheses

Table 10.1 shows how to mark unmatched quotes and parentheses in the argument of the %STR, %NRSTR, %QUOTE, and %NRQUOTE functions.

Table 10.1   Marking Unmatched Quotes and Parentheses

Notation	Meaning	Example
%'	unmatched single quote	%LET X=%STR(TR=A%'); quoted value stored: TR=A';
%"	unmatched double quote	%LET T=%STR(TITLE %"FIRST); quoted value stored: TITLE "FIRST
%(	unmatched left parenthesis	%LET A=%STR(LOG%(12); quoted value stored: LOG(12
%)	unmatched right parenthesis	%LET B=%STR(345%)); quoted value stored: 345)
%%	percent sign next to quote or parenthesis in text	%LET P=%STR(TITLE "20%%"); quoted value stored: TITLE "20%";

Items That May Require Quoting

Table 10.2 summarizes items that may require quoting in macro programs.

Table 10.2   Items That May Require Quoting and When Quoting Is Needed

Item	When Item Needs to Be Quoted	Remarks
+ − */ < > = ^¬~ | LE LT EQ NE GE GT AND OR NOT	when it should not be treated as an operator in the argument of an explicit or implicit %EVAL function	They are quoted by all quoting functions. One source of problems is the English words AND, OR, and NOT being interpreted as mnemonic operators by an implicit %EVAL. See **Table 10.3** for details.
blank	when a leading, trailing, or isolated blank is treated as a character rather than ignored	It is quoted by all quoting functions. See **Table 10.3** for details.
;	when it ends a macro program statement prematurely	It is quoted by all quoting functions. See **Table 10.3** for details.
, (comma)	when it should not indicate a new function argument, parameter, or parameter value	It is quoted by all quoting functions. See **Table 10.3** for details.
' " ()	when it is unmatched in the argument of the %STR-%NRSTR or %QUOTE-%NRQUOTE functions	There is no need to mark unmatched items in the arguments of the %BQUOTE-%NRBQUOTE and %SUPERQ functions. Using %BQUOTE-%NRBQUOTE is preferable to %QUOTE-%NRQUOTE when the value contains unmatched items. See **Table 10.3** for details.
%*name* &*name*	depends on what the expression resolves into	%NRSTR, %NRQUOTE, and %NRBQUOTE quote these patterns. To use %SUPERQ with a macro variable, omit the ampersand from *name*.

Comparison of Quoting Functions

Table 10.3 compares quoting functions to each other by the items they quote and the time the function takes effect.

Table 10.3   Comparison of Quoting Functions

Groups of Items That May Require Quoting	
Group	Items
A	$+ - ^* / < > = \neg \,\hat{}\, \sim \; ; , \mid$ blank AND, OR, NOT, EQ, NE, LE, LT, GE, GT
B	& %
C	unmatched, unmarked ' " ()

List of Functions		
Function	Affects Groups	Works at
%STR %NRSTR	A A, B	macro compilation
%QUOTE %NRQUOTE	A A, B	macro execution (after resolution)
%BQUOTE %NRBQUOTE	A, C A, B, C	macro execution (after resolution)
%SUPERQ	A, B, C	macro execution (prevents resolution)

MACRO
APPLICATIONS

Writing Utility Macros

Chapter 11
Writing Utility Macros

This chapter illustrates simple macros that can be used in many situations. The macros are grouped into several broad categories:

- user-written macro functions
- macros that supplement SAS functions
- macros that supplement SAS statements and SAS Display Manager System commands
- utility DATA steps and PROC steps
- a simple utility macro system.

Of course, you can write many other types of simple macros. These categories present macros that share some features. It may help you to know, when you approach a particular task, the general characteristics your macro will probably have.

Contents

WRITING MACROS FOR GENERAL USE

Simple, single-purpose macros like the ones shown in this chapter can provide you with a useful library of utility macros, especially if you use them in an autocall library. When you write macros for other people to use, you should take steps to keep your macros from interfering with their programs. The macros in this chapter illustrate most of the following rules:

- Use local macro variables whenever possible; create global macro variables only to contain values that need to be available outside the macro.
- Choose the names for global macro variables carefully. Users need to be able to remember the names (even if they seldom use the macro that generates them), and the macro names must not duplicate other global macro variable names.
- Avoid allowing a macro to issue "harmless" warning messages and notes. A person who does not know the structure of the macro does not know whether a message is harmless.
- If a macro generates part of a DATA step, create only the SAS variables that the user expects in the program. Use long SAS expressions instead of generating a series of assignment statements. If you must create other SAS variables, label them to indicate their origin and give them distinctive names that are not likely to duplicate variable names in the user's data set.
- Avoid creating SAS data sets, unless that is the purpose of the macro. If you must create a SAS data set, use a distinctive name that is not likely to duplicate a user's data set name. You can also include a PROC DATASETS step that deletes the data sets created earlier in the macro.
- Provide information about the intended use of the macro, what it requires, what it produces, and who wrote it, and provide a history of modifications. If you keep your utility macros in an autocall library, providing this information makes it easier for you or others to use and maintain your macros. The header portion of the macro VERIFY in the autocall library supplied by SAS Institute provides syntax information, a brief description, a usage example, and other notes about the macro definition that contains it, as shown here:

```
%*******************************************************************;
%*                                                                *;
%*  MACRO: VERIFY                                                  *;
%*                                                                *;
%*  USAGE: 1) %verify(argument,target)                            *;
%*                                                                *;
%*  DESCRIPTION:                                                   *;
%*    This macro returns the position of the first character in the *;
%*    argument that is not in the target value. If every character *;
%*    that is in the argument is also in the target value then this *;
%*    function returns a value of 0. The syntax for its use       *;
%*    is similar to that of native macro functions.               *;
%*                                                                *;
%*    Eg. %let i=%verify(&argtext,&targtext)                       *;
%*                                                                *;
%*  NOTES:                                                         *;
%*    Both values to this function must have non-zero lengths or an *;
%*    error message will be produced.                             *;
%*                                                                *;
%*******************************************************************;
```

USER-WRITTEN MACRO FUNCTIONS

User-written macro functions are macros that process arguments (usually given as parameter values) and generate a single piece of text. You can use user-written macro functions anywhere that you can use the functions supplied as part of the macro language. Most of the macros in the SAS autocall library are user-written macro functions.

Determining whether a Macro Variable Exists

Macro SYMCHK, shown here, checks to see if a macro variable is defined:

```
%macro symchk(name);
    %if %nrquote(&&&name)=%nrstr(&)&name %then
        %let yesno=NO;
    %else
        %let yesno=YES;
    &yesno
%mend symchk;
```

When you invoke macro SYMCHK, the parameter NAME is the name of a macro variable, not a macro variable reference. The following expression always yields a string consisting of a quoted ampersand followed by the value of NAME:

```
%nrstr(&)&name
```

Because the ampersand is quoted, this macro variable reference does not resolve. If NAME is not defined, the %IF condition becomes &NAME=&NAME, which is true, so SYMCHK assigns the value **NO** to macro variable YESNO, and the SAS System prints the following warning:

```
WARNING: Apparent symbolic reference macro-variable-name not resolved.
```

If the value of NAME is a defined macro variable, the left side of the %IF condition resolves to the macro variable value, the %IF condition is false, and SYMCHK assigns the value **YES** to macro variable YESNO. The following macro, MESSAGE, uses macro SYMCHK to conditionally write a message in the SAS log:

```
%macro message(varname);
    %if %symchk(&varname)=NO %then
      %put Macro variable &varname is not defined.;
    %else
      %put Macro variable &varname exists and has value: &&&varname;
%mend message;
```

Submitting the statements

```
%let x=This is a value.;
%message(x)
%message(y)
```

produces these lines in the SAS log:

```
%let x=This is a value.;
%message(x);
Macro variable x is defined and has value: This is a value.
%message(y);

WARNING: Apparent symbolic reference Y not resolved.
Macro variable y is not defined.
```

The attempt to resolve an undefined macro variable produces a warning in the SAS log. If you set system option NOSERROR before invoking macro MESSAGE, no warning appears when you attempt to resolve undefined macro variables.

Generating a List of Names

Several examples in this book generate a list of names. Macro NAMES, shown here, gives a general form in which you specify the number of names you want and, optionally, the prefix:

```
%macro names(number,prefix=v);
   %local i;
   %do i=1 %to &number;
      &prefix&i
   %end;
%mend names;
```

In macro NAMES, parameter NUMBER indicates the number of names to be generated. Parameter PREFIX gives the first part of the name so that you can avoid conflicts with other SAS names in a program. This example uses macro NAMES to generate a list of macro variable names in a %GLOBAL statement:

```
%global %names(10);
```

The complete %GLOBAL statement becomes

```
%global v1 v2 v3 v4 v5 v6 v7 v8 v9 v10;
```

Counting the Number of Times a Character Appears

Macro COUNTC counts the number of times a character appears in a value. Match the circled numbers to the explanations that follow.

```
%macro countc(target,char); ❶
   %local pos tot; ❷
   %let tot=0; ❸
   %do %until(&pos=0); ❹
      %let pos=%index(&target,&char);
      %if &pos ne 0 %then
         %do; ❺
            %let tot=%eval(&tot+1);
            %if &pos ne %length(&target) %then
               %let target=%qsubstr(&target,&pos+1);
            %else %let pos=0; ❻
         %end;
   %end;
   &tot ❼
%mend countc;
```

1. Parameter TARGET gives the value to be searched, and CHAR gives the character to be counted.
2. POS is the position of the value of CHAR within the value of TARGET, and TOT contains the number of times the character in CHAR occurs in the value of TARGET.
3. This statement initializes TOT to 0.
4. The %DO %UNTIL loop does the counting. The %INDEX function determines whether the value of CHAR is present within the value of TARGET.

5. If the character is present, the %DO group increments the value of TOT and produces a new string for the %INDEX function to search. Because the %DO %UNTIL statement checks its condition at the bottom of the loop, the loop is always executed at least once.
6. If the character being counted is the last character in the value of TARGET, the %LET statement assigns POS the value 0 rather than producing a new string to be searched. (Otherwise, the %QSUBSTR function would issue a harmless but confusing warning message because its second argument would be greater than the length of TARGET.)
7. When all occurrences of the character have been found (including 0 occurrences), macro COUNTC returns the value of TOT.

In macro COUNTC, macro variable POS contains the result of the %INDEX function. You could also write the %INDEX function each time it is needed instead of creating POS. However, if you need a macro expression more than once, it is more efficient to assign the result of the expression to a macro variable. Thus, each iteration of the %DO %UNTIL loop executes the %INDEX function once and uses the result four times.

In this example, you use macro COUNTC to count the number of single quotes in the value of macro variable X:

```
%let x=%str(TIME='9:15'T;);
%put ***%countc(&x,%str(%'))***;
```

The %PUT statement writes

```
***2***
```

Each time the %INDEX function locates a single quote, COUNTC produces a quoted substring of the current value of TARGET. In this example, the new substrings are

```
9:15'T;
T;
```

Since the %QSUBSTR function removes the significance of the single quote and the semicolon, they do not cause problems in the value TARGET.

Counting the Number of Words in a String

Macro WORDS counts the number of words in a character string and returns that value. Match the circled numbers to the paragraphs that follow.

```
%macro words(string); ❶
   %local count word; ❷
   %let count=1;
   %let word=%qscan(&string,&count,%str( )); ❸
   %do %while(&word ne); ❹
      %let count=%eval(&count+1);
      %let word=%qscan(&string,&count,%str( ));
   %end;
   %eval(&count-1) ❺
%mend words;
```

1. Parameter STRING contains the character string to be analyzed.
2. Macro variable COUNT contains a running total of the number of words in parameter STRING, and WORD temporarily contains each word identified in parameter STRING.
3. The %LET statement selects the first word in STRING using the %QSCAN function. The %QSCAN function quotes the value, including mnemonic operators such as AND and OR, so that the value does not cause problems for the implicit %EVAL function in the %DO %WHILE

condition. The %QSCAN function divides words only by blanks; therefore, in the following string the first word is A-:

```
A- B- AND C-
```

However, you can add more delimiters to the list if necessary. See Chapter 4, "Macro Functions," for more information on the %QSCAN function.

4. The %DO %WHILE loop executes as long as a word is present (that is, the value of WORD is not null). The first %LET statement increments the value of COUNT, and the second %LET statement selects the next word.

5. Because the value of COUNT is incremented before the %LET statement selects a new word, the value of COUNT is always one more than the number of words in the string. Therefore, the %EVAL function returns the number of words in the string.

The following macro, GVARS, uses macro WORDS to count the number of words in parameter STRING:

```
%macro gvars(string,vname=dsn);
   %local i j;
   %let i=%words(&string);
   %global %names(&i,prefix=&vname);
   %do j=1 %to &i;
      %let &vname&j=%qscan(&string,&j);
   %end;
%mend gvars;
```

Then, it uses macro NAMES (seen earlier in this chapter) to create that many global variables and uses a %DO loop to assign each word in STRING to a global variable. Since WORDS gives the number of words in STRING, the %DO loop iterates the right number of times.

MACROS THAT SUPPLEMENT SAS FUNCTIONS

Macros that supplement SAS functions are designed to be used as part of a SAS statement. They contain a SAS expression that is too long or inconvenient to program each time you need it. SAS variable names used in the expression are replaced by macro variable references. Each time you use the macro, you give the names of the SAS variables as parameter values in the macro call.

Because these macros issue a SAS expression, not a complete SAS statement, you can use them anywhere you use a SAS function. Note: You should enclose the expression in parentheses so that the expression remains a unit when used as part of another SAS expression.

Producing a Numeric Value from a Character Fractional Value

You can read data values containing fractions as a character variable and use macro FRAC, shown here, to create a numeric value from the character value:

```
%macro frac(var);
   (input(scan(&var,1,'/'),8.) / input(scan(&var,2,'/'),8.))
%mend frac;
```

Macro FRAC generates a SAS expression that reads the numerator and denominator of the fraction and performs the division. This example illustrates two uses of FRAC:

```
data test;
   input a $;
   f=%frac(a);
   inv=1/%frac(a);
   cards;
9/2
5/6
495/612
;
```

The SAS System sees these statements:

```
DATA TEST;
   INPUT A $;
   F=(INPUT(SCAN(A,1,'/'),8.) / INPUT(SCAN(A,2,'/'),8.));
   INV=1/(INPUT(SCAN(A,1,'/'),8.) / INPUT(SCAN(A,2,'/'),8.));
   CARDS;
9/2
5/6
495/612
;
```

Variable INV illustrates the reason for enclosing the expression in macro FRAC in parentheses. In the first execution of the DATA step, the value of INV is 1/(9/2) or .2222222. . . . Without the outer parentheses, the value would be 1/9/2 or .055555. . . .

You can begin to program a macro containing a long SAS expression as a DATA step containing a series of simple assignment statements. When the DATA step produces the correct result, condense the series of statements into a single statement with a long expression. Finally, replace the source variable's name with a macro variable reference; enclose the expression in parentheses and then in a macro definition; and define a macro parameter that creates the macro variable referenced. These stages show the development of macro FRAC:

```
/* program the calculation step by step */
data test1;
   input x $;
   a=scan(x,1,'/');
   b=scan(x,2,'/');
   c=input(a,8.);
   d=input(b,8.);
   e=c / d;
   put _all_;
   cards;
3/2
;
```

```
/* condense the steps */
data test2;
   input x $;
   c=input(scan(x,1,'/'),8.);
   d=input(scan(x,2,'/'),8.);
   e=c / d;
   put _all_;
   cards;
3/2
;


/* condense the steps further */
data test3;
   input x $;
   e=input(scan(x,1,'/'),8.) / input(scan(x,2,'/'),8.);
   put _all_;
   cards;
3/2
;


/* build the macro */
%macro frac(var);
   (input(scan(&var,1,'/'),8.) / input(scan(&var,2,'/'),8.))
%mend frac;
```

Producing the Lowercase Value of a Character String

Macro LOWCASE uses the DATA step function TRANSLATE to change uppercase
values in a character variable or string to lowercase values.

Macro LOWCASE complements the DATA step function UPCASE. Execution
of this macro results in a character value in which all uppercase alphabetic characters in the argument are lowercase, and all other characters are the same.

```
%macro lowcase(item);
    translate(&item,"abcdefghijklmnopqrstuvwxyz",
                    "ABCDEFGHIJKLMNOPQRSTUVWXYZ")
%mend lowcase;
```

The value you pass to LOWCASE as the argument must be either a quoted character string or the name of a DATA step variable containing a character value.

The following DATA step demonstrates one use for the LOWCASE function:

```
data weights;
   length name $ 20;
   input name $ weight;
   name = substr(name,1,1)||%lowcase(substr(name,2));
   put name weight;
cards;
JOE 155
RAOUL 147
KAMAL 115
JADWIGA 123
;
```

In this example, the value for DATA step variable NAME is all uppercase. The assignment statement preserves the first character of each value for NAME using the SUBSTR function. Then macro LOWCASE, together with the SUBSTR function, gets the lowercase equivalent for the rest of the value of NAME. On the right side of the assignment statement, the two parts are concatenated. The PUT statement writes the following in the SAS log:

```
Joe 155
Raoul 147
Kamal 115
Jadwiga 123
```

The main reason to use a macro to translate values from uppercase to lowercase is convenience. Macros such as LOWCASE save many keystrokes and are best utilized as autocall macros.

MACROS THAT SUPPLEMENT SAS STATEMENTS AND DISPLAY MANAGER COMMANDS

The macros in this section generate complete SAS statements or display manager commands. You can use them anywhere you use the SAS statements or commands they generate.

Renaming a Series of Variables

The following sections show two macros that rename a series of variables in a data set using two different methods: the RENAME statement and the RENAME= data set option.

RENAME Statement

Suppose you need to rename a long series of variables, for example, INFANT1–INFANT10 to CHILD1–CHILD10. Macro RENSTMT, shown here, generates the RENAME statement:

```
%macro renstmt(old=,new=,n=);
   %local i;
   rename
   %do i=1 %to &n;
       &old&i=&new&i
   %end;
   ;
%mend renstmt;
```

Macro RENSTMT generates the keyword RENAME, then the pairs of names in an iterative %DO loop, and then the semicolon. RENSTMT uses keyword parameters to avoid any confusion about which set of names refers to the existing names and which set gives the new ones.

You can use macro RENSTMT in a program such as this one:

```
data study;
   set uspop(keep=agemon84 infant1-infant10);
   agemon87=agemon84+36;
   %renstmt(old=infant,new=child,n=10)
run;
```

After macro execution, the SAS System sees these statements:

```
DATA STUDY;
   SET USPOP(KEEP=AGEMON84 INFANT1-INFANT10);
   AGEMON87=AGEMON84+36;
   RENAME  INFANT1=CHILD1 INFANT2=CHILD2 INFANT3=CHILD3 INFANT4=CHILD4
           INFANT5=CHILD5 INFANT6=CHILD6 INFANT7=CHILD7 INFANT8=CHILD8
           INFANT9=CHILD9 INFANT10=CHILD10
   ;
RUN;
```

RENAME= Data Set Option

You can also write a similar macro that generates a RENAME= data set option. Consider macro RENOPT, shown here:

```
%macro renopt(old=,new=,n=);
   rename=(
   %do i=1 %to &n;
      &old&i=&new&i
   %end;
   )
%mend renopt;
```

Use RENOPT as follows:

```
data study;
   set uspop(keep=agemon84 infant1-infant10 %renopt(old=infant,
             new=child,n=10));
   agemon87=agemon84+36;
run;
```

After macro execution, the SAS System sees these statements:

```
DATA STUDY;
   SET USPOP(KEEP=AGEMON84 INFANT1-INFANT10
   RENAME=(INFANT1=CHILD1 INFANT2=CHILD2 INFANT3=CHILD3
           INFANT4=CHILD4 INFANT5=CHILD5 INFANT6=CHILD6 INFANT7=CHILD7
           INFANT8=CHILD8 INFANT9=CHILD9 INFANT10=CHILD10) );
   AGEMON87=AGEMON84+36;
RUN;
```

Submitting a SAS Program with a Function Key

You can execute a SAS program in a display manager session by pressing a function key. First, define a macro containing the program you need and store it in your autocall library. Macro SALES, shown here, contains a simple SAS program:

```
%macro sales;
   pgm;
   submit "data sales;";
   submit "  infile in;";
   submit "  input dept $ revenue;";
   submit "  if upcase(dept)='TW';";
   submit "proc print;";
   submit "run;";
%mend sales;
```

The PGM display manager command ensures that you submit the program from the PROGRAM EDITOR window. Because text issued by a function key always goes through the display manager processor, use the display manager SUBMIT command to submit the SAS statements for execution. Then define a function key in the PROGRAM EDITOR window to invoke the macro. To do this, use the %KEYDEF command, as in the following example:

```
%keydef f6 '%sales'; /* assuming there is a key named f6 */
```

Note: Using the %KEYDEF statement correctly depends on your terminal and your operating system. See **%KEYDEF Statement** in Chapter 3, "Macro Program Statements," and the SAS documentation for your operating system for more information.

After you define function key 6 to be the invocation for macro SALES, pressing function key 6 anytime during a display manager SAS session executes macro SALES. Display manager sees these commands and submits the corresponding SAS statements:

```
PGM;
SUBMIT "data sales;";
SUBMIT "   infile in;";
SUBMIT "   input dept $ revenue;";
SUBMIT "   if upcase(dept)='TW';";
SUBMIT "proc print;";
SUBMIT "run;";
```

UTILITY DATA STEPS AND PROC STEPS

These macros package small DATA or PROC steps to do a variety of useful things. Because the macro contains a complete DATA or PROC step, you must invoke the macro as a separate step rather than within another DATA or PROC step. Macros in this category either produce a printed report or create a global macro variable containing the information calculated. You then use a macro variable reference to retrieve the information in another SAS step.

Formatting the Value of SYSDATE

Macro FDATE, shown here, assigns a format you specify to the value of SYSDATE:

```
%macro fdate(fmt);
   %global fdate;
   data _null_;
      call symput("fdate",left(put("&sysdate"d,&fmt)));
   run;
%mend fdate;
```

You can use macro FDATE as follows:

```
%fdate(worddate.)
title "Tests for &fdate";
```

If you execute this program on July 28, 1990, the SAS System sees the following program:

```
DATA _NULL_;
   CALL SYMPUT("FDATE",LEFT(PUT("28JUL90"D,WORDDATE.)));
RUN;
TITLE "Tests for July 28, 1990";
```

Determining the Number of Observations in a SAS Data Set

Macro NUMOBS uses a DATA _NULL_ step to retrieve the number of observations in a SAS data set and assign the value to a global macro variable. Match the circled numbers to the paragraphs that follow.

```
%macro numobs(dsn);
   %global num; ❶
   data _null_;
      if 0 then set &dsn nobs=count; ❷
      call symput('num',left(put(count,8.))); ❸
      stop;
   run;
%mend numobs;
```

1. Macro variable NUM contains the number of observations in the data set named in parameter DSN; it must be global so that the value is available after macro NUMOBS ceases execution.
2. Because the value of the NOBS= variable, COUNT, is available at DATA step compilation, you do not need to retrieve any records from the data set. The IF condition, IF 0, is never true; thus, the SET statement is never executed.
3. The CALL SYMPUT statement writes the value of COUNT as a character string and assigns that value to macro variable NUM. Because the PUT function makes an explicit numeric-to-character conversion, the SAS System does not produce a note that automatic numeric-to-character conversion has occurred. The LEFT function left-aligns the result of the PUT function so that the value of NUM does not contain leading blanks.

The following example uses NUMOBS within another macro, MERGIT. NUMOBS determines whether either of two data sets to be merged has zero observations. If either data set has zero observations, macro MERGIT does not perform the merge and prints warning messages.

```
%macro mergit(dsn1,dsn2,by=,new=);
   %local one two;
   %numobs(&dsn1)
   %let one=&num;
   %numobs(&dsn2)
   %let two=&num;
   %if &one ne 0 and &two ne 0 %then
      %do;
         data &new;
            merge &dsn1 &dsn2;
            %if &by ne %then %str(by &by;);
            run;
      %end;
   %else
      %do;
         %put WARNING: MERGE NOT PERFORMED.;
         %put &dsn1 HAS &one OBSERVATIONS, AND;
         %put &dsn2 HAS &two OBSERVATIONS.;
      %end;
%mend mergit;
```

Producing a Blank Calendar

Macro CAL produces a blank calendar covering the months you specify. Match the circled numbers to the paragraphs that follow.

```
%macro cal(start,stop,lines=6); ❶
   options nodate;
   title;
   data cal; ❷
   %local i;
   %do i=1 %to &lines-1; ❸
      x&i=' ';
      format x&i $char10.;
   %end;
   month="01&start"d;
   output;
   %if &stop ne %then
      %do; ❹
         month="01&stop"d;
         output;
      %end;
   proc calendar fill; ❺
      id month;
   run;
%mend cal;


%cal(feb90,aug90)
```

1. Parameter START contains the first month in the calendar; for a calendar with more than one month, parameter STOP contains the last month. The LINES= parameter gives the number of blank lines in each calendar cell. The default value, 6, is the maximum number of lines that the CALENDAR procedure prints when the value of the PAGESIZE= system option is 60.
2. The SAS data set is named CAL to remind the user that the CAL macro created it.
3. Because the CALENDAR procedure produces its cells according to the number of variables to be displayed, the %DO group generates the correct number of variables. Because PROC CALENDAR inserts one blank line between the day number and the first variable displayed, you need one fewer variable than the value of LINES (that is, &LINES−1). Each variable is given a format of $CHAR10., which produces a cell 12 spaces wide. Variable MONTH is the ID variable in PROC CALENDAR. The OUTPUT statement outputs an observation.
4. If the calendar covers two or more months, the value of STOP is not null, and the %DO group generates the SAS statements for a second observation.
5. The FILL option in the PROC CALENDAR statement produces calendars for months between the beginning and ending date that have no observations. You do not need a VAR statement in this PROC CALENDAR step because the CALENDAR procedure displays all variables in data set CAL except MONTH, the ID variable.

Parameter LINES illustrates allowing a user to enter a value that is easy to remember rather than the value the macro processor actually uses. The user assigns the number of lines in each calendar cell to LINES; the iterative %DO statement calculates the value to be used within the macro.

Determining whether a SAS Data Set Exists

At times you need to determine whether a particular data set exists. Macro EXIST, shown here, uses a DATA step with a SET statement and the automatic macro variable SYSERR to determine whether a particular SAS data set name is present in a SAS data library:

```
%macro exist(dsn);
   %global exist; ❶
      %if &dsn ne %then %str( ❷
         data _null_;
            if 0 then set &dsn; ❸
            stop;
         run;
      );
   %if &syserr=0 %then %let exist=yes; ❹
   %else %let exist=no;
%mend exist;
```

1. Macro EXIST first creates a global macro variable, EXIST, to contain information about the existence of the data set.
2. The bulk of the macro only executes if the parameter value you pass to it as a data set name is not null.
3. The DATA _NULL_ step contains a SET statement that never executes because the IF condition is always false. When the SAS System compiles the DATA step containing the SET statement, an error condition arises when the data set in the SET statement does not exist. When you use macro EXIST to check for a nonexisting data set, the SAS System generates the following error message in the SAS log:

   ```
   ERROR: File SAS-data-set-name does not exist.
   NOTE: The SAS System stopped processing this step because of errors.
   ```

   If the data set in the SET statement exists, no error messages appear in the SAS log.
4. The value of automatic macro variable SYSERR contains the return code set by SAS procedures. If SYSERR equals 0, execution of the last SAS process completed successfully and without warning messages. If SYSERR contains any value greater than 0, execution of the last SAS process did not successfully complete, or it completed with warning messages. Macro EXIST checks the value of SYSERR immediately after the DATA _NULL_ step to see if the compilation of the SET statement generated an error. Then, it assigns global macro variable EXIST an appropriate value, either **yes** or **no**. See **AUTOMATIC MACRO VARIABLES** in Chapter 2, "Macro Variables," for more information about automatic macro variable SYSERR.

As an example of using macro EXIST, suppose you regularly update master data sets with transaction data sets. Occasionally, however, there are no transactions and no transaction data set is created. Macro UPDT, shown here, uses macro

EXIST to test for the existence of a transaction data set before performing an update operation:

```
%macro updt(master,trans,by=id,out=newcurr);
    %exist(&trans)
    %if &exist=yes %then
        %do;
            proc sort data=&trans;
                by &by;
            run;
            data &out;
                update &master &trans;
                by &by;
            run;
        %end;
    %else %put UPDATE NOT PERFORMED--NO TRANSACTION DATA SET;
%mend updt;


%updt(in.current,daily)
```

Printing All SAS Data Sets in a SAS Data Library

Macro PRINTA prints all the SAS data sets in a SAS data library. Match the circled numbers to the paragraphs that follow.

```
%macro printa(libname,worklib=work);
    %local num i; ❶
    proc datasets library=&libname memtype=data; ❷
        contents out=&worklib..temp1(keep=memname) data=_all_ noprint;
    run;
    data _null_;
        set &worklib..temp1 end=final;
        by memname notsorted;
        if last.memname;
        n+1;
        if final then call symput('num',put(n,8.)); ❸
        call symput('v'||left(put(n,8.)),trim(memname)); ❹
    run; ❺
    %do i=1 %to &num; ❻
        proc print data=&libname..&&v&i;
            title "Data Set &libname..&&v&i";
        run;
    %end;
%mend printa;
```

1. The %LOCAL statement creates a macro variable to use as a loop index variable in macro PRINTA.
2. The CONTENTS statement of the DATASETS procedure produces a new data set containing the names of the SAS data sets in the library you specify in parameter LIBNAME. The CONTENTS statement produces the output data set in the WORK library by default, but you can specify another library with the WORKLIB= parameter.
3. The DATA step counts the number of unique data set names and assigns the number to macro variable NUM. The CALL SYMPUT statement creates a macro variable containing the total number of data sets in the library you specify only when the DATA step finds the final record in

the output data set TEMP1. The TEMP1 data set contains duplicate observations because the CONTENTS statement in PROC DATASETS creates one observation for each variable in each data set.

4. The DATA step also creates one macro variable for each unique value of variable MEMNAME in data set TEMP1. The CALL SYMPUT statement assigns the name of each SAS data set to a series of numbered global macro variables beginning with the prefix V. The TRIM function removes trailing blanks from the value of MEMNAME so that the trailing blanks do not become part of the macro variable's value. If the trailing blanks become part of the value, they appear as part of the TITLE statement later in the macro and cause the words in the title to seem shifted to the left.

5. The RUN statement forces the DATA step to execute before the %DO loop executes. This guarantees that the values of NUM and the macro variables containing data set names are available before the %DO loop starts to execute. Without the RUN statement, the DATA step executes when the SAS System encounters the first PROC PRINT statement, after the first reference to variable NUM in the macro, causing an error that stops the execution of the macro.

6. The iterative %DO statement issues a PROC PRINT step and a TITLE statement for each SAS data set described by the PROC CONTENTS step.

Note: This example shows how to execute one procedure on all data sets in a SAS data library. **Grouping Procedure Output Using BY Groups**, in the next section, shows how to pass a series of PROC steps into a macro. You can combine these techniques to write a macro that executes any number of procedures on all data sets in a SAS data library.

A SIMPLE UTILITY MACRO SYSTEM

A macro system is a series of several macros that work together to accomplish a task by each accomplishing a portion of the main task. Using a system of macros becomes more desirable when you attempt to solve relatively more complicated problems requiring more source code. It is easier to develop, test, maintain, and modify several small programs than one large one.

The following sections describe a system of four simple macros that define an input window, display the input window and accept input, and process a data set based on the input.

Grouping Procedure Output Using BY Groups

When you use the same BY statement with several procedures, the SAS System displays all output for one procedure before beginning the output for the next procedure. At times it is convenient to group procedure output according to BY groups. This section shows these four macros:

- Macro CREATEW creates a window to collect information about which procedures you want to run, which data set to use, and which BY variable to use.
- Macro DISPW displays the window created by the first macro and passes the information you enter to another macro.
- Macro SYMCHK, from earlier in this chapter, checks to see if a macro variable exists.
- Macro BYPROC invokes the other macros as needed and uses the information you supply to the other macros to group procedure output according to BY groups, with a title containing the BY value for each BY group being processed.

Creating an Input Window with the %WINDOW Statement

The %WINDOW statement provides an easy way to get information interactively in the following macro, CREATEW. Match the circled numbers to the paragraphs that follow.

```
%macro createw;
   %window procby
      group=first ❶
         #3 @8 "This system produces procedure output with"
         #4 @8 "all procedures for one BY group together."
         #6 @8 "Enter the BY variable:"
         #7 @8 byvar 35 attr=underline
         #10 @8 "Enter the data set name:"
         #11 @8 inds 35 attr=underline

      group=second ❷
         #3 @8 "Enter your SAS statements on the following lines."
         #4 @8 "Do not include a BY statement."
         #5 @15 "Move from line to line with the TAB key."
         #6 @8 "The last statement"
         #7 @12 "must " attr=highlight
         #8 @8 "be a RUN statement."
         #10 @8 line1 55 attr=underline
         #11 @8 line2 55 attr=underline
         #12 @8 line3 55 attr=underline
         #13 @8 line4 55 attr=underline
         #14 @8 line5 55 attr=underline
         #15 @8 line6 55 attr=underline
         ;
   %mend createw;
```

1. The first group of fields in window PROCBY accepts the name of the BY variable and the SAS data set you want to use.
2. The second group of fields accepts the PROC steps you want to run. You do not specify BY statements, and the last statement you enter must be a RUN statement. Otherwise, you enter the PROC steps just as you would in the PROGRAM EDITOR window.

Displaying a Window with the %DISPLAY Statement

You only need to define a macro window once during your SAS session. After you define a macro window, the window exists for the remainder of your session, and you can display it as many times as you need by using the %DISPLAY statement. The following macro, DISPW, displays macro window PROCBY and calculates information about what you entered in the fields of the window. Match the circled numbers to the paragraphs that follow.

```
%macro dispw;
   %local lci; ❶
   %display procby.first;
   %display procby.second blank;
```

```
        %let lci=6; ❷
        %do %until (&lcount ne);
           %if %bquote(&&line&lci) ne %then
              %let lcount=&lci;
           %else
              %let lci=%eval(&lci-1);
        %end;
     %mend createw;
```

1. The %LOCAL statement only localizes one macro variable, which it uses as a counter in a loop.
2. The macro that invokes DISPW will use your input to build a block of SAS code. This %DO loop finds out how many lines you filled out and passes the information to the invoking macro. The loop starts with the highest line number allowed (6) and works backward to find the last non-null line.

Checking a Global Condition with Macro SYMCHK

The simple macro system so far has a mechanism for creating a macro window to accept input, and a way to display the window and calculate the amount of input a user enters. Since you only want to invoke the macro that creates the window the first time you use this macro system, you need to set a global condition that spans many invocations to let you determine if a given invocation is the first one in a given session.

The following macro, SYMCHK, appears in **Determining whether a Macro Variable Exists** earlier in this chapter:

```
%macro symchk(name);
   %if %nrquote(&&&name)=%nrstr(&)&name %then
      %let yesno=NO;
   %else
      %let yesno=YES;
   &yesno
%mend symchk;
```

When you invoke macro SYMCHK, the parameter NAME is the name of a macro variable, not a macro variable reference. The expression

```
%nrstr(&)&name
```

always yields a string consisting of a quoted ampersand followed by the value of NAME. Because the ampersand is quoted, this macro variable reference does not resolve. If NAME is not defined, the %IF condition becomes &NAME=&NAME, which is true, so SYMCHK assigns the value **NO** to macro variable YESNO, and the SAS System prints the following warning:

```
WARNING: Apparent symbolic reference macro-variable-name not resolved.
```

If the value of NAME is a defined macro variable, the left side of the %IF condition resolves to the macro variable value, the %IF condition is false, and SYMCHK assigns the value **YES** to macro variable YESNO.

Generating Procedure Output for BY Groups

The following macro, BYPROC, invokes macro SYMCHK to see if this is the first invocation of the macro system during the current session. If it is the first invocation, macro BYPROC sets a global condition indicating it has been invoked and invokes macro CREATEW to create an input window. Macro BYPROC then invokes macro DISPW to prompt for BY group and data set information and produces the output for a series of SAS procedures for each BY group. BYPROC accomplishes this by doing the following:

- determining whether the BY variable is character or numeric
- sorting the SAS data set
- determining the number of BY groups in the SAS data set
- recording the value of the BY variable for each BY group in the data set
- executing all of the procedures you specify for each successive BY group by using a WHERE statement with macro variables to operate only on selected observations at each pass.

Match the circled numbers to the paragraphs that follow.

```
%macro byproc;
%local byvar bvtype inds
       line1 line2 line3 line4 line5 line6
       lcount index1 index2 index3
       prc_call where_st exe_code; ❶
%let yesno=%symchk(wn_exist); ❷
%if &yesno=NO %then
   %do;
      %global wn_exist;
      %createw
   %end;
%dispw
   proc contents data=&inds noprint out=temp (keep=name type); ❸
   data _null_;
      set temp;
      if name="%upcase(&byvar)" then
         call symput('bvtype',type); ❹
      run;
   proc sort data=&inds; ❺
      by &byvar;
   run;
   data _null_; ❻
      set &inds end=eof;
      by &byvar;
      if first.&byvar then
         do;
             index1+1;
             call symput('macvar'||left(index1),&byvar);
         end;
      if eof then call symput('tot',index1);
    run;
   %if &bvtype=2 %then
      %let where_st=%nrstr(
         where &byvar="&&macvar&index3";
      ); ❼
   %else
      %let where_st=%nrstr(
         where &byvar=&&macvar&index3;
      );
```

```
        %do index2=1 %to &lcount; ❽
            %let prc_call=%bquote(&&line&index2);
            %if %qscan(&prc_call,1)=proc %then
                %let exe_code=%bquote(&exe_code &prc_call &where_st);
            %else
                %let exe_code=%bquote(&exe_code &prc_call);
        %end;
        %do index3=1 %to &tot; ❾
            title "&byvar=&&macvar&index3";
            %unquote(&exe_code);
        %end;
        title;
    %mend byproc;
```

1. The %LOCAL statement ensures that the macro does not interfere with any existing global variables. It also provides variables for macro INWIND to access. These variables will have values assigned in macro INWIND:

BYVAR	contains the name of the BY variable.
BVTYPE	contains a **1** if the BY variable is numeric or a **2** if it is character.
INDS	contains the name of the SAS data set.
LINE1-LINE6	contain the PROC step statements.
LCOUNT	contains the number of PROC step statements entered.

The other local variables are

INDEX1-INDEX3	contain values controlling various %DO loops.
PRC_CALL	contains pieces of the PROC statements.
WHERE_ST	contains a WHERE statement.
EXE_CODE	contains the full complement of SAS code, including WHERE statements, to execute for each BY group.

2. The invocation of SYMCHK determines if global macro variable WN_EXIST exists. If it does not exist, a %DO group creates it with a %GLOBAL statement and invokes macro CREATEW. If global variable WN_EXIST exists, the %DO group does not execute. The invocation of macro DISPW occurs next.
3. The CONTENTS procedure creates the output data set TEMP containing the name of each variable in the data set you specify and whether that variable is numeric or character.
4. The CALL SYMPUT statement assigns to macro variable BVTYPE the value **1** if the BY variable is numeric or **2** if it is character. Using the PUT function in the CALL SYMPUT statement eliminates one implicit numeric-to-character conversion.
5. PROC SORT puts the data set in the order necessary to find out information about the BY groups and BY variable values.
6. The DATA _NULL_ step discovers all of the BY variable values and how many BY groups there are. At the beginning of each BY group, the first SYMPUT routine creates a macro variable containing each unique BY variable value. At the end of the data set, the second SYMPUT routine creates a macro variable with the total number of BY groups.
7. WHERE_ST contains a WHERE clause to control the procedures running later in the macro. The %NRSTR function quotes the value assigned to

WHERE_ST to prevent the macro processor from attempting to resolve the embedded references to macro variables. The assignment of the WHERE clause contains double quotes around the BY variable value if the BY variable is character, but no quotes if it is numeric.

8. The %DO loop iterates once for each line of input. If the first word of the input line is PROC, macro variable EXE_CODE is concatenated with the line and WHERE_ST (which contains the WHERE statement). Otherwise, EXE_CODE is concatenated with just the line.

9. The last loop iterates once for each BY group. All of the procedures you specified execute once for each BY group, and the WHERE statement the macro inserted in each procedure call causes the procedures to operate only on observations in the data set containing a particular value for the BY variable.

Running BYPROC

Suppose you have a data set named SALES, in which each observation contains information about the sale of a particular product. The variables in the data set include the following:

PRODUCT	contains a code for the product sold.
REP	contains a code for the salesperson making the sale.
GROSS	contains the dollar amount of the sale.
STATE	contains the state where the sale was made.

In this example, the values for STATE are either NC or SC. Since you like to look at summary information about your sales separated by state, this provides a perfect opportunity to run a few SAS procedures using macro BYPROC so the output for all procedures is grouped by state.

Suppose you invoke macro BYPROC like this:

```
%byproc
```

Display 11.1 shows the first window you see.

```
┌PROCBY─────────────────────────────────────────────────────────┐
│ Command ===>                                                   │
│                                                                │
│                                                                │
│          This system produces procedure output with           │
│          all procedures for one BY group together.            │
│                                                                │
│          Enter the BY variable:                                │
│          _____                  │
│                                                                │
│                                                                │
│          Enter the data set name:                              │
│          _____                  │
│                                                                │
│                                                                │
│                                                                │
│                                                                │
│                                                                │
│                                                                │
│                                                                │
│                                                                │
│                                                                │
│                                                                │
│                                                                │
│                                                                │
│                                                                │
│                                                                │
└────────────────────────────────────────────────────────────────┘
```

Display 11.1   First Input Window

Enter the name of the BY variable on the first line, and then use the TAB key to move the cursor to the second line to enter the data set name. In this example, say that you want to use the variable STATE and the data set SALES. **Display 11.2** shows the next window you see.

```
┌PROCBY─────────────────────────────────────────────────────────┐
│ Command ===>                                                   │
│                                                                │
│                                                                │
│                                                                │
│          Enter your SAS statements on the following lines.     │
│          Do not include a BY statement.                        │
│                  Move from line to line with the TAB key.      │
│          The last statement                                    │
│              must                                              │
│          be a RUN statement.                                   │
│                                                                │
│                                                                │
│              _____    │
│              _____    │
│              _____    │
│              _____    │
│              _____    │
│              _____    │
│                                                                │
│                                                                │
│                                                                │
│                                                                │
│                                                                │
│                                                                │
│                                                                │
│                                                                │
└────────────────────────────────────────────────────────────────┘
```

Display 11.2   Second Input Window

Using the TAB key to get from line to line until you are finished, enter the following lines:

```
proc freq;
    tables product*rep;
proc means min max range maxdec=2;
    var gross;
run;
```

Display 11.3 shows what the window looks like when you are finished.

```
┌PROCBY──────────────────────────────────────────────────────┐
│ Command ===>                                               │
│                                                            │
│                                                            │
│          Enter your SAS statements on the following lines. │
│          Do not include a BY statement.                    │
│                  Move from line to line with the TAB key.  │
│          The last statement                                │
│            must                                            │
│          be a RUN statement.                               │
│                                                            │
│          proc freq;                                        │
│              tables product*rep;                           │
│          proc means min max range maxdec=2;                │
│              var gross;                                     │
│          run;                                              │
│                                                            │
│                                                            │
│                                                            │
│                                                            │
│                                                            │
│                                                            │
│                                                            │
│                                                            │
└────────────────────────────────────────────────────────────┘
```

Display 11.3   Second Input Window with Completed Fields

Macro execution generates the following statements:

```
PROC SORT;
   BY STATE;
RUN;
DATA _NULL_;
   SET SALES END=EOF;
   BY STATE;
   IF FIRST.STATE THEN
      DO;
         COUNT+1;
         CALL SYMPUT('MACVAR'||LEFT(COUNT),&STATE);
      END;
   IF EOF THEN CALL SYMPUT('TOT',COUNT);
RUN;
TITLE "STATE=NC";
PROC FREQ;
   WHERE STATE="NC";
   TABLES PRODUCT*REP;
PROC MEANS MIN MAX RANGE MAXDEC=2;
   WHERE STATE="NC";
   VAR GROSS;
RUN;
TITLE "STATE=SC";
PROC FREQ;
   WHERE STATE="SC";
   TABLES PRODUCT*REP;
PROC MEANS MIN MAX RANGE MAXDEC=2;
   WHERE STATE="SC";
   VAR GROSS;
RUN;
TITLE;
```

APPENDICES

SAS® System Options Used with the Macro Facility

Reserved Words in the Macro Facility

Macro Efficiency and Debugging

278

SAS® System Options Used with the Macro Facility

This appendix discusses SAS system options used with the macro facility. Options discussed include:

General	Displaying Text	Autocall Facility
IMPLMAC	MLOGIC	MAUTOSOURCE
MACRO	MPRINT	MRECALL
MERROR	SYMBOLGEN	SASAUTOS=
SERROR		

Contents

GENERAL

The following system options control the general operation of the macro facility, including

- whether you can use statement-style macro invocations
- whether the macro facility is available
- whether an unrecognized macro name causes an error message
- whether an unrecognized macro variable reference causes an error message.

IMPLMAC: Allows statement-style macro calls

IMPLMAC | NOIMPLMAC

The IMPLMAC system option determines whether the macro processor recognizes a statement-style macro invocation (described in **Macro Invocations** in Chapter 3, "Macro Program Statements"). If you specify the IMPLMAC option, the macro processor examines the first word of every SAS statement to see whether it is a statement-style macro invocation. If the MAUTOSOURCE option is in effect, the macro processor also searches the autocall libraries for the member with the same name.

If you specify the MAUTOSOURCE option and the IMPLMAC option together, you should also specify the NOMRECALL option to improve operating efficiency. Using the NOMRECALL option with the MAUTOSOURCE and IMPLMAC options causes the macro processor to search the autocall libraries for potential autocall macros only the first time it encounters any particular keyword or variable name beginning a SAS statement.

You can specify the IMPLMAC option either at SAS invocation, in a configuration file, in an OPTIONS statement, or in the OPTIONS window of the SAS Display Manager System.

MACRO: Specifies whether the SAS macro language, the SYMGET function, and the SYMPUT routine are available

MACRO | NOMACRO

The MACRO system option determines whether the macro facility is available in a SAS program. If you specify the NOMACRO option, the SAS System compiles and executes your code a little faster, but most features of the macro facility are not available. You can specify the MACRO option only at SAS invocation or in a configuration file.

MERROR: Issues a warning message when a macro-like name does not match a macro keyword

MERROR | NOMERROR

The MERROR system option determines whether the macro processor issues the warning message

```
Warning: Apparent invocation of macro macro-name not resolved.
```

when it encounters the pattern %name but cannot find a macro of that name. You can specify the MERROR option either at SAS invocation, in a configuration file, in an OPTIONS statement, or in the OPTIONS window of display manager.

SERROR: Issues a warning message when a macro variable reference does not match a macro variable

SERROR | NOSERROR

The SERROR system option determines whether the macro processor issues the warning message

```
Warning: Apparent symbolic reference reference-name not resolved.
```

when it encounters the pattern &name but cannot find a macro variable of that name. You can specify the SERROR option either at SAS invocation, in a configuration file, in an OPTIONS statement, or in the OPTIONS window of display manager.

DISPLAYING TEXT

The following system options control whether the macro processor prints diagnostic messages to assist you in debugging your macros, including

- when any statement within a macro executes
- when any macro generates SAS source statements
- when any macro variable reference resolves.

MLOGIC: Traces execution of macro code

MLOGIC | NOMLOGIC

The MLOGIC system option specifies whether the macro processor prints a message whenever the SAS System executes any macro programming statement within a macro, completely tracing its execution. Setting the MLOGIC system option causes the macro processor to print messages revealing

- when a macro begins executing
- the value of any parameters
- when any program statement executes
- the status of any %IF or %DO condition
- when a macro stops executing.

You can specify the MLOGIC option either at SAS invocation, in a configuration file, in an OPTIONS statement, or in the OPTIONS window of display manager. Lines generated by the MLOGIC option are marked with the word MLOGIC and the name of the macro it is tracing in parentheses. The MLOGIC system option performs the same functions as the MTRACE system option of Release 6.03 of the SAS System.

The MLOGIC option is designed for debugging macros; note that using it can produce a great deal of output. See Appendix 3, "Macro Efficiency and Debugging," for an example of output from the MLOGIC system option.

MPRINT: Displays SAS statements generated by macro execution

MPRINT | NOMPRINT

The MPRINT system option specifies whether the macro processor displays SAS statements generated by macro execution in an easy-to-read form. Specifying the MPRINT option causes the statements to appear with macro variable references and macro expressions resolved. Each statement begins on a new line with one space separating words. You can specify the MPRINT option either at SAS invocation, in a configuration file, in an OPTIONS statement, or in the OPTIONS window of display manager. See Appendix 3 for an example of output from the MPRINT system option.

SYMBOLGEN: Displays results of resolving macro variable references

SYMBOLGEN | NOSYMBOLGEN

The SYMBOLGEN system option specifies whether the macro processor displays the result of resolving macro variable references. You can specify the SYMBOLGEN option either at SAS invocation, in a configuration file, in an OPTIONS statement, or in the OPTIONS window of display manager. See Appendix 3 for an example of output from the SYMBOLGEN system option.

AUTOCALL FACILITY

The following system options control the operation of the autocall facility, including

- whether the autocall facility features are available
- whether the autocall facility searches for a particular unrecognized macro only the first time you invoke it, or every time you invoke it
- which storage locations the autocall facility searches for autocall macros.

MAUTOSOURCE: Enables the macro autocall feature

MAUTOSOURCE | NOMAUTOSOURCE

The MAUTOSOURCE system option controls whether the autocall facility is available. If the MAUTOSOURCE option is in effect and you invoke a macro that has not been compiled in the current program, the macro processor searches each autocall library you specify with the SASAUTOS= system option for a member with the name you requested.

   Note: On operating systems that allow filenames with extensions, you must name autocall macro library members with a SAS-type extension, usually .SAS. Look at the autocall macros on your system provided by SAS Institute to determine whether names of library members containing macros must have a SAS-type extension at your site.

   You can specify the MAUTOSOURCE option either at SAS invocation, in a configuration file, in an OPTIONS statement, or in the OPTIONS window of display manager. See **Setting SAS System Options to Use the Autocall Facility** in Chapter 7, "The Autocall Facility," for instructions on finding and viewing autocall libraries supplied by SAS Institute.

MRECALL: Searches autocall libraries for a member not found during an earlier search

MRECALL | NOMRECALL

The MRECALL system option determines whether the macro processor searches the autocall libraries you specify with the SASAUTOS= system option for a member that was not found in a previous search. If the MRECALL option is in effect, the macro processor searches the libraries for an undefined macro name each time you invoke that macro. If the NOMRECALL option is in effect, the macro processor searches only once. The main use of the MRECALL option is to recover from an error in which you autocall a macro from a library that is not available and need to invoke that macro again when the library is available.

You can specify the MRECALL option either at SAS invocation, in a configuration file, in an OPTIONS statement, or in the OPTIONS window of display manager.

SASAUTOS=: Specifies one or more autocall libraries

SASAUTOS=*library-specification* |
        (*library-specification-1*, . . . ,*library-specification-n*)

The SASAUTOS= system option specifies one or more autocall libraries. *Library-specification* can be one of the following:

- a SAS fileref.
- a quoted string describing the name of an aggregate storage location on your operating system.
- a concatenated list of filerefs and quoted filenames enclosed in parentheses and separated by either blanks or commas. Concatenated lists can contain any mixture of filerefs and quoted filenames in any order. See **Improving Autocall Efficiency** in Chapter 7 for a discussion of how the autocall facility uses these lists.

Note: See the SAS documentation for your operating system for complete details on specifying the physical names of external files, including details about using operating-system-specific filerefs.

You can specify the SASAUTOS= option either at SAS invocation, in a configuration file, in an OPTIONS statement, or in the OPTIONS window of display manager.

Reserved Words in the Macro Facility

The following list gives reserved words in the macro facility. A *reserved word* is a name that is used now or may be used in the future by an internal component of the macro facility. Do not use a reserved word as the name of a macro, a macro variable, or a macro label.

Note: Do not use any name beginning with the letters SYS for a macro or a macro variable.

ABEND	ELSE	MACRO	STOP
ABORT	END	MEND	STR
ACT	EVAL	METASYM	SUBSTR
ACTIVATE	FILE	NRBQUOTE	SUPERQ
BQUOTE	GLOBAL	NRQUOTE	SYSEXEC
BY	GO	NRSTR	SYSGET
CLEAR	GOTO	ON	SYSRPUT
CLOSE	IF	OPEN	THEN
CMS	INC	PAUSE	TO
COMANDR	INCLUDE	PUT	TSO
COPY	INDEX	QSCAN	UNQUOTE
DEACT	INFILE	QSUBSTR	UNSTR
DEL	INPUT	QUOTE	UNTIL
DELETE	KEYDEF	QUPCASE	UPCASE
DISPLAY	LENGTH	RESOLVE	WHILE
DMIDSPLY	LET	RETURN	WINDOW
DMISPLIT	LIST	RUN	
DO	LISTM	SAVE	
EDIT	LOCAL	SCAN	

If you define a macro using a reserved name, the macro processor issues a warning, and your macro is neither compiled nor available for execution.

Appendix 3
Macro Efficiency and Debugging

This appendix describes opportunities to improve operating efficiency when you design, write, or use macros. It also presents some practical advice for debugging macros, including demonstrations of the system options you can use to assist you with debugging.

Contents

MACRO EFFICIENCY

The macro processing facility of the SAS System offers opportunities for the efficient processing of information. You can improve the efficiency of your macros by doing the following:

- using SAS efficiency features and writing efficient SAS code
- using sound programming techniques
- providing for human resource efficiency
- knowing when to use macro features.

SAS Efficiency Features and Efficient SAS Code

Although both are important, efficient basic SAS code usually has more impact on the efficiency of a program than an efficient macro. When you use the macro facility to generate SAS code, the result is only as efficient as the code you cause the macro facility to generate. You should first concentrate on developing efficient SAS code and then make the macro itself efficient.

For example, a common macro program is one that generates multiple DATA steps, where the only difference between each step is a filename or a data set name. Instead of using a macro to generate multiple DATA steps, you can use the stored program facility to compile and store a DATA step, and use a macro to pass values, such as filenames or data set names, that change for each run. You save the compilation of each DATA step and improve your processing efficiency. See Appendix 3, "Stored Program Facility," in *SAS Language: Reference, Version 6, First Edition* for a description of the stored program facility.

Sound Programming Techniques

You can apply these general programming techniques and principles to your macro programs to improve their processing efficiency:

- Avoid resolving expressions within a loop. Try to resolve all expressions outside of a loop, assigning the value to a variable. Any comparisons or calculations you need to make within the loop can then use the variable instead of re-evaluating the expression in each cycle. This applies to both macro programming and SAS DATA step programming.
- Keep the number of variables you use to a minimum. This minimizes the chance of work region overflow and its associated input/output overhead.
- Use local variables rather than global variables whenever possible. Use macro variables to communicate information between DATA steps or PROC steps rather than using information stored in files or data sets. By using macro variables rather than files or data sets, you save file reading and writing overhead.

Human Resource Efficiency

You can apply these general programming techniques and principles to your programs to improve the efficiency with which you or other programmers can use and maintain them:

- Use programming structure. Use indention and blank lines to visually separate your macro program modules from each other and from the SAS statements that they generate.
- Provide internal documentation. Use comments in your macros generously. Remember to use the macro comment statement when you

document your macros. See Chapter 3, "Macro Program Statements," for a discussion of the %*comment statement.

- When you write macros, remember that shorter programs may not be more efficient if they are less clear, especially if somebody may have to spend time analyzing them later on.
- In multihost environments, use macro features to write applications that are portable between machines. You can use the automatic macro variable SYSSCP to enable your programs to determine the current operating system and then provide for conditional execution of operating-system-specific code based on the result. By using this technique, you only have to maintain one flexible program, rather than one for each operating system at your site.

Tips for Using Macro Features

You can use these features of the macro facility to improve processing efficiency:

- Use the autocall facility to run tested macros so that you compile only the macros you need and avoid having to use the %INCLUDE statement or the INCLUDE display manager command during your SAS session.
- Always specify the NOMRECALL system option unless you need to recompile a corrected macro.
- Remember that the macro facility is a text processor. Avoid using the macro facility to do arithmetic whenever possible to avoid the implicit character-to-numeric conversions that decrease processing efficiency.
- Only specify the IMPLMAC and MAUTOSOURCE system options together when you know you will use an autocall library containing statement-style macros. Keep statement-style autocall macros in a separate library to make it more obvious when you use statement-style autocall macros.
- Specify the NOMACRO system option if you are about to run a large SAS program that does not contain any macro references, any macro variable references, the SYMPUT routine, or the SYMGET function. Remember that the NOMACRO system option does not affect your ability to use the %INCLUDE statement in a SAS program or session.
- Use macro statements in open code rather than compiling entire macros if you can accomplish the same thing. You save the compilation overhead.

DEBUGGING MACROS

Debugging is the process of finding and correcting errors in program code. You can simplify debugging your macros by taking the following steps:

- identifying common errors
- separating macro errors from SAS statement errors
- displaying text to debug macros
- debugging errors in macro invocations
- debugging errors in macro variable references.

Identifying Common Errors

Before you begin a full-scale debugging project, check for these common errors:

- having the system option NOMACRO in effect rather than MACRO.
- having the system option NOMAUTOSOURCE in effect rather than MAUTOSOURCE if you are using the autocall facility.

- omitting the ampersand from a macro variable reference or adding an ampersand where one is not needed.
- omitting the percent sign from a macro language keyword, especially macro language keywords that correspond to DATA step keywords. For example, it is easy to write %DO WHILE instead of %DO %WHILE.
- using an ampersand in place of a percent sign or vice versa.

Separating Macro Errors from SAS Statement Errors

Error messages with numbers, such as the following, come from the SAS statements generated by executing a macro:

```
Error 180-322: Statement is not valid or it is used out of proper order.
```

First, use the MPRINT option and the SYMBOLGEN option to determine what text is being generated incorrectly. If necessary, use the MLOGIC option to further trace text generated by executing a macro so you can more easily locate the part of the macro that is generating the incorrect text.

Error messages without numbers, such as the following, come from the macro processor:

```
Error: There is no %IF statement for the %ELSE.
       A dummy macro will be compiled.
```

Specifying the MPRINT and SYMBOLGEN options does not help if only macro error messages are present.

One way to approach errors from the macro processor is to add %PUT statements to display the values of macro variables at various stages and indicate that particular macros have started and finished execution. The MLOGIC option should also be helpful since it causes the macro processor to print a message when any macro statement within a macro executes.

See the next section, **Displaying Text to Debug Macros**, for a discussion of using the MLOGIC, MPRINT and SYMBOLGEN system options to help debug macro programs.

If using the macro debugging options brings you no closer to a solution, but you suspect there is a problem with SAS source statements rather than with the macro itself, do the following:

1. Route the SAS log to a permanent external file.
2. Specify the MPRINT option so that the macro processor generates a readable copy of the SAS statements that the macro produces.
3. Invoke the macro again.
4. Edit the external file where you sent the log, removing extraneous elements such as line labels and headings, so that you are left with the SAS code produced by your macro.
5. Execute the SAS program in that file.
6. If the program does not execute successfully, debug the SAS statements before debugging the macro any further.

Displaying Text to Debug Macros

The way the macro processor displays text generated by the execution of macros and by the resolution of macro variable references is controlled by the three SAS system options MLOGIC, MPRINT, and SYMBOLGEN.

General guidelines for using these system options include the following:

- The MPRINT option shows all SAS statements generated by macro code; use MPRINT to help locate problems from errors generated by the SAS compiler.
- The SYMBOLGEN option shows when each symbolic substitution and macro variable reference resolution occurs; use SYMBOLGEN to help locate problems with macro variable reference resolution.
- The MLOGIC option shows when each statement within a macro executes; use MLOGIC to help locate problems with the way a macro executes, especially to check %IF conditions and %DO loops.

The following sections describe the system options you can use to display text useful in debugging macros. Each section gives an example of the text you get from using a particular option. **Specifying the MLOGIC, MPRINT, and SYMBOLGEN Options** shows an example of the output you get when you specify all of the text display system options simultaneously. Each example uses the following program:

```
filename scores 'file-specification';

%macro names(dsn,infile,number,prefix=v);
   %local i;
   %if %upcase(&prefix)=SYS %then
      %do;
         %put WARNING: Prefix SYS is reserved. Default prefix used.;
         %let prefix=v;
      %end;
   data &dsn;
      infile &infile;
      input
   %do i=1 %to &number;
      &prefix&i
   %end;
      ;
   run;
%mend names;

title "Today is &sysday";

%names(tstscors,scores,3,prefix=sys)
```

In this example, the invocation deliberately uses the reserved variable prefix SYS in order to demonstrate the macro's complete capabilities.

Specifying No Display Options

Specifying no display options produces the SAS log shown in **Output A3.1**.

Output A3.1   No Display Options

```
5          filename scores 'FILE-SPECIFICATION';
6
7          %macro names(dsn,infile,number,prefix=v);
8             %local i;
9             %if %upcase(&prefix)=SYS %then
10               %do;
11                  %put WARNING: Prefix SYS is reserved. Default prefix used.;
12                  %let prefix=v;
13               %end;
14            data &dsn;
15               infile &infile;
16               input
17            %do i=1 %to &number;
18               &prefix&i
19            %end;
20               ;
21            run;
22         %mend names;
23
24         title "Today is &sysday";
25
26         %names(tstscors,scores,3,prefix=sys)
WARNING: Prefix SYS is reserved. Default prefix used.

NOTE: The infile SCORES is:
      Dsname=FILE-SPECIFICATION

NOTE: 4 records were read from the infile SCORES.
NOTE: The data set WORK.TSTSCORS has 4 observations and 3 variables.
```

Specifying the MPRINT Option

Specifying the MPRINT system option causes the SAS System to display all the SAS code your macro generates. Specify MPRINT if you get a numbered error message or unexpected program results without an error message. If the MPRINT option helps you determine that incorrect SAS source statements are causing your errors, you may need to use the MLOGIC option to find out why your macro generates incorrect SAS source statements.

Specifying the MPRINT option produces **Output A3.2**.

Output A3.2   MPRINT System Option Output

```
23
24         options mprint;
25
26         title "Today is &sysday";
27
28         %names(tstscors,scores,3,prefix=sys)
WARNING: Prefix SYS is reserved. Default prefix used.
MPRINT(NAMES):    DATA TSTSCORS;
MPRINT(NAMES):    INFILE SCORES;
MPRINT(NAMES):    INPUT V1 V2 V3 ;
MPRINT(NAMES):    RUN;

NOTE: The infile SCORES is:
      Dsname=FILE-SPECIFICATION

NOTE: 4 records were read from the infile SCORES.
NOTE: The data set WORK.TSTSCORS has 4 observations and 3 variables.
```

The SAS log contains the SAS statements generated by invoking macro NAMES. The generated statements are marked with the tag MPRINT and the name of the macro that generated them in parentheses.

Specifying the SYMBOLGEN Option

Specifying the SYMBOLGEN system option causes the SAS System to display each macro variable reference resolution, either within macros or in open code. Specify SYMBOLGEN if you think macro variable references are resolving to values you do not expect.

Output A3.3 shows the result of specifying the SYMBOLGEN option.

Output A3.3   SYMBOLGEN System Option Output

```
23
24              options symbolgen;
25
SYMBOLGEN:  Macro variable SYSDAY resolves to Tuesday
26              title "Today is &sysday";
27
28              %names(tstscors,scores,3,prefix=sys)
SYMBOLGEN:  Macro variable PREFIX resolves to sys
WARNING: Prefix SYS is reserved. Default prefix used.
SYMBOLGEN:  Macro variable DSN resolves to tstscors
SYMBOLGEN:  Macro variable INFILE resolves to scores
SYMBOLGEN:  Macro variable NUMBER resolves to 3
SYMBOLGEN:  Macro variable PREFIX resolves to v
SYMBOLGEN:  Macro variable I resolves to 1
SYMBOLGEN:  Macro variable PREFIX resolves to v
SYMBOLGEN:  Macro variable I resolves to 2
SYMBOLGEN:  Macro variable PREFIX resolves to v
SYMBOLGEN:  Macro variable I resolves to 3

NOTE: The infile SCORES is:
      Dsname=FILE-SPECIFICATION

NOTE: 4 records were read from the infile SCORES.
NOTE: The data set WORK.TSTSCORS has 4 observations and 3 variables.
```

In this example, you can see the macro processor resolving each macro variable reference it encounters. The name of each macro variable and the value that each reference resolution provides are clearly marked. If you just need to look at resolved references, using the SYMBOLGEN option gives you that information.

In the preceding example, you can tell that the variable PREFIX resolves to the value **sys** immediately before the %PUT statement produces a warning message. In other cases, determining when macro variable resolution occurs relative to the execution of other macro statements or the production of SAS code requires you to combine the SYMBOLGEN option with the MLOGIC option or the MPRINT option.

Specifying the MLOGIC Option

Specifying the MLOGIC system option causes the SAS System to display a message whenever any macro program statement executes from within a macro. Specify MLOGIC if you think logical conditions in your macro are not correctly structured or the order of macro statement execution is the cause of the problem.

Output A3.4 shows the output you get using the MLOGIC option.

Output A3.4 MLOGIC System Option Output

```
23
24          options mlogic;
25
26          title "Today is &sysday";
27
28          %names(tstscors,scores,3,prefix=sys)
MLOGIC(NAMES):  Beginning execution.
MLOGIC(NAMES):  Parameter DSN has value tstscors
MLOGIC(NAMES):  Parameter INFILE has value scores
MLOGIC(NAMES):  Parameter NUMBER has value 3
MLOGIC(NAMES):  Parameter PREFIX has value sys
MLOGIC(NAMES):  %LOCAL  I
MLOGIC(NAMES):  %IF condition %upcase(&prefix)=SYS is TRUE
MLOGIC(NAMES):  %PUT WARNING: Prefix SYS is reserved. Default prefix used.
WARNING: Prefix SYS is reserved. Default prefix used.
MLOGIC(NAMES):  %LET (variable name is PREFIX)
MLOGIC(NAMES):  %DO loop beginning; index variable I; start value is 1; stop
                value is 3; by value is 1.
MLOGIC(NAMES):  %DO loop index variable I is now 2; loop will  iterate again.
MLOGIC(NAMES):  %DO loop index variable I is now 3; loop will  iterate again.
MLOGIC(NAMES):  %DO loop index variable I is now 4; loop will not iterate again.

NOTE: The infile SCORES is:
      Dsname=FILE-SPECIFICATION

NOTE: 4 records were read from the infile SCORES.
NOTE: The data set WORK.TSTSCORS has 4 observations and 3 variables.

MLOGIC(NAMES):  Ending execution.
```

Lines generated by the MLOGIC option are marked with the word MLOGIC and the name of the macro it is tracing in parentheses. Note that the MLOGIC option produces text that explicitly traces parameter values, the %IF condition, the %DO loop, and all other statements.

Specifying the MLOGIC, MPRINT, and SYMBOLGEN Options

When you combine the MLOGIC, MPRINT, and SYMBOLGEN options, the timing of the macro variable reference resolution and the production of SAS statements by the macro is quite clear. You can tell when every statement executes, what logical steps the macro processor takes, and the results of each step. **Output A3.5** shows the result of specifying the MLOGIC, MPRINT, and SYMBOLGEN options all at the same time.

Output A3.5   MLOGIC, MPRINT, and SYMBOLGEN System Options Output

```
23
24          options mprint symbolgen mlogic;
25
SYMBOLGEN:  Macro variable SYSDAY resolves to Tuesday
26          title "Today is &sysday";
27
28          %names(tstscors,scores,3,prefix=sys)
MLOGIC(NAMES):  Beginning execution.
MLOGIC(NAMES):  Parameter DSN has value tstscors
MLOGIC(NAMES):  Parameter INFILE has value scores
MLOGIC(NAMES):  Parameter NUMBER has value 3
MLOGIC(NAMES):  Parameter PREFIX has value sys
MLOGIC(NAMES):  %LOCAL  I
SYMBOLGEN:  Macro variable PREFIX resolves to sys
MLOGIC(NAMES):  %IF condition %upcase(&prefix)=SYS is TRUE
MLOGIC(NAMES):  %PUT WARNING: Prefix SYS is reserved. Default prefix used.
WARNING: Prefix SYS is reserved. Default prefix used.
MLOGIC(NAMES):  %LET (variable name is PREFIX)
SYMBOLGEN:  Macro variable DSN resolves to tstscors
MPRINT(NAMES):    DATA TSTSCORS;
SYMBOLGEN:  Macro variable INFILE resolves to scores
MPRINT(NAMES):    INFILE SCORES;
SYMBOLGEN:  Macro variable NUMBER resolves to 3
MLOGIC(NAMES):  %DO loop beginning; index variable I; start value is 1; stop
                value is 3; by value is 1.
SYMBOLGEN:  Macro variable PREFIX resolves to v
SYMBOLGEN:  Macro variable I resolves to 1
MLOGIC(NAMES):  %DO loop index variable I is now 2; loop will  iterate again.
SYMBOLGEN:  Macro variable PREFIX resolves to v
SYMBOLGEN:  Macro variable I resolves to 2
MLOGIC(NAMES):  %DO loop index variable I is now 3; loop will  iterate again.
SYMBOLGEN:  Macro variable PREFIX resolves to v
SYMBOLGEN:  Macro variable I resolves to 3
MLOGIC(NAMES):  %DO loop index variable I is now 4; loop will not iterate again.
MPRINT(NAMES):    INPUT V1 V2 V3 ;
MPRINT(NAMES):    RUN;

NOTE: The infile SCORES is:
      Dsname=FILE-SPECIFICATION

NOTE: 4 records were read from the infile SCORES.
NOTE: The data set WORK.TSTSCORS has 4 observations and 3 variables.

MLOGIC(NAMES):  Ending execution.
```

Note that combining the MLOGIC, SYMBOLGEN, and MPRINT options produces a detailed picture of macro execution but generates many separate lines of text. In larger macros, the amount of text produced can be overwhelming, especially in macros with other macro invocations nested within them.

Debugging Errors in Macro Invocations

If you invoke a macro and nothing happens, there are several possible explanations:

1. The macro may be running but not doing what you expect. Specify the MLOGIC and MPRINT system options to see if the macro executes as you think it should.

2. You may have mistyped the %MEND statement. If the macro processor does not recognize the end of a macro definition, the macro processor treats all subsequent statements as part of the macro definition. In an interactive session, submit several %MEND statements; when you get the following error message, you have successfully ended the macro definition and can resume your SAS session:

   ```
   Error 180-322: Statement is not valid or it is used out of proper order.
   ```

3. If you defined the macro with parameters in an interactive session and you have omitted all parameter values in the invocation, the macro processor must verify that the list of values is not being submitted on a

later line before it executes the macro. Submitting blanks or null lines is not sufficient; you must submit another word (or token). Placing an empty set of parentheses after the invocation is a simple way to indicate the end of an invocation when you omit the parameter values, as in the following example:

```
%macro demo(first=a,second=b);
    %put First is &first and second is &second;
    %mend demo;
%demo()
```

4. If your macro accepts input from a terminal with a %INPUT statement, you can become trapped in a loop if you forget to close an expression with a right parenthesis. You are then submitting macro invocations to the input loop rather than to the macro processor. Enter several right parentheses and semicolons, and you may be able to close the expression causing the looping. Again, receiving an error message indicates that the session is no longer paralyzed.

Debugging Errors in Resolving Macro Variable References

Problems with resolving macro variable references usually fall into one of the following categories:

- The reference does not resolve.
- The reference resolves, but the macro processor does not use the resolved value.
- The reference resolves, but you do not realize that it has resolved.

Use a %PUT Statement

To find out which of these is the problem, use a %PUT statement at various points in your macro or program to write a prominent message where you expect the reference to resolve, as in the following:

```
%PUT ******* THE VALUE OF LOANS IS &LOANS *******;
```

Set the SERROR system option, submit the program again, and look at the result of the %PUT statement.

Case 1: Reference recognized, resolution not possible   If the text written by the %PUT statement appears without change and the following warning is present, the macro processor recognized a macro variable reference but could not resolve it:

```
WARNING: Apparent symbolic reference LOANS not resolved.
******* THE VALUE OF LOANS IS &LOANS *******
```

Check for the following problems:

- misspelling the name of the macro variable.
- assigning the variable a value with the SYMPUT routine, but referencing the variable before the DATA step executes.
- creating the variable inside a macro and referencing it outside the environment of the macro. You must create the variable in a %GLOBAL statement before you assign it a value in order to place the variable in the global referencing environment.

  Since you cannot use a macro parameter in a %GLOBAL statement, you must use a %GLOBAL statement to first define a new variable and then assign the parameter value to the new variable in order to make a parameter value global. See **Referencing Environments** in Chapter 2, "Macro Variables," for a complete discussion of how and when macro variables become available during macro execution.

Case 2:   Reference not recognized   If the reference is not resolved in the text written by the %PUT statement and there is no warning message, as shown here, the macro processor did not recognize the reference:

```
******* THE VALUE OF LOANS IS &LOANS *******
```

Check for the following problems:

- referencing a macro variable without having the system option MACRO in effect.
- enclosing a reference in single quotes. Macro variable references in single quotes do not resolve; to allow the reference to resolve, enclose it in double quotes instead of single quotes.
- placing the reference in lines following a CARDS or PARMCARDS statement; macro variable references are not valid in those positions.

Case 3:   Resolution to a null value   If the reference disappears on the text written by the %PUT statement, as shown here, the macro variable reference resolved to a null value:

```
******* THE VALUE OF LOANS IS  *******
```

If you expected a different value, check for the following problems:

- not giving the variable a value. A macro variable used in a %GLOBAL statement or as a macro parameter has a value of null until you explicitly give it a value.
- creating a variable in a %GLOBAL statement and giving it a value with the SYMPUT routine, but referencing it before the DATA step containing the SYMPUT routine executes. Until the DATA step executes, the macro variable has the null value that the %GLOBAL statement gave it. You may need to make the DATA step complete within the referencing environment of the macro by adding a RUN statement to the code that it produces, or you may need to move the reference. See Chapter 6, "DATA Step Interfaces," for a complete discussion of the SYMPUT routine.

Check the Placement of Macro Variable References

You can use a macro variable reference anywhere except in the lines following a CARDS or a PARMCARDS statement. Remember that the value to which the macro variable reference resolves must be valid at the location where you place it.

Don't be concerned about using macro variable references in SAS code where a numeric value usually is required. Even though macro variable values represent characters, they are not character strings in the sense that the DATA step uses the term. Characters in the macro facility include numbers, letters, and special symbols. If the value of a macro variable is a number, the SAS System sees only the number. Since macro activity takes place during the compilation of SAS code, the value is substituted, and the SAS compiler never knows that a macro variable existed.

Distinguish between the %PUT and PUT Statements

Be careful about using macro variable references in DATA step PUT statements. Consider the following examples:

```
*This works;
%let value=xyz;
%put &value;

*This produces a note;
data a;
   put &value;
run;
```

In the first part of the example, the %PUT statement writes the text string **xyz** in the SAS log. The string **xyz** is not used in any other way by the SAS System.

In the second part of the example, the SAS System compiles and executes a DATA step. While the PUT statement is being compiled, the reference &VALUE is resolved, and its value, **xyz**, is passed to the DATA step compiler as a part of the PUT statement. The SAS System sees the following DATA step:

```
DATA A;
   PUT XYZ;
RUN;
```

The text XYZ is a valid SAS name, and the SAS System treats a valid SAS name in a PUT statement as a variable name. Therefore, the DATA step produces a note that XYZ is an uninitialized variable, and the PUT statement writes a missing value, as in the following:

```
NOTE: Variable XYZ is uninitialized.

NOTE: The data set WORK.A has 1 observations and 1 variables.
```

If you had created a variable named XYZ earlier in the DATA step in this example, the SAS System would print its value or values with the PUT statement.

If you want XYZ to represent a character literal rather than a DATA step variable name, use the syntax for character literals (that is, enclose the value in double quotes). Remember that you must use double quotes in order for the reference to resolve. The following example shows the correct form:

```
%let value=xyz;
%put &value;

* Correct way to produce a character literal;
* with a macro variable reference and a DATA step PUT;
data a;
   put "&value";
run;
```

Glossary

This glossary defines some terms used in this book. See the **Index** for references to the pages where these items are discussed.

argument
> a string used by a macro function.

ASCII
> the acronym for the American Standard Code for Information Interchange. ASCII is a 7-bit coded character set (8 bits when a parity check bit is included) used for information interchange among data processing and communication systems. The ASCII set consists of graphic (printable) and control (nonprintable) characters.

autocall facility
> a feature of the SAS System that enables you to store the source statements that define a macro and invoke the macro as needed, without having to include the definition in your program.

automatic macro variable
> a macro variable defined by the SAS System rather than by the user.

calling a macro
> See the entry for macro invocation.

compilation
> the process of checking syntax and translating a portion of a program into a form that the computer can execute.

computed %GOTO destination
> a destination in a %GOTO statement that is created by resolving a macro expression and is therefore determined at macro execution rather than at macro compilation.

constant text
> strings stored as part of a macro or as a macro variable's value in open code from which the macro processor generates text to be used as SAS statements, display manager commands, or other macro program statements. Constant text is also called model text.

conversational macro
> a macro that displays messages to the user and accepts input from the user during its execution.

current referencing environment
> the referencing environment in which macro processor activity is taking place.

DATA step interface
> a DATA step CALL routine or function that interacts with the macro processor while a DATA step is executing, not while a DATA step is being compiled.

dummy macro
> a macro that the macro processor compiles but does not store.

EBCDIC
> the acronym for Extended Binary Coded Decimal Interchange code. EBCDIC is an 8-bit character coding scheme. The EBCDIC character set

uses the 256 possible 8-bit patterns to represent a selection of graphic (printable) and control (nonprintable) codes. The following operating systems supported by the SAS System use the EBCDIC collating sequence: CMS, MVS, and VSE.

execution
the process of performing the actions defined in a portion of a program (such as a DATA or PROC step or a macro).

forward scan
the technique the macro processor uses to resolve macro variable references. Forward scan consists of reading and resolving a string until the processor encounters a character that cannot be part of a macro variable reference or cannot resolve into part of a macro variable reference (for example, a blank). When forward scan is interrupted, the macro processor rescans the string, beginning with the first item resolved in the previous scan. When a scan produces no changes, scanning ceases.

global macro variable
a macro variable that, once created, can be referenced in any referencing environment in a SAS program, except where blocked by a local macro variable of the same name. A global macro variable exists until the end of the program.

global referencing environment
the outermost referencing environment, that is, the entire SAS job or session.

input stack
the most recently read line of input from a SAS program and any text generated by the macro processor that is awaiting processing by the word scanner.

integer arithmetic
arithmetic that uses only integers (numbers not containing a decimal point).

invoking a macro
See the entry for macro invocation.

keyword parameter
a macro parameter defined with an equal sign after the parameter name, as in *parameter-name*=.

local macro variable
a macro variable created within a macro that is available only within that macro and macros invoked from within that macro. A local macro variable ceases to exist when the macro creating it ceases execution.

local referencing environment
the referencing environment associated with the execution of an individual macro.

macro
a member of a catalog in the WORK library containing compiled macro program statements and stored text. A macro can be executed to generate SAS statements, display manager commands, and other macro program statements; to write messages to the SAS log; to accept input; to create or change the values of macro variables; and to perform other activities.

macro boundary
    the point that divides the word queue into the section that can contain
    quoted tokens and the section that cannot.

macro call
    See the entry for macro invocation.

macro compilation
    the process of converting a macro definition from the statements you
    enter into a form that is ready for the macro processor to use and
    storing the result for later use in the SAS job or session.

macro execution
    the process of following the instructions given by macro program
    statements to generate text that can become SAS statements, display
    manager commands, and other macro program statements; to write
    messages to the SAS log; to accept input; to create or change the values
    of macro variables; and to perform other activities.

macro expression
    a sequence of macro operators and operands, where any item stored as
    text can be an operand and where operators include arithmetic and
    logical operators, grouping parentheses, and macro functions.

macro facility
    a portion of the SAS System used for extending and customizing the SAS
    System and for reducing the amount of text that must be entered to do
    common tasks. It consists of the macro processor and the macro
    language.

macro invocation
    an instruction to the macro processor to execute a macro; it is also
    known as a macro call. A macro invocation can either be name-style
    (%name) or statement-style (name;) depending on how the macro was
    defined.

macro language
    the programming language you use to communicate with the macro
    processor.

macro parameter
    a local macro variable defined in parentheses in the %MACRO
    statement.

macro processor
    the portion of the SAS System that compiles and executes macros and
    macro program statements.

macro quoting
    See the entry for quoting.

macro variable
    a variable belonging to the macro language whose value is a string that
    remains constant until you change it. A macro variable is also called a
    symbolic variable.

macro variable reference
    the name of a macro variable preceded by an ampersand (&name) that
    the macro processor replaces with the value of the macro variable
    named.

mnemonic operator
    an arithmetic or logical operator composed of letters rather than symbols
    (for example, EQ rather than =).

model text
See the entry for constant text.

name-style macro invocation
See the entry for macro invocation.

null value
a value consisting of 0 characters.

open code
the part of a SAS program outside any macro definition.

parameter
See the entry for macro parameter.

positional parameter
a parameter that is defined by name only and whose value is assigned by matching the parameter in a particular position in the %MACRO statement with the value in the corresponding position (delimited by commas) in the macro invocation.

quoting
the process that causes the macro processor to treat certain items as text rather than as symbols in the macro language. Quoting is also called removing the significance of an item.

quoting function
a macro language function that performs quoting on its argument.

recursive execution
execution that occurs when a macro, while executing, invokes itself or invokes another macro(s) that invokes the original macro.

referencing environment
the scope of a macro variable's availability.

reserved word
a name that is used or may be used in the future by an internal component of the macro facility.

resolving a macro variable reference
the process of replacing a macro variable reference on the input stack with the value of that macro variable. This process is also called symbolic substitution.

returned value
a string resulting from the execution of a macro function.

SAS compilation
the process of converting statements in the SAS language from the form in which you enter them into a form ready for the SAS System to use.

SAS execution
the process of following the instructions given by SAS statements to perform an action.

statement-style macro
a macro defined with the STMT option in the %MACRO statement.

step boundary
a point in a SAS program at which the SAS System recognizes that a DATA or PROC step is complete. It consists of either a RUN statement; a QUIT statement in an interactive procedure; a semicolon following data lines; the word DATA or PROC indicating the beginning of the next step; an ENDSAS statement; or the end of a noninteractive program.

string
> any group of characters.

symbol table
> the area in which the macro processor stores all macro variables and macro statement labels for a particular referencing environment.

symbolic substitution
> See the entry for resolving a macro variable reference.

symbolic variable
> See the entry for macro variable.

token
> the unit in the SAS language or the macro language into which input must be broken in order to be processed by the SAS System. Tokens (also called words) include items that look more or less like English words (such as variable names) and items that do not (such as mathematical operators and semicolons).

tokenizer
> the part of the word scanner that breaks input into tokens (also called words).

unquoting
> the process of restoring the meaning of a quoted item.

word
> See the entry for token.

word queue
> the portion of the SAS System in which the word scanner examines and processes tokens (words) before making the tokens available to the SAS compiler.

word scanner
> a portion of the SAS System that examines all tokens (words) in a SAS program and moves the tokens to the portion of the SAS System that requested them. The word scanner triggers the macro processor to examine all *%name* and *&name* patterns in a program.

Index

R

S

Your Turn

If you have comments or suggestions about the SAS macro facility or the *SAS Guide to Macro Processing, Version 6, Second Edition*, please send us your ideas on a photocopy of this page.

Please return the photocopy to the Publications Division (for comments about this book) or the Technical Support Division (for suggestions about the software) at SAS Institute Inc., SAS Campus Drive, Cary, NC 27513.